ACROSS THE BORDER

ACROSS THE BORDER

RURAL DEVELOPMENT IN MEXICO AND RECENT
MIGRATION TO THE UNITED STATES

Harry E. Cross
James A. Sandos

INSTITUTE OF GOVERNMENTAL STUDIES
University of California, Berkeley   1981

Harry E. Cross is Research Scientist, Battelle Memorial Institute

James A. Sandos is Associate Professor of History, University of Redlands

Copyright ©1981 by the Regents of the University of California
All rights reserved

Second Printing 1982

Designed by Joan Lichterman; cover design by Shelley Jones
Typesetting by Ann Flanagan Typography, Berkeley, California
Cover photograph courtesy of U.S. National Archives and Record Service

Library of Congress Cataloging in Publication Data

Cross, Harry E.
  Across the border.

    1. Agriculture—Economic aspects—Mexico.
2. Mexico—Emigration and immigration. 3. Mexicans—
United States. I. Sandos, James A. II. Title.
HD 1792.C7   331.12′791   81-6276
ISBN 0-87772-280-3   AACR2

To Paul S. Taylor

Contents

Appendix

Illustrations

Foreword

Authors Harry Cross and James Sandos brought excellent credentials to their joint writing of this book. Both are trained historians who have done substantial investigative work in Mexico: Harry Cross with his inquiry into life and labor on haciendas in Zacatecas and San Luis Potosí, and Jim Sandos with his strong interest in the Mexican Revolution (1910-1940). Between them they have written more than 20 articles and monographs on Latin American history, from the colonial era to the present.

In 1978 they decided to combine resources for an in-depth examination of immigration and related issues, trying to take a genuinely binational and biregional approach to a fascinating if troubling international phenomenon. Not only did this mean rewriting the history of Mexican agricultural development in light of its relationship to migration and agriculture in the southwestern United States, but also it meant a rigorous restudy of virtually all relevant social science research done in the U.S. and Mexico since 1969, attempting to separate the wheat from the chaff on these complex and thorny issues.

The two authors have also brought other qualifications to their sensitive work on immigration. From age five to 23, Sandos lived and worked in the vicinity of Fresno, and during part of the Bracero Era (1960 and 1961) labored in the San Joaquin valley fields, coming into daily contact with Mexican workers and sleeping in bracero camps. At about the same time, Harry Cross lived on a ranch near Victorville, California, where he also came into contact with many braceros. In short, beyond their professional interest, the authors have a deep and abiding personal interest in the phenomena they are studying.

Knowing of our Institute's work in policy research, especially on issues of particular concern to California, in the spring of 1979 the authors approached us with a work plan and a 30-page initial draft. Finding much merit in their proposal, we expressed definite interest in publication possibilities and assisted them in finding support. The Pericles Foundation in Walnut Creek, California, stepped in on short notice and provided crucial financial help that summer.

In the fall of 1979, when their initial draft was substantially complete, it underwent an unusually rigorous peer review, partly because of the controversial nature of the subject. With flying colors it passed this critical reading by a number of eminent scholars of varied backgrounds, who also made many suggestions to guide the authors and editors in preparing the manuscript for publication. After significant revision, the authors candidly confided their hope to have written something that would stand the test of time, and perhaps be regarded as in the same league with earlier writings of Manuel Gamio and Paul S. Taylor (to whom this book is dedicated). Judging from the peer review comments and from our own editorial work with the manuscript, we believe they have fulfilled their aspiration.

In any event, the Institute of Governmental Studies is most pleased to publish this unique study of Mexican immigration, a source of interest, puzzlement, and concern on both sides of the border. We believe it is an important book that will help many readers look at immigration and related phenomena in a new light, and will also assist policymakers in both Mexico and the United States to deal with the issues in more enlightened, constructive, and effective ways.

                                                              Stanley Scott
                                                              Assistant Director

Preface

The unprecedented proliferation of Mexicans migrating to the United States in the decade of the 1970s has brought the migration issue to the forefront of national concern in both countries. Despite a growing literature on this compelling subject, the phenomenon has not been fully explained even though it touches virtually every aspect of national and personal life north and south of the border. Involved are such diverse issues as inflation, the use of social services, media responsibility, cultural identity, job competition, and unemployment. Proposed solutions suggest another constellation of issues ranging from rural development strategies in Mexico to law enforcement programs in the United States. This massive movement of people carries with it myriad human problems, and ready solutions are not at hand. It is impossible to understand the massive movement without an historical and binational perspective, which is also an essential component of problemsolving. Our purpose is to provide such a context.

Mexican migration is not simply a contemporary human event. It is another unfolding of a much larger picture that began to emerge a century ago. The interweaving of long-term historical forces in both countries has produced an interdependence that is not adequately appreciated. Historical studies have tended to view past events with little regard for their organic relationship to the present. Conversely, contemporary studies often give the impression that Mexican migration is almost entirely a recent development. But the migration is a much more complicated and continuing series of phenomena that need to be better understood. Rarely are we afforded such an opportunity to demonstrate how detailed knowledge and awareness of the past are essential to devising sound, long-term policy for the future.

For over 130 years, two strikingly different countries have shared 2,000 miles of common border. To the north, a highly industrialized, technologically advanced society emerged within an Anglo-Saxon cultural milieu.

A persistent characteristic of the American system has been a strong demand for inexpensive labor. To the south, a much older Latin tradition gave rise to a different kind of society. Unlike its northern neighbor, political independence for Mexico did not lead to economic independence. A measure of economic autonomy was finally attained in the 1940s, but only after Mexico had experienced major social upheaval and after the United States had committed itself to a world war.

In the three decades prior to 1940, the demand for labor in the United States, coupled with the lack of opportunity and political turmoil in rural Mexico, caused Mexicans to migrate northward, sometimes in massive numbers. In 1940, with agrarian reform far advanced, Mexico reached a crossroads in its alternatives for national economic development. The country chose a strategy whose by-product was the continued displacement of people in the countryside. Migration from the countryside to Mexican cities or to the United States, accelerated by an unforeseen population explosion, became an accepted, and sometimes encouraged, national policy. The evolution of this strategy resulted in an uneven development of the rural infrastructure among the regions of Mexico. It caused those areas of Mexico most seriously affected by the previous 30 years of strife to continue to export people. The continued unequal development of agriculture through the 1970s has meant an historical continuity in those regions chiefly responsible for out-migration. Not surprisingly, the Mexican states that contributed the bulk of migrants to the United States in the 1920s continued to do so in the 1970s.

The states of Durango, Guanajuato, Jalisco, Michoacán, San Luis Potosí, and Zacatecas have traditionally formed the core region of "sending" states (see map).* In the 1920s, this region contributed about 70 percent of all Mexican migrants to the United States.[1] Recent research indicates the region still directly sends more than half of all Mexican migrants to this country.[2] Indirectly, it is responsible for a proportion equal to that of the 1920s by virtue of a staged northward migration.

Detailed knowledge about the development of the "sending" region—not previously available—forms the core of material presented in the first five chapters of this book. The historical analysis presented in these five chapters is indispensable to a full grasp of matters dealt with in the rest of the book.

The primary questions we pose are: Why has this migration principally originated from one specific region of Mexico, and what factors have caused the region consistently to provide a high level of migration for over 70 years?

The sixth chapter of the book critically examines evidence of the contemporary impact of migration, and the focus thus shifts to the United States. Our inquiry relates to the key questions of numbers, job displacement, social services utilization, and cultural interchanges. The seventh and final chapter offers policy recommendations for both the United States and Mexico. We have tried to formulate recommendations that are consistent with the historical development of the sending and receiving regions, and that relate realistically to what we know of contemporary impact. In short, we based our policy formulation on two essential elements: historical understanding and an assessment of current knowledge.

---

*Several regional distinctions are made throughout the text. In Chapter 1, the North Center refers to the states of Zacatecas, San Luis Potosí, and the northern portions of Jalisco and Guanajuato. In Chapter 2 and thereafter, this original sending region is expanded to include the rest of the states of Guanajuato, Jalisco, and to add the states of Michoacán and Durango. Central Mexico is defined as the Federal District, the State of Mexico, and those states contiguous to the State of Mexico, including part of Michoacán. By North Mexico we mean the states bordering on the U.S., as indicated on the map.

Acknowledgments

We wish to thank our parents. They best know the reasons why.

Valuable criticism of our initial draft of this manuscript came from more than a dozen readers representing many fields. The spectrum of expertise ranged from that of farmers to governmental advisors and policy implementers. Scholars in the academic community contributed insights from the disciplines of history, economics, agricultural economics, anthropology, and public administration. Our readers are distinguished and we thank them in alphabetical order: Vernon M. Briggs, Jr., Woodrow Borah, Manuel L. Carlos, Norris Clement, Walter Fogel, Lloyd L. Gallardo, Ralph Guzmán, Susan Hayes, James D. Kitchen, Jack Lloyd, Philip L. Martin, William P. McGreevey, Joseph Nalven, Howard Twining, and James W. Wilkie. We, not they, are responsible for any remaining inaccuracies.

Our study would not have been possible without the indispensable financial assistance of several sympathetic individuals and institutions. The Tinker Foundation provided support in the form of a postdoctoral fellowship for some of the archival research and writing on Mexico for the period before 1940. The Center for Latin American Studies at the University of California, Berkeley, under its director Woodrow Borah, kindly provided the research facilities necessary to produce the first draft. During the hectic final stages of research and writing, work was greatly stimulated and facilitated by support from the Battelle Memorial Institute's Population and Development Policy Program and its director, William P. McGreevey. The Pericles Foundation under the directorship of Warren Breed contributed vital support at precisely the moment it appeared that the project might not be completed for want of funds. Finally, essential editorial assistance was generously provided by the Institute of Governmental Studies at UC Berkeley, and its assistant director, Stanley Scott. Marta Sanchez and Joan Bolduc provided bibliographic support, and Joan Lichterman was production editor. Our heartfelt thanks go to all of these people.

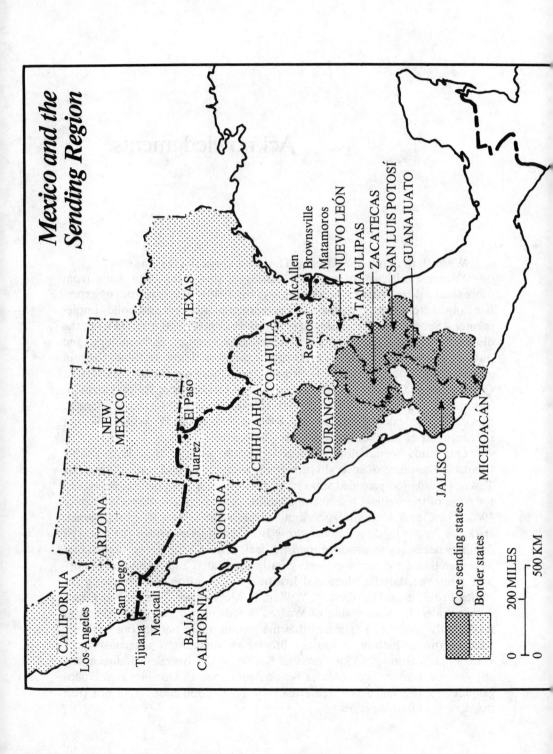

Mexico and the Sending Region

Los Angeles
San Diego
Tijuana
Mexicali

CALIFORNIA

BAJA CALIFORNIA

ARIZONA

NEW MEXICO

El Paso
Juarez

SONORA

CHIHUAHUA

TEXAS

COAHUILA

DURANGO

JALISCO

MICHOACÁN

McAllen
Reynosa

Brownsville
Matamoros

NUEVO LEÓN

TAMAULIPAS

ZACATECAS

SAN LUIS POTOSÍ

GUANAJUATO

Core sending states

Border states

0   200 MILES
0   500 KM

1

Rural Development in North Central Mexico, 1880–1940

In order to understand fully the current Mexican migration phenomenon, we must look to rural Mexican history. This section addresses the relationship between rural change and migration in North Central Mexico during 1880–1940.

The character of Mexico in pre-Columbian times was largely determined by human migration. For centuries, nomadic peoples wandered over the countryside and eventually settled in the rich basins of central and southern Mexico. The North Center, with its arid plains and mountains, was left vacant or sparsely populated by nonsedentary war-like Indians commonly called *chichimecas*. The region had its beginnings as a modern political unit as a result of another significant migration—the large-scale movement of Europeans into the New World in the sixteenth century. Spaniards in search of precious metals discovered massive deposits of silver ores in the 1540s, and populated the North Center in a matter of decades. The chichimecas were largely subdued or driven out altogether, and in their place grew up large estates, called *haciendas*, which supplied livestock and other agricultural products to the silver mines and budding cities.

As the mining industry flourished and the demand for a variety of goods and commodities increased, the great haciendas of North Central Mexico multiplied. Ranchos and small communities grew up in the inter-

1

stices. They did not compete with the haciendas, but instead complemented the latters' activities by providing human resources and by engaging in the least-profitable agricultural activities. Thus, haciendas dominated the countryside and the rural economy in North Central Mexico from the late sixteenth century until the beginning of our period in the late nineteenth century.

The fortunes of haciendas as economic, social, and political units varied over the decades, according to business and especially silver-mining cycles, and to a lesser extent the vicissitudes of Mexico's political climate. Their fortunes swung between success and failure with more regularity than has been supposed. By the end of the nineteenth century, however, highly stable political conditions (the Porfirian dictatorship) and a concerted national policy aimed at economic expansion created an environment that permitted haciendas in the North Center to prosper. By 1900, most haciendas in the region were highly productive. A balance between demand and supply for labor meant that unemployment was low and wages were adequate by the standards of the day.

Forty years later, in 1940, the hacienda system in the North Center had been destroyed, along with the social and economic relationships that had given the old order a measure of vitality. Revolution and rebellion (1913–1929) caused the displacement of large numbers of rural dwellers, most of whom migrated to Mexican cities or to the North. The structure of the new order established in the 1930s failed to meet rural needs and thus perpetuated the process of labor displacement and migration that persists to this day. The North Center of Mexico, which today directly contributes one half of illegal migrants to the United States, provides a logical point for inquiry.[1] By studying the North Center (1880–1940), we not only view the historical creation of the migration process, but we also come to comprehend the inadequacies of contemporary rural development in Mexico.

The North Center, 1880–1912

Land

The North Center encompassed most of the states of San Luis Potosí, Zacatecas, and the northern reaches of Jalisco and Guanajuato (see map). It largely comprised the middle portion of Mexico's physiographically diverse Central Meseta. Many of the haciendas in the region were found on this semiarid plateau at elevations of roughly 2,000 meters. The climate and terrain at this elevation favored livestock raising and cultivation of certain staple crops, especially maize, the Mexican equivalent of corn. On the Hacienda del Maguey in Zacatecas, for example, the principal activity was sheep raising.[2] Wool and tallow accounted for the chief marketable products. At the Hacienda de Bledos in southern San Luis Potosí, better soil and an excellent irrigation system allowed more diversification in production. Besides sheep, Bledos grew large quantities of wheat, maize, beans, and chile, and also produced dairy goods, alcoholic beverages, and leather.[3]

Fertile lowland valleys at about 1,000 meters elevation enjoyed a more humid climate and greater rainfall; estates in these areas prospered by growing several semitropical cash crops. Sugar proved the most profitable, followed in no particular order by fruits, fibers, and staples. These haciendas also raised livestock. For instance, the Hacienda de Estancita possessed extensive cane fields, five small sugar mills, 9,000 head of cattle, and over 16,000 goats.[4] Although some of the output of the lowland haciendas found its way into the international marketplace, the majority of all hacienda surplus supplied regional and local markets.[5]

Population

In the late nineteenth century, the North Center had over a million inhabitants, or about a tenth of Mexico's total population. This preindustrial society was overwhelmingly rural; over three-quarters of the inhabitants lived in locations of less than 1,500 people. The average rural site in this region averaged only 200 people, and nearly all of them derived their living from agriculture. More than 60 percent of the region's rural population resided on haciendas, while the remainder occupied small hamlets and villages *(ranchos)* adjacent to the haciendas.[6] Many of those not living directly on hacienda lands were associated with the estates as temporary laborers, sharecroppers, or as renters. At the turn of the century, therefore, the "common man" of the North Center found himself a *peón* working on an hacienda, or a *ranchero* dependent upon the hacienda for supplementary income. The remainder survived through a variety of subsistence activities.

Labor

Despite differences in size, environment, and output, all North Central haciendas shared one common feature: their labor system. This invariably involved some combination of permanent and temporary employees. Permanent laborers, called *acomodados,* were dominant in the nineteenth century. Their conditions of employment included a guaranteed monthly salary, and a ration of maize sufficient to cover the needs of an average family. The maize ration was a particular benefit for the permanent workers. Not only did it supply them and their families with 75 percent of their food requirements, but it also protected them against the constantly fluctuating maize prices in local markets. Besides receiving most of their food, permanent laborers also enjoyed such perquisites as grazing and planting rights, and some form of free housing. Of all hacienda laborers, therefore, the acomodados had the most favorable terms of employment.[7]

Temporary employees *(alquilados)* who worked on a daily basis for a wage or contracted employment by the job *(contratistas)* were less secure than acomodados. They generally received no ration and had fewer perquisites. Temporary work was often seasonal, and hence full employment proved rare for daily workers. To balance these disadvantages, however, temporary laborers received a higher wage than their permanent counterparts. Particularly on the highland estates, temporary workers accounted for a small proportion of the total number of employees. On the Rancho Grande Hacienda, for example, only a third of the work positions were classified as temporary in the early twentieth century. These alquilados and contratistas were drawn from the haciendas' resident populations, or from the inhabitants of nearby ranchos.[8]

A final component of the hacienda labor system comprised the sharecroppers and renters. Although of minor importance on many North Central haciendas during the nineteenth century, this sector expanded greatly following the Mexican Revolution of 1910. Because sharecropping and tenant farming were high-risk, low-profit propositions, those engaged in these activities were among the most disadvantaged of the rural population. These farmers depended entirely on primitive agricultural techniques and on rainfall for their economic survival. In this area of Mexico, one could at least count on insufficient rainfall one year out of three. As a result, sharecroppers and tenants often found themselves in debt to the hacienda and to other local creditors. In some years, it was not unusual for some sharecroppers to have no income. But the haciendas needed these farmers to guarantee a sufficient supply of staples, so they rarely pressured for repayment, choosing instead to view the losses as a necessary subsidy.[9]

In short, depending on the needs and financial condition of the hacienda, a variable mixture of permanent and temporary laborers made up the workforce. The exact proportions in each category changed over time and from hacienda to hacienda. Changing labor demands during the course of the year promoted the lateral movement of nonpermanent workers and tenants from category to category. For example, on some haciendas such as the Hacienda del Pozo del Carmen in San Luis Potosí, sharecroppers regularly spent portions of the year working as alquilados.[10] The flexible nature of labor utilization on haciendas increased the opportunities for employment for rural inhabitants.

Conventional wisdom asserts that the bonding agent for this rural labor system was debt peonage, a condition in which a laborer is held in perpetual servitude through continual credit advances by the hacienda.[11] But recent research in the account records of more than two dozen North Center haciendas has revealed no cases of what could be called debt peonage. The relative incidence of indebtedness proved very low in many cases and nonexistent in others. On the Hacienda del Maguey, for instance, only 9 percent of the 179 low-income laborers found themselves in debt at the end of 1883. Those in debt owed an average of three weeks' wages. Thirty years later, in 1913, 17 out of the estate's 200 employees owed less than two weeks' wages.[12] At Bledos, the average debt per laborer declined from three weeks' wages in the 1880s to just seven days' money wages in 1900–1910.[13] In sum, then, the North Center remained virtually free of debt peonage before 1910. Hacienda owners and administrators simply did not make use of credit advances to attract and maintain a labor force.

If indebtedness was insignificant, then it follows that the haciendas' company stores *(tiendas de rayas),* the sources of advances, were not the exploitative institutions commonly portrayed. Much checking and comparing of prices has revealed no example of noticeable and continued overcharging by haciendas. On the contrary, hacienda stores often supplied commodities to its employees at less than local market prices, confirming the assertion that administrators did not gouge residents.[14] The contemporary attitude regarding company stores seems best expressed by one of the region's largest landholders, who wrote the following private instructions to his sons in 1905:

> Without taking advantage of the employees, one can expect a marginal profit by selling commodities to them at market prices, or perhaps even less. The hacendado [hacienda owner] should take care to exploit the earth, not the people.[15]

Despite these practices, rural life in prerevolutionary North Central Mexico was far from idyllic. Most peones did not own land although nearly all of them enjoyed some measure of access to pastures and cultivable plots. Daily wage earners, tenants, and agrarians accepted underemployment as a fact of life. But unemployment remained low during the last two decades of the nineteenth century because of growing demand for labor in the region's mining, transportation, and budding agribusiness sectors.

An apparently favorable employment picture should not, however, obscure the deterioration in rural life caused by a decline in real wages. As population increased from 9.4 million to 15.2 million between 1877 and 1910, wages remained virtually static. Conversely, commodity prices generally rose as Mexico's export economy expanded during the same period.[16]

6	ACROSS THE BORDER

Despite the erosion of living standards, the average family's income was still sufficient to provide its basic needs. In fact, when the Revolution came to the North Center in 1913, real wages were at their highest in a decade, and the countryside clearly did not seethe for drastic solutions to its problems.[17]

The Years of Destruction, 1913–1929

Revolution, 1913–1920

The cumulative effects of the Revolution (1913-1920) and the religious uprising of the Cristeros (1926-1929) destroyed the economic vitality of the old order. Stability gave way to instability and the once-familiar became strange. For nearly two decades, the people of the North Center, derided by the combatants as *pacíficos,* lived in uncertainty, expecting and fearing violence.[18] For parts of the rural North Center, the Mexican Revolution of 1910 meant destruction, pure and simple. Despite some precursor activities in the capital of San Luis Potosí, the thrust of the upheaval came from the country's northernmost states, namely Sonora, Chihuahua, and Coahuila. The violence and destruction that accompanied the Revolution did not originate locally, but rather was visited upon the North Center by combatants from hundreds of miles away.

The holocaust primarily followed the railroad lines. Since major trunk lines transversed San Luis Potosí, Zacatecas, and the northern reaches of Jalisco and Guanajuato, these areas suffered greatly.[19] Northerners wanted Mexico City and the political power of government, and the North Center, lying in between, had the geographical misfortune to become the principal battleground. Armies and bands of revolutionaries temporarily occupied nearly all of the haciendas in San Luis Potosí and Zacatecas. They destroyed property, carried off and sold or consumed most of the area's livestock, and pillaged sugar mills and mescal manufactories.

As a result, by 1917 operations had come to a halt on all large haciendas.[20] This in turn meant a drastic loss of employment for the rural masses in those two states. Many peasants migrated to other parts of Mexico during these years, some emigrated to the United States, but most simply attempted to eke out an existence by hunting, gathering, and subsistence farming. Needless to say, living conditions deteriorated disastrously. The price of maize rose tenfold and living standards in terms of real wages for those still fortunate enough to be employed declined by some 75 percent between 1913 and 1916. In Zacatecas and San Luis Potosí, we estimate net capital losses in agriculture of 50 percent of fixed assets, and perhaps 75 percent of variable assets.[21] Thus when peace came in 1920, landowners lacked the financial resources to return their operations to previous production levels.

In more general terms, a variety of conditions eroded the quality of rural life in the North Center areas affected by the Revolution. In addition to the outright destruction of assets, capital left agriculture either by migration to large Mexican cities or by emigration from the country, mainly to the United States.[22] Moreover, revolutionary factions issued paper scrip, the value of which varied with the fortunes of war and politics. For the masses, this fiat money contributed to lower real wages, higher prices, and an inflationary bind that only intensified each time one army replaced another in the field.[23] Marauding revolutionaries, bandits, and dispossessed rural workers depleted herds, burned fields, seized grain, and created a climate of uncertainty that led to crop shortfalls due to reduced plantings. Many landowners abandoned their haciendas and sought the safety of the city. Violent death and epidemic disease accompanied the economic misery that plagued the countryside.[24]

Faced with myriad problems, and with little agricultural financing available from a preoccupied government, hacendados who resumed operations in the 1920s relied heavily upon sharecropping and renting. In this manner, landowners shifted some of the burden of capital investment and risk onto former peones and peasant farmers. While the high risks of agriculture could be equally shared by landlord and sharecropper, the risks incurred by the landowner who rented his pastureland became negligible. The production system changed rapidly, therefore, from being almost totally financed by the landowner to one in which the costs were partially borne by those who could least afford them.[25]

As a result of this shift in production, the haciendas' permanent labor force virtually disappeared. On the Hacienda de Santa Teresa in San Luis Potosí, for example, permanent laborers accounted for 58 percent of all wage payments in 1910. By 1927, their share of all wages had fallen to 14 percent.[26] Santa Teresa was but one example of many. In Guanajuato, a list in the municipal archive dated 1925 enumerated 135 permanent laborers (acomodados or *peones acasillados*) on over 40 haciendas, or an average of only 3.4 acomodados per estate. A century earlier, the highland hacienda of Duarte alone maintained 34 permanent workers.[27] With the elimination of acomodado positions during the Revolution and after, the most secure rural jobs became unavailable to the rural working population.

Another important result of the change in the structure of rural production was a rise in the incidence of indebtedness far above prerevolutionary levels. The shift to sharecropping and temporary laborers meant that daily wage earners now had to rely on the few opportunities offered directly by haciendas, and upon the periodic requirements of the largely impoverished sharecroppers and tenants. Wages rose little in the 1920s and commodity prices remained high. Thus, not only was there a loss in employment opportunities, but also the cost of living remained high. The result was a worsening financial condition for the average peasant family. The average debt on the Hacienda de Santa Teresa quadrupled between 1908 and 1928, to about three months' wages. At Bledos and Pozo del Carmen, overall indebtedness increased by 500 percent from 1917 to 1928.[28]

Besides altering the relationship of hacienda to worker, rural restructuring also affected the regional labor market adversely. Not only did demand for labor drop precipitously, but also only poorer quality jobs were offered. Static agricultural production and the highest rates of population growth in the region's history only exacerbated the plight of agricultural workers. An index of productivity based on staples, livestock, and sugar showed no rise in output during the 1920s. But population growth, which had averaged well under 1 percent annually in the nineteenth century, rose to over 2 percent in the 1920s.[29] Instead of doubling every 100 years, the population of the North Center began a process of doubling every 25 or 30 years. Employment opportunities did not begin to keep pace with the new additions to the labor force.

Rebellion, 1926–1929

The new revolutionary government that had emerged by 1917 found itself in no position genuinely to help the North Center even if it had been so inclined. The United States, Mexico's dominant trade partner, erroneously considered the new Mexican government to be Bolshevik, and so denied loans for any purpose.[30] In fact, both Mexico and Russia faced the 1920s internally devastated by civil war, and needing capital goods, foreign loans, and with limited means for rewarding the victors with what modest surplus remained.[31]

Fortunately for the Mexican peasantry, no Soviet-style collectivization was attempted. Instead, the revolutionary government concerned itself with three immediate tasks: the restitution of land titles wrongfully taken before 1910, rewarding the victorious generals in an attempt to buy peace, and imposing control over the Roman Catholic Church. The implementation of the anticlerical provisions of the Constitution of 1917 were designed to remove a long-perceived bottleneck to modernization. The revolutionary government seriously underestimated the resistance its policy would provoke. The peasantry of the North Center interpreted this anticlericalism as an attack upon the sacred, a subversion to be met with force if necessary.[32] Erupting in 1926, the Cristero movement, the rebellion so named for the slogan, "¡viva Cristo Rey!," fought the government for three long years. Rebellion in the name of religion brought together frustrated peasants from Michoacán and Durango, along with those of the North Center, into open conflict with the revolutionary government. San Luis Potosí provided the Cristeros with a refuge.[33]

The Cristero war cost the region 40,000 lives and the Mexican Army lost an additional 60,000 in a protracted guerrilla conflict which neither side proved strong enough to win decisively. Brutality and severity on both sides marked the struggle.[34] In the little community of Arandas, Jalisco, for example, on three occasions whose duration totalled more than a year, the rural inhabitants were rounded up and brought into town, while federal troops stripped the countryside of anything of value.[35] When an armistice was reached in June 1929, and religious services resumed, the Army began to massacre those who had turned in their arms.[36] For the already weakened North Center, the Cristero war meant further devastation. To sum up, revolution arrived in the North Center in 1913, and a desultory peace was not achieved until 1920. Then in 1926 the rural inhabitants took up arms to defend their religion, and the North Center expressed its violence in a rebellion for the old ways. In short, the North Center bore the brunt of the Revolution, and later lost the Rebellion. Its rural society and economy had been shredded in the 16 years from 1913 to 1929.

The Beginnings of Large-Scale Migration, 1913–1929

Internal Migration

The alternative to the hardships of revolution and rebellion in the rural North Center was simply to migrate to other regions offering better employment opportunities. Indeed, perhaps one-fifth of the population moved out of the region permanently in the years 1910–1930.[37] Their destinations were Mexico City, three or four of the country's northern border states, and the southwestern United States, including California. Mexico City provided the inhabitants of the North Center with physical safety, and new opportunities for capital investment for the more affluent. Thus, while there were only 278 people from Zacatecas and San Luis Potosí in Mexico City in 1910, their number had grown to over 20,000 in 1930.[38] If the well-to-do sought refuge in the nation's capital, the rural poor generally looked to the border states and to the United States for new opportunities. The cotton fields of Coahuila attracted many migrants, and by 1930 a seventh of Coahuila's population consisted of immigrants from the North Center.[39] Similarly, Tamaulipas with its cotton fields and easy access to the United States had drawn over a tenth of its population from the states of San Luis Potosí and Zacatecas alone.[40]

Migration to the United States

Thousands of those Mexicans displaced from the North Center's agricultural sector simply continued on to the United States, where they found work in the newly irrigated fields of the Southwest and the growing industries of the Midwest. From the lower Rio Grande valley in Texas to California's Imperial valley, large-scale irrigation projects brought millions of acres into production after 1910. Ironically, much of the water that made these developments possible was, or had been, Mexican.[41] Land under irrigation in California grew by over two million acres between 1909 and 1929, while in Texas, the single decade of 1909–1919 witnessed a 317 percent increase in irrigated land.[42] A further expansion of the railroads and resultant lower transportation costs enhanced the marketability of this part of the Sunbelt's agricultural products, and stimulated unprecedented increases in output. The availability of inexpensive labor from Mexico completed the successful economic integration in the Southwest. By 1930, 200,000 persons born in Mexico lived and worked in California legally. At least 90 percent of these had immigrated to California during the period 1910–1929, and most worked in agriculture. Evidence suggests that similar trends occurred elsewhere. In northeastern Colorado, the number of Mexican laborers in the sugar beet fields increased from 1,002 in 1909, or 9.4 percent of the total work force, to 14,313, or 59.0 percent in 1927.[43]

The industrial centers of the Midwest also attracted Mexican immigrants in the 1920s. An extensive survey in 1928 conducted in four large industrial plants in the Chicago and Calumet region revealed that 75.7 percent of the more than 2,000 Mexican workers had entered the United States after 1921. Half of these workers came from Mexico's North Center.[44]

Given the high demand for cheap labor in the United States and the expulsive forces of violence and economic displacement in Mexico, it was not surprising that hundreds of thousands of Mexican nationals chose to seek a new life north of the border. But unlike today, their migration, whether legal or illegal, was not hindered by such barriers as fences, border patrols, or legal quotas. The Mexican Revolution and the Cristero Rebellion caused two waves of northward migration. As a result, from 1900 to 1930 an estimated 1.5 million Mexicans, or one-tenth of Mexico's entire population, migrated to the United States.[45]

Response: Indecision and Crisis, 1930–1940

Mexican Agrarian Reform

Government efforts to reconstitute the rural structure actually intensified problems in the countryside further. The *ejido,* communal property that could be worked either individually or collectively, became the basic element of restructuring. During the Revolution a commitment had been made to return communal landholdings that had been wrongfully taken. A strong and increasingly influential element in the postrevolutionary government favored outright land redistribution, regardless of antecedents. Central to the thinking behind such reform lay the assumption that peones were land hungry, and that redistribution would purchase at least rural peace if not goodwill.[46] In retrospect, we can discern a general policy of land distribution as appeasement for rural unrest regardless of local demand for land. Thus the North Center, which had witnessed much of the revolutionary fighting, experienced a dramatic increase in per capita ejido holdings during the 1920s. Following the Cristero Rebellion, the dividing up of haciendas continued in those areas that had given aid and comfort to the Cristeros, and took off at a dizzying pace in Guanajuato, Jalisco, and Michoacán, which had actively fought the government. The increase in *ejidatarios* (communal farmers) expressed as a percentage of the agriculturally active population illustrates the pattern. From 1930 to 1940, ejidatarios in Durango, San Luis Potosí, and Zacatecas increased by 113 percent, while those in Guanajuato, Jalisco, and Michoacán grew by 217 percent.[47]

When active reformers led by President Lázaro Cárdenas gained power in the 1930s, they envisioned rural development in terms of genuine land reform and an expanding rural infrastructure. They sought to create a strong landholding peasantry and to eliminate the Revolution's institutionalized enemy, the hacendado class. Both goals were to be achieved by expropriation and redistribution of all remaining hacienda lands. Many hacendados panicked at the prospect of government intervention, subdivided their property, and sold parcels. By 1940, 50 percent of the arable lands of San Luis Potosí, Zacatecas, and Guanajuato was held in ejidos. Many haciendas had been broken up either voluntarily or by the government, and those haciendas that remained intact were paralyzed by both lack of capital and the fear of expropriation.[48]

The Shortcomings
of Land Redistribution

The transformation of relatively efficient, surplus-producing agricultural units into small, inefficient plots permanently expanded the subsistence sector. While land hunger may have motivated the majority of peasants elsewhere, a different attitude prevailed among rural workers in the North Center. Many peones realized that breaking up haciendas—either to make ejidos or to parcel them out and sell them off—coupled with rising population, meant less for everyone. As one man in the village of Huecorio, Michoacán recalled:

Before the Revolution and before we were given land, we lived
better. We were fewer in number and we all worked on the haciendas
and sugar mills, and we ate well.... Now, we have land but not
enough work.[49]

His experience proved anything but unique. In 1930, the average daily
income of ejidatarios, who averaged only 3 hectares of arable land each in
this region, ranged from a low of 2.5 cents in Zacatecas to 12 cents in Jalisco,
with the average less than a dime. At the same time agricultural work in
California paid from 10 to 100 times as much.[50] The low return on ejidal
labor meant that many ejidatarios had to seek wage work or engage in cottage
industry in order to survive.

To many villagers in Erongaricuarío, Michoacán, "the ejido was one
of the worst things that could have happened to the village."[51] In San Luis
Potosí, 160 heads of households living on the Hacienda de Santa Teresa
petitioned the government to stop the breakup of the estate. Their petition
in part read, "We find our economic arrangements satisfactory and do not
desire a change...the land is so poor that if we are transformed into
ejidatarios, we will not be able to support ourselves." Their protest was of
no avail and Santa Teresa's 46,000 hectares passed into ejidal or private land.[52]

Resistance to subdividing the hacienda in the North Center must be
seen within the context of the preceding rural devastation which engendered
fear of any further change. Moreover, the Mexican government made only
feeble attempts to support the haphazard parceling of haciendas with the
credit and technology necessary to make small plots productive.[53] In Tonalá,
Jalisco, for example, the Hacienda de Arroyo de Enmedio, which had some
irrigated lands, was parceled out to several communities in 1927. Up to that
time the irrigated areas had yielded two annual crops: wheat in the dry season,
and maize in the rainy season. After partition, the five communities receiving
land proved unable cooperatively to manage the waterworks, and the fields
formerly irrigated went dry. Henceforth successful cultivation depended on
natural rainfall, and wheat production ceased.[54] Similarly, irrigated hacienda
lands in San Luis Potosí fell into disuse when ejidatarios failed to maintain
the extensive waterworks.[55] In Tzintzuntzan, Michoacán, a governmental
agricultural extension agent arrived around 1935 and taught a man how to
compost manure. From the Revolution to the mid-1960s that was the only
visit to the village by a government agricultural technician.[56] In the North
Center the Mexican government gave the people more individual plots, but
offered little or no rural credit, technological advice, or water with which to
make those plots productive.[57] Government alteration of the structure of
agriculture in the North Center, coupled with a lack of financial support to
sustain the transition, had the net effect of perpetuating the agricultural
inefficiency caused by the Revolution. In short, for most of the rural pop-

ulation, revolution, rebellion, and government reform meant subsistence agriculture.

In the wake of the international Depression, flight to the United States became a less attractive alternative for Mexican rural dwellers. For Mexico as a whole the Depression adversely affected the world demand for Mexican exports, thereby constricting the Mexican economy's most dynamic sector. In four short years from 1928 to 1932, Mexico's gross domestic product fell by over one-fifth. The Depression generally lowered agricultural prices. Not surprisingly then, the production of the basic commodities that occupied the majority of the rural sector in the North and West Center also declined, increasing unemployment and underemployment.[58]

Depression in the United States

In the United States' Southwest the Depression caused a drastic decline in agricultural production and wages. Shipments of cantaloupes and heads of lettuce from California's Imperial valley fell by more than 50 percent between 1929 and 1933. Mexican laborers in the Southwest United States bore the brunt of financial hard times. Their wages in California agriculture, which had averaged 35 cents an hour in the peak year of 1928, fell to 14 cents five years later. American citizens, some of whom had formerly shunned agricultural employment, began migrating and competing with Mexicans for the few jobs in the fields. By 1933, even after massive deportation of Mexicans, there were still more than two workers available for every farm job in California.[59]

A further consequence of economic scarcity involved a rising hostility toward Mexican workers. Politicians, growers, and businessmen who had welcomed Mexican migrants for two decades suddenly began calling for restrictive measures. Repatriation to state of origin became the short-term solution. From 1929 to 1933, 400,000 Mexicans were sent back to Mexico, among them many American citizens. A brief examination of the destinations of those repatriated revealed that three-fourths of them came from the border states (Nuevo León, Coahuila, and Chihuahua for 41.4 percent) and from the North and West Center (33.8 percent). Many repatriates sent to the states adjacent to the United States had originated from the North Center during the Revolution. Returnees quickly spread the word of lessened economic opportunity and increased discrimination in the United States, thereby discouraging others from seeking economic refuge north of the border.[60]

But for the repatriate, life in Mexico meant a decline in living standards and employment opportunities. Rural population rose by over 15 percent during the 1930s. This natural growth was further augmented by the repatriates themselves, who in the region comprising the North Center swelled the rural labor force by 10 percent in just a few short years.[61] At the same time, the value of per capita agricultural production declined precipitously as inflation and devaluation of the peso racked the countryside. Maize prices doubled in the North Center and production lingered behind prerevolutionary levels. Throughout the 1920s and 1930s, Mexico had to import large quantities of maize and wheat to sustain its population.[62]

A growing labor pool, static agricultural output, and the elimination of the United States as an alternate source of employment translated into drastic increases in unemployment, underemployment, and subsistence activities. Real wages may have risen temporarily during the early 1930s thanks to depressed maize prices, but the short-term benefits were far outweighed by losses of employment and market opportunities caused by the Depression.[63] Some rural inhabitants responded to these worsening conditions as they had in the previous decade by seeking work in the cities. Between 1930 and 1940, for example, 250,000 emigrants, mostly from rural Mexico, settled permanently in Mexico City.[64] But for the most part the rural community residents chose to weather the storm in their home state and perhaps receive a small parcel of land through an ejido grant.[65]

The census data tell a revealing story about their plight. In the states of San Luis Potosí and Zacatecas, an estimated 96,000 males entered the job market in 1930–1939. During the same period only 36,000 new jobs were created, meaning that as many as 60,000 people joined the rolls of the unemployed in this decade alone.[66]

The North Center in 1940:
Forty Years of Change

In 1940, the population of Mexico's North Center remained overwhelmingly rural, perhaps the only significant characteristic that had not changed after 1900. At the turn of the century, nearly two-thirds of the North Center's inhabitants resided on haciendas, the highest proportion in Mexico. The destruction of the hacienda and the rural infrastructure caused by the Revolution, the Rebellion, and governmental campaign, therefore, had its most drastic social and economic consequences in the North Center. In 1940 the country produced less maize and beans, the staples of rural diet, than it had in 1900.[67] The cultivation of cash crops and the growing of cane and agave, with their by-products of sugar, mescal, brandy and fibers, diminished or ceased altogether.

Planting of foodstuffs for subsistence became almost the exclusive goal of agriculture. The structure of agriculture had changed and with it so had productivity. The hacienda as a vital premodern economic institution had been undermined by destruction, division into ejidos, or outright parceling.

With the withering away of the hacienda went the acomodado position, the old order's most secure employment. In short, loss of agricultural vitality in the primary sector meant loss of employment opportunities. Moreover, the underemployment already structurally inherent in the hacienda system became a more widespread feature of the new rural structure now dominated by ejidos and ranchos.[68] Unemployment rose, not simply because the hacienda was destroyed, but also because the hacienda was not replaced by anything else as effective or vital.

By 1940, this fundamental alteration in land tenure had resulted in pervasive subsistence farming and economic dislocation. Significant population increase by natural reproduction, compounded by repatriates from the United States, intensified pressure upon land already being used inefficiently. There were more mouths to feed and fewer resources to do it with than in 1900. The government had failed to deliver the agricultural credit, the water, and the technological assistance necessary to complement its socioeconomic transformation of the countryside. Migration to the larger Mexican cities or to the United States became the principal adjustment mechanism for responding to the altered rural environment. In the 1930s, migration was temporarily halted by the U.S. programs to restrict Mexicans from immigrating, and the Mexican government's measures to redistribute land, which discouraged internal migration. Migration resumed in the 1940s and 1950s, and became institutionalized in rural Mexican life with the agreements known collectively as the bracero program.

2

Mexico and the
Green Revolution,
1940–1965

Before turning to the institutionalization of U.S. migration in Mexican life, we will discuss further the forces that made large numbers of Mexicans available for the U.S. labor market. The focus continues to be upon agriculture since, as we have already shown, rural agriculture and its changing structure produced most of the migrants.

The economic policies of the reformist presidency of Cárdenas (1934–1940) focused primarily upon the rural sector, which it hoped to transform by land redistribution and increased public investment in the rural infrastructure. At best these programs had debatable success, and at worst, were nonexistent. In some areas, such as the North Center, rural reform actually destroyed the production system and decreased employment opportunities.

Aggregate national data, however, seemed to portray the ejido as doing well. Thus a statistic often cited reveals that by 1940, ejidos controlled 48 percent of the nation's cultivable land, and produced 51 percent of the total value of agricultural output.[1] Proponents of land reform argued that the data clearly demonstrated communal land holdings to be as, or more, productive than privately held lands. But the first ejidos had been granted some of the very best cropland in Mexico, and should have done well. Moreover, many highly productive haciendas had reduced operations or ceased, so the ejidos' appearance of ascendancy may have been misleading.

In any event, staple crop production in 1940 still did not surpass that of prerevolutionary times. Productivity remained at premodern levels, with Mexico ranking 79th in 1940 on a world scale of maize producers—one of the worst records on the globe.[2] Further, Mexico experienced chronic shortages of basic foodstuffs throughout the 1930s, especially of wheat, and some observers went so far as to suggest that portions of the Mexican population might face starvation.[3] In short, the production of both ejido and hacienda after the 1934–1940 reforms was dismal.

The widespread and rapid pace of land reform, coupled with declining per capita agricultural production, brought a reaction from Mexico's governing circles. With the presidency of Avila Camacho beginning in 1940, the country's leaders consciously abandoned rural reform in favor of urban industrialization. The new emphasis on industrialization was to be accompanied by modernization of the agricultural sector. In the new scenario, agriculture was not the rural development intended by Cárdenas, but an increase in productivity in order to subsidize industrial growth.[4]

Mexico's subsequent governments were highly successful in effecting increases in agricultural production. In effect, a production revolution occurred, now popularly called the Green Revolution, which dramatically increased agricultural output. But it also perpetuated the endemic displacement of rural labor begun after the Revolution of 1910. The modernization of Mexican agriculture was a highly stratified process. The benefits of the Green Revolution accrued only to those having the land, capital, and initiative to take advantage of the new methods. The mass of Mexican farmers were bypassed by modernization. As was true of the spoils of the Mexican Revolution, distribution of the Green Revolution's rewards was highly selective.

The Green Revolution

Mexico's Green Revolution originated with a joint United States-Mexico technical program specifically designed to raise agricultural productivity. With the blessings of both governments, in 1943 the Rockefeller Foundation sent a group of highly qualified scientists to work with Mexico's Office of Special Studies in the Ministry of Agriculture. The stated purpose of the cooperative effort was to increase crop yields by developing new seed strains, improving soil by using fertilizers, and controlling insects and disease. The Mexican government was to back the joint endeavor by providing the necessary rural infrastructure: irrigation projects, transportation improvements, and capital. The combined venture reached a peak in the mid-1950s, when the Office of Special Studies employed 18 U.S. scientists and over 100 Mexican specialists at a total cost of $1.6 million annually.[5] When one considers aggregate figures, the results of the program are remarkable, and it fully deserves the name "revolution."

Real growth rates are particularly indicative of agricultural-sector advances. While the early 1940s witnessed sluggish growth of less than 2 percent per year, the new technology and new investment soon sent growth rates soaring. In four years, 1947–1950, agricultural production increased at the unprecedented rate of 9.4 percent annually. It slowed slightly in the 1950s, but still registered a rate of 7.1 percent for 1952–1958.[6] Overall, Mexican agriculture grew at 6.3 percent per year for 1940–1960—equal to the highest rates in the world.[7]

It is difficult to pinpoint the proportional contributions of the many factors accounting for the Green Revolution. The list would certainly include improved farm management, increased education, and mechanization. But perhaps more important was the development of high-yield, disease-resistant strains of seeds, which provided Mexican farmers with the means to increase output. The Mexican government complemented these developments by supplying large amounts of agricultural credit, and initiating massive irrigation projects. Government funds expended for irrigation increased sevenfold during the 1940s, to more than 10 million pesos annually. During the peak year of 1954, the Ministry of Hydraulic Resources spent 23.8 million pesos on various projects.[8]

Largely because of these efforts, the amount of irrigated land doubled between 1940 and 1960, and seasonal land under cultivation grew by 60 percent.[9] Table 1 indicates the irrigation program.

Government sponsorship of irrigation projects was supplemented by investments in research and extension, in livestock, and in forestry. Total public investment in the agricultural sector grew from 1.2 billion pesos in 1941–1946 to 8.4 billion pesos in 1959–1964.[10] Private investment in agriculture paralleled public investment during the same period. A formidable expansion of credit accompanied the growth of investment. Even in constant pesos, the availability of all credit to the rural agricultural sector rose 15-fold from 1947 to 1966.[11] Besides investment and credit, there were important advances in the rural transportation system, with many hitherto inaccessible areas being linked to national markets. A vigorous construction program in the 1940s and 1950s more than quintupled the kilometers of paved highway, from 4,781 in 1940 to over 27,000 in 1960.[12]

The aggregate results of the massive irrigation projects, technical advances, credit expansion, and transportation improvements were impressive. The production of maize—Mexico's most important food crop in terms of volume, value, and hectares—increased over 500 percent in the 30-year period from 1940 to 1970. In 1940, maize output amounted to only 1.6 million metric tons, but by 1968 the figure reached 9.0 million.[13]

During the same period, population grew by some 250 percent, but

TABLE 1

Newly Created Irrigated Lands
Mexico, 1926–1958

Period	Government-Sponsored New Hectares	Total Irrigated Farmland
1926–1946	419,867	1,343,359
1947–1952	386,668	2,206,527
1953–1958	565,767	3,317,616

Source: México, Secretaría de Recursos Hidráulicos, *Informe de Labores, 1974–75* (México, 1975), Appendix 5–2.

maize production neverthess far outstripped population growth.[14] The production increase was of great importance to Mexico, since half of all its arable land was devoted to maize, the cultivation of which supported more than half of the rural population. In addition, the traditional combination of maize and *frijoles* (beans) provides about 75 percent of the total caloric intake in the countryside.[15] Given the key role of maize in Mexican life, this doubling of per capita output was a remarkable achievement.

Other staples also showed geometric increases in production. Wheat harvests rose from about half a million tons in 1940 to over two million tons 30 years later.[16] Annual bean harvests doubled between 1950 and 1970, and sorghum output increased 14-fold to 2.7 million tons during the same two decades.[17] Much of this increase was accomplished by bringing more hectares of land into production, but equally significant was the research on seed strains by the Rockefeller-supported Office of Special Studies. The use of improved seeds, coupled with fertilizers and irrigation, helped raise productivity far beyond pre-1940 levels.

Wheat benefited the most from the combination of new inputs. Yields per hectare fluctuated between 650 and 850 kilograms during the 1925–1944 period.[18] Beginning in the late 1940s, yields began a consistent upward trend, breaking the 1,000 kilograms per hectare mark in 1953. In just 10 more years, wheat productivity doubled to over 2,000 kilograms per hectare. At the present writing, they have nearly doubled once again, to 4,000 kilograms per hectare.[19]

While maize harvests have not enjoyed such spectacular yield increases, as noted above (see Table 2), productivity has nevertheless increased remarkably, breaking out of a centuries-old pattern that antedated the coming of the Spaniards in 1519.[20] Lagging behind wheat, maize yields did not begin

TABLE 2

Maize and Wheat, Total Average Annual Production and Yields
Mexico, 1940–1964

	Maize		Wheat	
Period	Tons	Yields (kg/ha)	Tons	Yields (kg/ha)
1940–44	2,050,255	602	425,212	754
1945–49	2,557,797	719	417,891	838
1950–54	3,591,505	777	639,900	960
1955–59	4,842,371	837	1,214,263	1,358
1960–64	6,665,449	1,021	1,445,349	1,835

Source: Alcántara, *Modernizing Mexican Agriculture...*, tables 38 and 39, pp. 110–113.

to rise until the 1950s. By 1955–59, harvests were averaging 837 kilograms
per hectare, compared to 602 in 1940–44. Productivity reached the 1,000
kilogram per hectare level in 1964. Other food crops experienced similar
favorable rises in productivity.[21]

In short, by 1965 productivity had been transformed by the combined
effects of the changes associated with the Green Revolution. In the Mexican
view, the program initiated a scant 20 years earlier had been a dramatic
success. Outside the country, admirers of Mexico's progress went so far as
to label the development the "Mexican Miracle."[22] Food production, which
had fallen to dangerously low levels in the 1930s, surpassed population growth
so much that Mexico began to export large quantities of grains by the 1960s.[23]
Increasing agricultural productivity gained Mexico a worldwide reputation
as a model developing country. When the agricultural successes of 1945–1965
were combined with one of the highest rates of industrial growth in Latin
America, it seemed as if Mexico had indeed gotten off the treadmill of
dependency.

Modernization vs. Development

In Mexico there has been a tendency to equate agricultural production
with rural development.[24] By such reasoning, rising national productivity
must mean that the whole sector is improving. This majority opinion assumes
that the benefits of the production increases have been enjoyed by all. But
in fact the opposite occurred. The way the Green Revolution was implemented

exacerbated some traditional problems and produced new structural deficiencies in the agricultural sector. These weaknesses increasingly plagued rural Mexico.

Instead of leading to broad-based, evenly distributed improvements, agricultural progress since the 1940s has been very unequal. The gains of the "Mexican Miracle" have not brought a more equitable distribution of income, but instead have tended to concentrate income and benefits by class and region. The poorer levels of rural society—especially in the region of the sending states—have been pushed increasingly into a marginal position. To understand this better, it is helpful to examine the ways the production revolution benefited certain regions and levels of society at the expense of others.

Irrigation and Wheat

It has been said that the Green Revolution was largely biological and chemical. But political, social, and economic forces determined the way the technologies were applied. Consequently the program favored certain crops over others, and especially favored wheat over maize. Though equal sums were expended upon research on the two crops in the first years of the Rockefeller program, wheat received the most immediate benefits.[25] The U.S.-developed technical package adapted for Mexican agriculture was best suited for flat, relatively large-unit, irrigated land. Thus, implementation occurred most rapidly on wheat farms. By the early 1950s, new seed strains had been introduced in all of Mexico's major wheat-producing areas. With the addition of fertilizers, mechanization, and more available credit, wheat production and yields doubled in a decade, although the cultivated area increased only by one half.[26]

The modernization of wheat growing was immeasurably aided by the fact that the farmers who grew this crop in Mexico were better educated and more affluent than the maize-producing farmers. Their affluence was based in part on the larger size of their land units, which contrasted with the ejidal holdings.

As noted earlier, Mexico's agrarian reforms of the 1920s and 1930s distributed land in small parcels. In Guanajuato, for example, ejidatarios who received cropland between 1915 and 1945 averaged about 5 hectares per recipient.[27] This pattern continued through the 1960s, so that by the mid-1960s the average irrigated ejido parcel, considered to be the best communal land available, amounted to 4.54 hectares.[28] Consequently ejidal lands were for the most part not easily adaptable to raising wheat.

Privately held lands, on the other hand, were much larger, despite a long-standing government prohibition limiting the maximum size of cropland farms to 100 hectares. By the mid-1960s, the most affluent 56 percent of all private irrigated holdings in Mexico averaged 68 hectares in area, while the same proportion of ejido farms averaged only 10 hectares each.[29] Given the 100-hectare limitation, it became a common practice for Mexican landowners to divide their holdings within their family, thereby maintaining the integrity of their land. As a result, relatively large-scale irrigated farms persisted in Mexico, and now dominate some of the most productive agricultural areas. In the Yaqui River valley in Sonora, for example, average farm size has recently been estimated at 500 hectares, with many units of over 1,000 hectares.[30] These were the landholdings and areas that enjoyed the immediate benefits of the Green Revolution.

When the Mexican government initiated its drive toward agricultural modernization in the 1940s, one of its principal decisions was allocation of investment to irrigation projects. To make these investments where the returns would be highest, the government concentrated irrigation projects in northern Mexico along the Pacific coast, in Baja California near the Colorado River, and along the lower Rio Grande basin. During 1941–1970, the four northern states of Baja California, Sinaloa, Sonora, and Tamaulipas received 47.2 percent of all public funds allocated for new irrigation lands (see Appendix 3). These expenditures occurred despite the fact that the four states contained only 9.3 percent of the nation's total population in 1960.

In contrast, the six sending states, with 24.8 percent of total population, received only 15 percent of irrigation investment.[31] The four northern states had acquired nearly a million hectares of newly created irrigated lands by 1970, while the much more populous sending states had to be content with only 200,000 hectares.[32] Thus the creation of new irrigated lands benefited the North Pacific and the Northeast far more than the Center.

Most of the newly created cropland was not distributed to ejidatarios and small farmers, but was purchased in maximum allowable units (100 hectares) by politicians, businessmen, and federal employees. Consequently the private agricultural sector grew much faster than did the communal holdings. In Sonora, for example, ejidos accounted for 40 percent of cropland in 1940, but 10 years later their proportion had fallen to 17 percent.[33] Clearly, the distribution of the benefits of irrigation after 1940 did not favor small holders and ejidatarios.

Dry Farming and Maize

Unlike wheat, maize is grown almost exclusively on seasonal or rainfed cropland. Maize-producing farms are invariably small, and are concentrated in the central Mexican plateau stretching from Zacatecas through Guanajuato and Michoacán down to the state of Puebla.[34] For the most part, the six

THE GREEN REVOLUTION, 1940–1965

sending states are included within this populous, maize-producing belt. In 1960, maize was the principal crop of an estimated two million families, representing nearly a third of Mexico's total population. Farm size averaged only 3 hectares, irrigation in these holdings was nearly unknown, and economies of scale were virtually out of the question.[35]

Except for a few pockets of fertile, irrigated cropland, the soils in the maize-producing region are of uneven quality and yields are generally low. In the 1960s, for example, maize yields on ejidos of less than 5 hectares were under 950 kilograms per hectare, whereas irrigated lands in the Guanajuato Bajío produced maize yields of 3,500 kilograms per hectare.[36] But Bajío productivity was a rare exception rather than the general rule in the core sending states, and low productivity and small-sized landholdings continued to persist through the 1960s.

Unequal Distribution of Benefits

Data for regions in Mexico are difficult to come by, and figures for individual states are equally scarce. Nevertheless, information on regional productivity in Table 3 illustrates the comparative agricultural advantages and disadvantages just described.

In the North Pacific, which received the greatest benefits from the Green Revolution, maize and wheat productivity far surpassed that of the Center. In maize production, not only are the North Pacific yields more than 62 percent higher than those of the Center, but the rate of increase in yields between 1940 and 1960 was also greater. The comparative advantages of

TABLE 3

Maize and Wheat Yields by Region
1940–1960 (kilograms per hectare)

	North Pacific	North	Bajío	Central	All Mexico
Maize					
1940	871	464	543	580	610
1960	1,256	682	786	776	839
Wheat					
1940	1,121	735	642	463	760
1960	1,638	1,258	1,116	964	1,342

Source: Alcántara, *Modernizing Mexican Agriculture...*, from Table 12, p. 41.

economies of scale and access to water are also evident in the figures for wheat productivity. In looking at the data in Table 3, it should be borne in mind that the existence of some irrigated areas along with a few scattered but productive wheat farms within the Center (including the North Center) pushes the *overall* averages upward. Thus, in fact, the majority of farms in the sending states had yields far below those indicated in the table.[37]

Factors other than small farm size, poor soil, and lack of water also held back the agricultural sector in the core sending states. Whereas new wheat strains were rapidly dispersed among the nation's larger farms, improved maize seeds and their utilization encountered more difficulties. One of the main problems related to the kind of improved seeds developed by the Office of Special Studies. During the late 1940s and early 1950s, it produced two types of higher-yield seeds: hybrids and open-pollinated varieties. Hybrids could produce up to 70 percent more than the traditional maize seed, while the open-pollinated varieties raised yields by 50 percent.[38]

The hybrids yielded more maize, but their effectiveness was limited because productivity lasted only through one planting. Moreover, hybrids responded best when utilized in conjunction with fertilizers and adequate water. Most small Mexican farms in the 1950s lacked both prerequisites. Open-pollinated varieties, on the other hand, were relatively permanent, and thus could be used year after year, once having been disseminated. In short, the open-pollinated varieties, even though they produced less than hybrids, were more suited to Mexico's maize-production structure.

In addition, it was beyond the capability of the Ministry of Agriculture to supply enough seed annually for all farmers. Despite these drawbacks, the Office of Special Studies opted to produce only hybrids, because their short-term goal was to maximize total output. By 1956, therefore, hybrid maize comprised 96 percent of the seeds that government agencies made available to the country's farmers.[39] Since the hybrids' special requirements, noted above, made them most suitable for irrigated lands, most Mexican maize farmers were excluded from the production benefits of new high-yield seeds.

The limited use of new seed strains was also related to a general problem of information diffusion. The Mexican government supported agricultural research in the 1940s and 1950s, but it proceeded very slowly with agricultural education programs.[40] Data on extension personnel clearly demonstrate the government's apparent lack of concern for conveying new techniques through extension programs. In 1953, the Ministry of Agriculture employed only 49 extension agents for the whole country. By the early 1960s, there were still only 197 agents assigned to Mexico's 36 agricultural districts. Moreover, only 30 of these (15 percent) worked in the six sending states, although they contained 28 percent of the nation's rural population.[41] With a grossly understaffed extension service, farmers were largely left on their own to utilize the new technologies. Consequently the educated and moneyed farmers, who had the resources, knowledge, and initiative to seek out new techniques and seeds, were the ones who received most of the benefits from the maize improvements.

Other institutional constraints prohibited most Mexican farmers from sharing the benefits of the production revolution. One of the key requirements for semicommercial and commercial farmers is credit, and the government has supplied large amounts of it to the rural population over the years.[42] This was done by funneling money into private banks for disbursement, and by creating national banks for farmers, including ejidatarios. But the methods of credit distribution were strongly biased in favor of larger, solvent landowners, especially in the case of private banks. Simply, banks did not loan to small farmers because of the risky nature of their operations.[43] Reliance upon rainfall for water, and lack of technical improvements, made small-scale maize farming an unattractive investment. Consequently, large-scale commercial businesses with new technology, effective organization, and water, received the lion's share of government-guaranteed private-sector loans to agriculture.

National banks for communal landholders, who work about half of the country's agricultural land, have been more successful in facilitating rural credit. But much of this credit has been mismanaged, and the basis on which some of it was extended to small farmers worked to their disadvantage. Thus short-term loans under standard repayment agreements forced many less efficient farmers into debt, and ultimately closed off access to any credit whatsoever.[44] Further, many urban-oriented bank bureaucrats, empowered to make loan decisions, were untrained and lacked knowledge about the special needs of small farmers. Consequently they made unreasonable demands of their clients.

The national government used the ejido banks to implement agricultural production policy. Often, this meant the disbursement of credit with stipulations ranging from the crop to be grown to the day of the sowing. Such requirements, often formulated in the comfort of a Mexico City office, limited much-needed flexibility for small-scale agricultural producers. Finally, despite the fact that ejido lands grew by 25 million hectares in the decade of the 1960s, total loans of the principal ejidal bank remained constant in real value.[45]

The distribution of machinery resembled the distribution of credit. Ejidatarios and small farmers tended to pay higher unit costs for vehicles and machines, because of the cumbersome bureaucracy that controlled their sale. Middlemen who brokered machinery for the credit banks often took advantage of small farmers, charging higher-than-market prices.

Large-scale farmers, with their cooperative buying associations, made more efficient purchases at lower prices. Encouraged by middlemen and bank officials, many small farmers bought more machinery than necessary, overextending themselves, as well as underutilizing important capital equipment.[46] Finally, tractors are simply less efficient financially when used on small plots than they are on large spreads, and also in the long run tend to reduce employment.

There was another, even more serious, issue in the government's participation in agricultural modernization: corruption. One of the key inputs for the Green Revolution has been fertilizers. Fertilizer distribution illustrates the disadvantages that most farmers face in dealing with government and commercial interests. As with farm machinery, fertilizer distribution for small farmers has been dominated by middlemen, both inside and outside the government. There were many opportunities for subverting intended methods of sale, and there is no way to know the extent of such practices. But they were thought to have been widespread: in the 1950s complaints of adulteration, high prices, and black markets proliferated. One knowledgeable observer stated that it was common practice for credit-granting banks to insist on the use of fertilizers, and to sell farmers adulterated products. Similar practices also resulted in fertilizer overuse, to the detriment of some areas, and to the disadvantage of other areas where users were unable to obtain enough.

Other venal customs included altering receipts for goods sold to farmers, and charging higher-than-market prices for fertilizer and other key inputs.[47] The most important effect of corruption was to increase the cost of farming. For the organized large-scale farmer, the adverse effects of corruptive practices could be avoided, or at least minimized, through effective political demands and higher profit margins. The small farmer, on the other hand, operating with a limited margin, suffered the most from the high costs of farming in an unequal system.

Income Distribution

The discussion has presented a selected sample of the kinds of problems confronting Mexican agriculture during the development and implementation of the modernization program. Taken together, the disadvantages besetting the small farmer in Mexico raised the costs of his inputs. Large-scale commercial farmers relied much less upon government agencies and intermediaries, and thus paid less for their essential inputs. Consequently the ratio of costs to final selling price was more favorable for large-scale commercial farmers than it was for small farmers. Furthermore, the comparative disadvantages of maize-growing versus wheat-growing extended to other commercial crops such as cotton, sorghum, and sugar.

Whatever comparisons are made, the general picture is clear: while the modernization of Mexican agriculture after 1940 dramatically increased production, it sustained and sharpened the dual nature of the agricultural sector. Commercial farms with irrigated croplands flourished and grew, while smaller traditional farms relying upon maize and rainfall suffered relative income losses. During 1940–1965, most of the rural sector in the six sending states fell into the latter category, and thus was excluded from many of the benefits of Mexico's development strategy.

A variety of statistical analyses illustrate the comparative losses suffered by much of the rural sector after 1940. A few examples will suffice to make the point here. National income distribution suggests relative declines for the lowest income group in Mexico, which included more than 80 percent of all farmers. The 1950s was an especially unfavorable decade for the lower 50 percent of Mexican families: their share of total personal income fell from 19.1 percent in 1950 to 15.6 percent in 1957.[48] It is not a coincidence that agricultural modernization had its most significant impact in this decade. While the proportion of total income for the lower half of the Mexican population rose from 15.6 percent in 1957 to 18.3 percent in the late 1960s, the proportion was still below the 1950 figure.[49] In any event, these figures clearly do not suggest relative betterment for the rural population.

Equally revealing are figures developed by Clark Reynolds, who calculated rural/urban income shares for 1940–1965. The rural agricultural share of gross domestic product dropped from 22 percent in 1940 to 16 percent in 1965. This happened despite the fact that the economically active population in agriculture increased from 3.8 millions in 1940 to about 6 millions 25 years later.[50]

Changes in income distribution also show up in differences between agricultural and nonagricultural earnings. Data for 1960 and 1968 in Table 4 demonstrate that average monthly incomes for agricultural families did not even approach half of that of nonagricultural families.

TABLE 4
Average Monthly Family Income
(pesos)

Income Source	1960	1968
Agricultural	356	1,136
Nonagricultural	800	2,731
Agricultural as % of nonagricultural	44.5%	41.6%

Source: 1960, CDIA, *Estructura Agraria,* p. 189; 1968, Grindle, *Bureaucrats, Politicians, and Peasants...,* p. 80, from 1971 Banco de México study.

Further, the relative position of farm families versus nonfarm families deteriorated over the decade of the sixties, and agricultural-sector income diminished in comparison to the remainder of the country during the flowering of the Green Revolution. The relative diminution of income was felt most keenly by the majority of the agriculturists whose farming techniques remained basically unchanged, but the effects were widespread, since about half of Mexico's population relied on agricultural activities for income.

The comparative losses in income saw much regional variation. As we have implied, an analysis of income distribution in the six sending states should show that the region suffered relative setbacks during the period of agricultural modernization. Unfortunately, however, regional data on Mexico are not readily available, and researchers must rely upon data based on territorial divisions determined by Mexican government agencies. It is also unfortunate that, despite their common history and characteristics, the six sending states have never been included in the same statistical reporting unit.[51] Nevertheless, existing regional data used with caution demonstrate that in the past 40 years the rural sectors in the sending states have fallen behind the rest of the nation in economic benefits.

An excellent study completed by Ifigenia M. de Navarrete in 1960 found that families in North and Central Mexico in 1956 averaged monthly incomes of 675 and 464 pesos respectively. (According to her designation, the North and the Center of Mexico each contain three of the six sending states.) Both of these earnings figures were below the national average. In contrast, the Federal District and the North Pacific had average incomes of over 1,200 pesos monthly per family. Navarrete also calculated the numbers of families by region with monthly incomes of less than 300 pesos ($24 U.S.), and discovered that two-thirds of these families, considered to be living at subsistence or below, resided in the North and Center.[52] Given the differences in rural and urban incomes previously discussed, there is little doubt that most of these subsistence families were peasants.

Another way to measure regional agricultural income is to examine changes in per capita agricultural production. Between 1940 and 1960, for the statistical reporting units used by the government, per capita agricultural output increased by 119 percent for all of Mexico. It rose by 200 percent in the North Pacific, and by 102 percent in the North—in this case including the states of Durango, San Luis Potosí, and Zacatecas. It grew by only 81 percent in the Center, with more than a third of the nation's population.[53]

Crop production followed a similar trend during the same period. In the 1950s harvests increased in the North Pacific by 192 percent, whereas they rose only 53 percent in the Center, including Guanajuato, Jalisco, and Michoacán.

An examination of the structure of Mexican crop production reveals the causes of the regional discrepancies in agricultural production and income.

In the six sending states—Durango, Guanajuato, Jalisco, Michoacán, San Luis Potosí, and Zacatecas—maize comprised the principal crop. Indeed, in 1951–1963 these six states alone grew 43.1 percent of all Mexican maize. In contrast, the states of Sonora and Sinaloa, major beneficiaries of the Green Revolution, accounted for only 3.8 percent of maize production, even though their yields were more than twice those of the sending region. This contrasts sharply with wheat. Thus while Sonora and Sinaloa grew more than half of Mexico's wheat, the sending states produced less than a fifth of the total harvest.[54] These regional differences were reflected in the profitability and wellbeing of the individual farms.

Perhaps the best expression of comparative profitability is in Table 5, which contrasts the peso value of productivity per worker for maize and wheat in 1960.

TABLE 5

Product per Person/Day of Labor
by Crop and by Land Holding
1960 (in pesos)

Crop	Private More Than 5 Hectares	Private Less than 5 Hectares	Ejidos
Maize	21.58	21.67	21.37
Wheat	108.47	78.90	76.63

Source: CDIA, *Estructura Agraria...*, p. 1117.

Whatever the size of landholdings, wheat raising was a much more lucrative activity than maize growing. At a minimum, the wheat business generated 3.5 times the profits of maize production. Further, since wheat productivity far outstripped maize after 1960, maize growing fell even further behind wheat growing in relative profitability, and agricultural-sector income distribution became even more skewed.[55] This development did not pass unnoticed by the masses of Mexican farmers.

The relative losses in rural income in the sending states, and the comparative advantages of large-scale commercial farms over the majority of semicommercial and subsistence farms, meant that the small holder had less and less incentive to grow his crops. Moreover, the lack of incentive was especially acute in the sending states. These circumstances would have been highly unfavorable even if not accompanied by substantial population growth.

The Effects of Population Growth

Following the Mexican Revolution, a sharp decline in the death rate and a rise in the birth rate sent Mexico's population on an upward spiral that has now barely begun to show signs of slowing. At the outset of the Green Revolution in the early 1940s, the country had about 20 million inhabitants. By 1950 population had grown by 6 million, and during the height of the production revolution in 1960, Mexico's population reached 35 million.[56] At the same time, the compound rate of population growth increased from 1.7 percent in 1930–40 to 3.1 in 1950–60.[57] Despite a substantial process of urbanization during these years, rural populations living in villages of less than 2,500 still grew from 12.7 million in 1940 to 17.2 million in 1960. In the six sending states, rural population rose by 1.2 million people.[58] But even these figures are somewhat understated, since a multitude of highly rural populations live in towns and villages of more than 2,500. It should also be noted that rural families are usually larger than urban families; consequently population growth has a greater relative impact on the countryside.[59]

Population pressure on the agricultural sector, especially in the sending states, exacerbated the already deteriorating condition of the rural populace. A relative loss of exploitable land meant that the economically active population in agriculture increased faster than new lands were brought into production, and discrepancy between supply and demand increased the numbers of landless laborers. Thus, the number of economically active persons in agriculture per parcel of land grew from 1.59 in 1940 to 2.27 in 1960.[60] By the latter year, landless day laborers supported half of all agricultural families in Mexico, and their ranks had swollen to over 3 million workers. The lot of these landless people did not materially improve during the period of the Green Revolution. Instead, the rural minimum wage declined by 6 percent in real terms between 1940 and 1960, despite the fact that agricultural yields, production, and gross income skyrocketed during the same years.[61]

Unemployment and Underemployment

The increase in the supply of agricultural workers and small landholders also contributed to higher rates of underemployment and unemployment. Loss of employment opportunities was particularly acute in the maize-growing sector where relative profitability for small farmers declined.

Ejidatarios provide a representative picture of growing underemployment in the rural sector. With small parcel sizes and low productivity, these farmers rarely worked year-round. Research in the early 1960s showed that in San Luis Potosí, ejidatarios in one area worked an average of about 50 days per year.[62] In Jalisco, farmers with less than 10 hectares relying upon rainfall fared better than their San Luis Potosí counterparts, but still toiled only 111 days per year on their ejidos. For working less than 50 percent of available work days, these farmers earned the equivalent of only $269 each. Ejidatarios in Taretan, Michoacán, labored an average of 167 days on their 3.7-hectare plots but earned only $316, showing the lowest daily return of the survey.[63]

These figures are characteristic of subsistence farming. And indeed, despite the Green Revolution, the practice of subsistence farming, which received its impetus after the Mexican Revolution, continued unabated through the 1960s. In 1950, 54 percent of all farms in Mexico operated at below subsistence level (less than $80 U.S. in annual production) and accounted for 7 percent of the total value of agricultural production. Ten years later in 1960, the below-subsistence sector had declined slightly to 50 percent of the total, but its share of production dropped to 4 percent.[64] This trend appears to have continued through 1970. Despite considerable inflation, 77 percent of all persons economically active in agriculture earned less than $40 per month. These earnings contrast to the industrial sector, where only 17.5 percent of the workers fared so poorly.[65]

Another indication of the small farmer's decline was the increasing trend for ejidatarios to rent their lands, in spite of government prohibitions preventing the alienation of communal lands in any form. In one Michoacán community, renters controlled 80 percent of all ejidal lands in 1967. At a similar time in Guanajuato, perhaps as much as 30 percent of ejidal plots were rented to enterprising farmers who had the resources to make the land productive. Indeed, the practice of renting communal land has given rise to a practice called *caciquismo ejidal* (ejidal bossism) in which one or two individuals take majority control over village lands.[66]

Unemployment and underemployment also struck the landless sector. According to a recent massive study by Mexican economists, landless laborers worked an average of 190 days annually in 1950. By 1960, the number of days worked had fallen to 100, or only about 40 percent of the total possible. Real wages declined correspondingly as income for landless agricultural laborers dropped by 18 percent in the same decade.[67] Carried through to 1970, the figures suggest a continuing deterioration in the countryside.

The effects of declining real wages and lessened employment opportunities were not lost on many rural inhabitants as thousands sought jobs outside the agricultural sector. Indeed, in the sending region, the decade of the 1960s witnessed a loss of 384,000 agricultural workers, both landed and landless.[68] Conditions appeared no better in the beginning of the 1970s. One researcher concluded that, "...in 1970...over four-fifths of all the rural cultivators in Mexico, as well as an even larger proportion of landless laborers, could not meet the basic needs of their families with the proceeds of their parcels or their wage labor alone."[69]

Response: Urbanization and Migration

The unbalanced development of the countryside engendered by Green Revolution policies merely exacerbated structural weaknesses already developed during 1910–1940. High rates of population growth further limited rural opportunities in the 1940s and 1950s. The response of the rural populace was—as it had been during the Mexican Revolution and after—to migrate to other areas with greater employment potential. This migration, which grew along with the spectacular increases in agricultural production, followed several patterns.

One pattern involved migration and urbanization within state boundaries. Between 1940 and 1970, all of the sending states significantly reduced the *proportion* of population living in centers of less than 2,500 inhabitants. In 1940, roughly 70 percent of all people lived in the countryside. By 1970, however, less than half the population in the sending states lived in rural locations.[70] To describe this phenomenon in another way, between 1940 and 1960 the state of San Luis Potosí increased its rural population by 37 percent, while the state's capital grew by 113 percent.[71] The majority of the capital's gain was a direct result of rural/urban migration within the state, and most of those who migrated were agriculturalists.[72]

While migration and urbanization within individual states was significant, it was also a highly interregional movement. Consequently a few metropolitan areas of Mexico began to receive massive numbers of migrants after 1940. The best example is Mexico City, with one of the most phenomenal growth rates of any city in the world. Its 1940 population of 1.6 million nearly tripled in 20 years to 4.7 million, far outstripping national population growth. Similarly, Guadalajara in Jalisco tripled in population during 1940–1960, while León in Guanajuato grew 2.5-fold.[73] Large numbers of Mexico City's population increase came from the six sending states. By 1960, a total of 656,000 people from the sending region had taken up residence in the Distrito Federal, comprising 14 percent of the population of the nation's capital.[74]

The exodus continued unabated during the 1960s. Net out-migration from the sending states amounted to over 700,000 people in the decade, and this emigration occurred despite the fact that two major receiving cities (Guadalajara and León) are located within the region.[75] Actual rural/urban migration during this period may have topped one million, if it included the interregional movement into Guadalajara and other local cities.

Moreover, migration was not confined to the cities of central Mexico.

Another migratory pattern brought tens of thousands of rural dwellers from the sending region into Mexico's northern border states. Table 6 gives percentages of out-migrants from the sending states whose destinations were the border states. Despite the magnetic attraction of Mexico City and other large urban centers in Mexico, it is clear that many migrants from the sending region chose to seek their futures in the North.

TABLE 6

Percent of Total Out-Migration to Border States
1960

Sending States	Percent to Border States
Durango	64.7
Guanajuato	18.3
Michoacán	14.6
Jalisco	29.6
San Luis Potosí	64.1
Zacatecas	48.3

Note: See Table 7 for border states.
Source: México, *VIII censo general. . . 1960.*

Since the Mexican Revolution, the Mexican North has grown at a much faster rate than other regions save the Federal District. Much of this growth originated in the sending region. (See Table 7.)

Although 26 Mexican states send migrants to the border area, only six of these—the sending states—account for over 50 percent of the in-migration. Since the 1940s, the North of Mexico has enjoyed rates of economic prosperity unknown in other regions of the country. Thus it is not surprising that the North attracted thousands of emigrants during 1940-1970. And in light of the earlier analysis of Mexican agricultural development, it is also not surprising that so many of these migrants came from a region largely deprived of economic opportunity—the six sending states.

To sum up, we have discussed the disproportionate contribution of the sending region to the population growth of central Mexican cities and to the border states. This disproportionate contribution was the direct result of the dual development of agriculture after 1940. In a seeming inverse relationship,

TABLE 7

Total In-Migration to Border States from Sending Region
and Percent of Total In-Migration
1950–1970

	1950		1970	
Receiving State	Number	Total In-Migration (%)	Number	Total In-Migration (%)
Baja California	65,420	48.1	186,480	54.0
Coahuila	103,678	72.6	91,015	66.2
Chihuahua	67,963	66.5	108,690	66.0
Nuevo León	68,849	50.7	210,799	52.7
Sonora	16,630	26.6	50,712	31.2
Tamaulipas	95,890	43.2	140,095	44.0
Totals	418,430	52.2%	787,791	51.6%

Note: The six core sending states include: Durango, Guanajuato, Jalisco, Michoacán, San Luis Potosí, and Zacatecas.
Sources: México, *Séptimo censo general. . .1950,* and México, *IX censo general. . .1970.*

which was accentuated as the Green Revolution ran its course, aggregate increases in production were accompanied by the displacement of rural workers from the sending region.

The flow from the sending states was, however, greater than the receiving capacity of Mexico's cities and the North. Consequently, opportunities for a livelihood beyond the Mexican border attracted huge numbers of rural inhabitants from the sending region. The following chapter traces and analyzes the pattern of migration to the United States, a central theme of this study.

3

Institutionalizing Migration, 1940–1965

During the Bracero Era (1942–1964), migration to the United States became institutionalized as an important part of rural life in the sending states. Migration, not the ejido, proved to be Mexico's "way out"[1] of its development crisis of the mid-twentieth century. The new conservative political order—described by one writer as "neo-científico" in its similarity to late Porfirian rule[2]—concentrated on industrial growth and selective agricultural improvement.[3] The Green Revolution, discussed in the previous chapter, brought spectacular results, but benefited relatively few. Whether this was deliberately chosen as a long-term strategy, or simply comprised ad hoc measures for short-term solutions, the Mexican government in practice allocated more than 50 percent of its bracero contracts to rural residents of the sending states, an area that then accounted for only about 25 percent of Mexico's rural population.[4]

This selective exodus of surplus population from the overpopulated and impoverished sending region, brought short-term peace in the countryside. It also institutionalized migration through legal contracting, augmented and confirmed de facto by the accompanying illegal migration, and by desertion of braceros once in the U.S. The bracero program must be considered in some detail to illustrate its impact on both countries, an impact which has not hitherto been fully appreciated.

U.S. Labor Demand and Law

As the U.S. entered World War II, American agribusiness feared that the drain on its labor supply would jeopardize harvests. Industry also feared labor shortages as America mobilized for war.[5] As a result, the national executives of both countries concluded informal agreements to provide Mexican labor. Later, in 1951, the U.S. Congress passed Public Law 78 (PL 78) to regulate formally the recruitment, placement, and treatment of Mexican nationals as American field laborers. With various extensions, PL 78 remained in effect until Congress voted against further extensions in May 1963, permitting it to lapse on December 31, 1964.[6] During the life of the bracero program, more than 4.6 million contracts were issued to Mexicans to work in American agriculture.[7]

It is often overlooked that additional legal agreements were also concluded, augmenting and extending the bracero program into areas other than agriculture. By the end of 1944, 118,471 braceros had been brought into American agriculture, predominantly in the Southwest. But at the same time more than 80,000 additional Mexican nationals had been contracted for work on railroads in the U.S. Thus nearly 200,000 Mexicans legally entered the U.S. to work from 1942 through 1944, of whom 40 percent took nonfarm jobs. Moreover, of 137,405 Mexican laborers who left Mexico during a 20-month period in this same era, only four in 10 returned.[8] More than 60 percent of the workers in this initial phase came from the six sending states.[9]

Labor Recruitment in Mexico

Recruitment procedures of the Bracero Era forced the rural poor into contact with lower-level Mexican administrative officials on a scale not previously experienced, adding to their general woe. The need to bribe merely to get routine bureaucratic work accomplished intensified dramatically as potential workers needed official papers even to compete for jobs in the U.S., and the only way the papers could be obtained involved giving the appropriate *mordida* (bribe) to the right official.

Another phenomenon which ordinarily occasions no remark is the fact that while procedures are established and forms printed, many people do without them. Both the mordida and an unawareness of the correct formal procedures caused many of the desperate jobless to take informal action. This contributed to the massing of tens of thousands of men at selected departure points, usually overloading the local facilities. Conditions at these sites were frequently miserable. At Hermosillo, Sonora, some 12,000 men hoping for work camped out in a city park. At the little crossroads of

Empalme, Sonora, a staging center for braceros coming to California in the late 1940s and 1950s, it was common for 25,000 men to gather at the peak of the contracting season. Men would wait in line for days, not daring to leave to eat or to relieve themselves lest they miss a chance to work. Empalme could scarcely accommodate the migrants, since it normally housed only 10,000 people.[10]

What process produced these conditions? The formal process included a decision by the Mexican Ministry of the Interior to designate the areas of Mexico with surplus labor. Quotas were drawn up and assigned to the various states. State governments parceled out requirements among local magistrates, who in turn issued *permisos* to locals desiring work in the U.S. The prospective laborer obtained his permiso by paying a bribe, and was then sent to one of the migration centers for actual selection.[11] On various occasions more than 50,000 men flocked to the national stadium in Mexico City, hoping to be chosen as a bracero.[12]

But even when a man with a permiso arrived at a migration center, his prospects for employment still were not assured. Another set of officials needed bribing. Faced with a surplus of candidates, these local officials sold places in line. Those who could not pay had to wait or consider entering the U.S. illegally.

Those with permisos at the migration station also confronted another group, the *libres,* usually penniless people like themselves, but who had come without papers. The libres outnumbered the permisos, and waited virtually without prospect of being called. Some did find a quasi-legal way out. In Sonora they could work on large farms and ranchos for 15 days at low wages in return for being placed on a *lista* at the migration center. Placement on the lista meant certain employment in the U.S. and eliminated the need to pay a mordida. Libres welcomed this opportunity since otherwise they had to wait an average of two or three months to be selected as a bracero.[13]

The Illegal Corollary:
The Undocumented Bracero

Mexicans engaged in acquiring bracero papers and a place in line often had to borrow money to get started. Those with some security, such as a house, usually pledged it against an advance of approximately 300 pesos. Such short-term loans, often made by local money lenders, customarily bore an interest rate of 5 percent a *month*.[14] But by the time he arrived at the migration center, even a man with a permiso may have exhausted his ready cash. In some cases even employment would not alleviate indebtedness. Thus some contracts were issued for such a short period that the man taking one could not earn enough to repay the original loan, let alone save.[15]

Since the border proved readily passable, the costs in time, energy, and money involved in dealing with the formal system could be easily circumvented by illegal crossing. For a few pesos the novice could hire a guide to lead him to the border, and if necessary he could be ferried across for a few pesos more.[16] Cost differences between following the rules of the game and simply ignoring them provided powerful incentives for the poor to enter the United States without papers.

Naturally, the "undocumented bracero" did not need to limit his employment to agriculture. Available evidence strongly suggests that throughout the Bracero Era large numbers of illegals, either those who entered without papers or those who deserted following expiration of a bracero contract, worked in a variety of occupations. In 1949, for example, the secretary of the El Paso Central Labor Union estimated that illegal workers from Mexico constituted from 29 percent to 43 percent of the city's total labor force.[17] American fear again mounted in the 1950s, and at one time manifested itself in the form of "Operation Wetback." During 1954, an augmented Border Patrol in a military-style maneuver apprehended and deported more than one million Mexicans whom the Immigration and Naturalization Service (INS) determined had entered illegally.[18] Despite such spectacular examples of increased law enforcement, Mexicans continued to enter without papers. In California's Imperial valley in the early 1960s, nearly two-thirds of the agricultural crops were harvested by Mexican-born laborers, half of whom were in the country illegally.[19]

U.S. Labor Markets

Dynamism characterized the labor markets in the Bracero Era. The relationship of U.S. labor demand and supply varied with U.S. participation in World War II and the Korean conflict, and with the changing structure of agriculture and industry, as mechanization began selectively to displace members of the workforce. As difficult as it is to measure with precision the magnitude of demand, the evidence shows that the level generally remained high throughout the period.

War mobilization initially meant a dramatic loss of farm labor. In early 1943, the U.S. Bureau of Agricultural Economics estimated that 2.8 million workers had left agriculture over the previous three years.[20] Mexicans came to take their places. Again during the Korean conflict, U.S. agriculturalists anticipated manpower losses, and again braceros filled those jobs. One Mexican source estimated that between 1943 and 1953 one million braceros went to the U.S., accompanied by another million without papers.[21] But the peak period for bracero labor was between 1956 and 1960, when an average of 443,000 contracts were issued annually.[22] In all, braceros worked in 27 of the continental states of the U.S., but California was the state of preference because of higher demand, higher wages, and better treatment than elsewhere.[23]

Some impressions of factors affecting the farm labor market can be based on the experience of the major states using braceros: California and Texas.[24] Examining relevant features of California agriculture requires focusing on the changes between productivity per acre and per unit labor cost. In general the output of California farms can be classified in the categories of field and vegetable crops, fruits, and nuts.[25] Cotton was the most important labor-demanding crop at the beginning of the Bracero Era. Cotton required irrigation and therefore needed more man-hours per acre than dry-farming. Thus irrigated cropland in combination with a scarcity of machinery produced a strong demand for hand labor.

But the Bracero Era also coincided with the introduction of new, commercially marketable mechanical devices, chief among which were the cotton stripper and the cotton picker. The latter device was steadily adopted in California, so that during the 1951-1952 season more than half of California's cotton was harvested by machine.[26] In absolute terms, the numbers of mechanical pickers rose from 400 in 1948 to 5,500 in 1952, a prodigious 13-fold increase.[27] The number of man-weeks needed to harvest a bale of cotton fell from 1.28 to .74 in the same period,[28] a figure further reflected in the decline of maximum harvest laborers in cotton by 19.4 percent.[29] Thus cotton yields increased while labor costs decreased.

In Texas, a different set of conditions prevailed. Cotton, the crop initially demanding the greatest amount of labor, was mechanized far more slowly than in California. The harvest cycle began in the lower Rio Grande valley in July, and ended on the High Plains in late December.[30] The High Plains quickly adopted the cotton stripper, which especially suited the storm-resistant plants cultivated there. Nevertheless, by 1953 less than a quarter of Texas cotton was machine harvested, only half the percentage of the California crop.[31] Consequently the demand for hand labor persisted longer and at higher levels in Texas than in California. But overall wages in cotton in Texas had declined by 11 percent following World War II.[32] That average figure masked regional variations, since the same tasks performed in the lower Rio Grande valley commanded $0.75 to $3.00 an hour more in other parts of the state.[33]

In the late 1950s, Texans began to accelerate the mechanization of cotton. Anticipating that the time could come when legal foreign labor would be unavailable, farmers began buying spindle pickers and stripper harvesters. By 1960, over half the state's cotton was harvested by machine, a figure that rose to 90 percent in 1964, the last year of the bracero program. Within two years, 95 percent of the cotton in Texas was being taken from the fields by machine.[34] But the results did not benefit the domestic worker. In 1966 a Texas state report observed:

> An unfortunate corollary of this development [mechanization to reduce dependence on foreign workers] was, however, that it affected our domestic migrants as well, depriving them of their major field of agricultural employment and income at the very time when they might have expected to gain the benefits resulting from the elimination of competition from the alien [sic] labor.[35]

In California, cotton workers displaced by mechanization found other crops to harvest. Table grapes, lettuce, strawberries, tomatoes, and citrus fruits all demanded hand labor, and all expanded significantly from the early 1950s to the mid-1960s. In 1965, California produced 40 percent in value of all fruit and nut harvests and 35 percent of all fresh and processed vegetables in the United States.[36] Mexicans harvested these crops. Two years before the bracero program ended, Mexicans constituted nearly 90 percent of the temporary workforce in tomatoes,[37] 71 percent in lettuce, and 82 percent in lemons.[38]

The California tomato industry illustrates the bracero-related adjustment made in the early '50s and suggests its consequences. Not until 1952 did braceros begin to figure significantly in the canning-tomato harvests.[39] They worked at fairly constant wages for several years. In Ventura County, for example, the wage index did not change between 1953 and 1959.[40] Mechanization took longer to enter the industry, so that by the end of the bracero program only 25 percent of canning tomatoes were harvested by machine.[41] We will return to developments in processing tomatoes in the post-Bracero Era in another section, but here we must note two things. First, enough labor was available for these work-intensive crops and second, with real wages remaining constant over time, the farmers enjoyed lower labor costs.

The tomato-processing industry, with its steady shift to Mexican workers during the Bracero Era, tells us two things about California agriculture in the period. First, lower labor costs meant increased employer profits and decreased labor income. With wages fairly constant and the cost of living rising, real wages for farmworkers declined. While it would be impossible to prove that the availability of Mexican workers depressed farm wages, it would be equally impossible to prove that such availability had no effect. Wages for several California crops reached a plateau between 1948 and 1964, and to the employer that meant savings.[42] Some of those savings were turned back into agribusiness in the form of machinery investments. Ironically, declining real wages for Mexicans helped to finance the mechanization that contributed to their later displacement from agriculture.

Second, constant farm wages, with their real income losses over time, made farmwork unattractive to citizen workers. As long as sufficient Mexican labor was available to work at the prevailing wage, there was no reason to increase wages. Such a condition suggests, but does not prove, that Mexicans displaced citizen workers in agriculture over time. As we shall see later, at the conclusion of the Bracero Era only the law about braceros had changed, not the demand for their labor and the profits that their labor meant to their employers.

If Mexicans laboring in California and elsewhere were actually working themselves out of future jobs, they had scant hope for an alternative in Mexico. Most of the braceros, having come from the sending region which was the most critical of the Revolution, were unwanted at home and considered potentially dangerous there.

National Mexico:
The Politics of Blame

In Mexico, since 1915 disaffection with the victors of the Revolution has been constant if relatively quiet. In that year, Mariano Azuela, a former physician with the medical corps of Pancho Villa's famed *División del Norte* and lifelong resident of Lagos de Moreno, Jalisco, shared with an indifferent world his personal experiences and pessimistic vision of the Revolution by publishing his novel *Los de Abajo* (The Underdogs) in an obscure newspaper in El Paso, Texas.

Los de Abajo did not come to general intellectual attention and acclamation in Mexico until 1924, but since then it has become generally acknowledged as *the* novel of the Revolution.[43] Azuela saw at first hand the physical and moral destruction that touched rural and urban dwellers in the battlefields of the North Center. Such criticism of the Revolution has been nullified by the ruling party by enshrining Azuela as a critic of Pancho Villa, rather than of the entire Revolution, thus illustrating the skill of the "Revolutionary Family"[44] in fending off blame.

Another example of the "politics of blame" concerns governmental responses to political discord in the sending region just prior to and during World War II. Once ended, the frustration and violence that had led to the Cristero uprisings of the 1920s lay quiet for less than 10 years. In 1937 a political party was formed, seeking to give ideological expression to the religious feelings of the rural poor, as well as to openly oppose the government's land practices. They were known as the *Sinarquistas* and their political party, the PNS, was a serious challenge to the government. Although founded in León, Guanajuato, the PNS drew adherents from the rest of central Mexico, especially Michoacán and Jalisco. Party leaders, drawn from the professional classes, adopted the simple lifestyle of the Franciscan monks who had originally Christianized the area, and went to rural villages to live and organize the peasants. By 1941 they claimed 500,000 followers, and by 1944 over 900,000.[45]

Sinarquista complaints that the Revolution had impoverished rural central Mexico were true. In avowing protection for the church, the Sinarquistas openly appealed to the deep conviction of many poor that the sacred should not be attacked. At the same time, the authoritarian structure of the party caused it to be viewed by outsiders as an extension of the fascism of Spain's Falangist movement.[46]

The Mexican government moved against the Sinarquistas cautiously. The government found itself limited both by the popular following the movement attracted, and by its own absorption in international problems attendant on Mexico's nationalization of the petroleum industry in 1938. Foreign companies, mainly American and British, successfully urged their governments to impose an embargo on Mexican petroleum exports. The industry faced serious difficulties, which were significantly alleviated by British entry into World War II, and later removed by American involvement.[47] The Allies needed oil. They also feared subversion in the hemisphere. American reporters and visitors, aided by Mexican investigations, began to perceive German and possibly Nazi influence behind the Sinarquistas. One influential newspaperwoman wrote in 1942 that, *"The Sinarquistas may easily become the most dangerous fifth column in the Americas."*[48]

World War II and the United States gave the Mexican government the means to demolish its opposition. In 1940 the Sinarquistas had strongly supported the candidate who opposed the ruling party. Subsequently there had been some clashes, and blood spilt on both sides. In 1942, when the President of the Republic watched 15,000 union members and governmental officials demonstrate in his favor in Mexico City, simultaneously in León, Guanajuato, an alleged group of 80,000 Sinarquistas rallied for their movement.[49] On June 22, 1944 the Mexican government used charges of subversion to justify drastic action against the Sinarquistas. It outlawed the PNS, forbade public meetings, and suppressed the newspaper. All this was done on the grounds of national security. The Sinarquistas went underground, but did not go away. Nearly a year later, some 50,000 Sinarquistas assembled in León to demonstrate their power.[50]

While the Mexican government moved to deny the party national juridical existence, it had simultaneously worked to destroy the movement's base by exporting its manpower. The labor contracts for braceros, as pointed out earlier, heavily favored the sending region, the area of greatest Sinarquista support. Unable to provide rural opportunity for the braceros in Mexico, the government sought that opportunity in the United States.

Nearly two-thirds of the braceros came from areas of Sinarquista activity.[51] Thus, for the government, encouraging migration meant rural peace through American agriculture. By this twofold approach to the Sinarquista apparatus and its rural source of support, the Mexican government rendered the movement moribund by the early 1950s. All that remained was PAN, the Partido Acción Nacional, a splinter group from the Sinarquistas, which has since become the contemporary loyal opposition.[52]

Rural Mexico:
The Socioeconomic Impact

The bracero program profoundly altered rural life in the sending region by institutionalizing migration to the United States as an accepted and expected life experience. The families of rural North and West Central Mexico found the money to survive, and in some cases to prosper, on the earnings of a family member working in "the North," either as a documented bracero or as an illegal laborer. The percentage of working-age males who made the trip to the United States between 1942 and 1964 often proved surprising. In Tzintzuntzan, Michoacán, 50 percent of the adult males had been to the U.S. by 1960, many of them on 10 or more occasions.[53] Other village studies yielded similar results: "most able-bodied village men" from Las Animas, Zacatecas, participated;[54] San José de Gracia in Michoacán frequently sent 20 percent of its workforce in a given year;[55] by 1962 Huecorio, Michoacán, had seen a third of its adult male population obtain work experience in "the North";[56] an anonymous village in West Central Mexico had sent 53 percent of its male laborers,[57] and 34 percent of the households in another unnamed community in Michoacán had a family member who had worked as a bracero. A field study of nine villages in Jalisco found that "just about everybody went."[58]

From a social standpoint the education received and transmitted by the documented and undocumented bracero had a twofold effect. The Mexican migrant learned directly the process of traveling to the border, crossing it, and finding work. He learned new social mores as well, and became familiar with American foods, money, alcoholic beverages,[59] housing, and entertainment. The more enterprising learned some English, and saw their opportunities expand. Above all, the bracero learned directly what he could and could not do, and learned not to fear the journey. Indirectly, on his return, the bracero taught his family and friends what it had been like through his stories, his spending patterns, and his financial support of his family.

During the 22-year period, more than 4.6 million contracts were issued.[60] Discounting for repeaters by dividing by three, we estimate a new number of actual documented braceros at one million for the era. If we follow the conventional wisdom that the number of undocumented entrants equalled those with papers,[61] this gives an overall minimum of two million men who learned to work in the U.S. during the contracting years. Allowing for two other males in a family (brother, cousin, nephew, son), then these two million workers influenced at least four million other male Mexicans,[62] preparing by example a new generation of migrants who began entering the job market as the bracero program formally came to an end. (See Table 8.)

Both documented and undocumented braceros remitted part of their earnings to their families in Mexico. The Mexican government attempted to track postal money orders processed through the Banco Nacional, and their records show that more than 7 billion pesos came to Mexico over the course of the Mexican labor program.[63] Such a figure is far too low to approximate the total remitted, as it was customary for men to save while working and to return to Mexico with a lump sum. One observer noted that from 1948 to 1960 the average bracero saved from 8,000 to 10,000 pesos for each year that he worked in the U.S.[64] Obviously, then, the 7-billion-peso figure represents an undercount, and may be short by 50 to 90 percent.

TABLE 8

Minimum Number of Braceros Sent to the United States by Origin, Selected Years 1942-1964

States	1942-1944	1953-1954	1960-1964
Durango	1,438	61,004	62,048
Guanajuato	19,848	58,761	132,263
Jalisco	8,202	54,458	110,054
Michoacán	34,069	48,371	143,527
San Luis Potosí	7,718	23,560	58,456
Zacatecas	7,619	56,962	91,831
Total, Six Sending States	78,894	303,116	598,179
Total Mexico	137,405	494,435	1,163,054
Percent from Sending Area	57.4%	61.3%	51.4%

Note: The numbers above represent minimum figures because they reflect only permisos issued by the Mexican government. They do not include the libres who secured bracero positions at the migration center. Further, the figures do not include those many bracero candidates from the sending states who traveled to Mexico City and obtained papers there.

Sources: Whetten, *Rural Mexico,* Table 51, p. 269 for 1942-1944; Lázaro Salinas, *La Emigración de Braceros,* Appendices 1 and 2, unpaginated, 1953-1954; México, *Anuario Estadístico...1964-1965,* cuadro 3.29, pp. 118-119, for 1960-1964.

The opportunity to use this windfall income to develop the rural structure of the sending states was lost, due to shortcomings of Mexican national development policy during the Green Revolution. While examples can be found of braceros investing in renewable resources, the list is quickly exhausted. In the fertile Bajío region of Guanajuato, three ejidatarios pooled their bracero savings and bought a tractor. They rented the vehicle out as well as their services to other ejidatarios whose plots were too small to permit personally financed mechanization.[65] The fact that legally ejidatarios could not become braceros[66] testifies to the straitened circumstances many of them faced in their daily struggle for survival. In a village in Michoacán one man saved enough from his bracero earnings to open a small store, another purchased an American sewing machine and became a tailor to escape agriculture, and yet another bought an irrigation pump and tripled his production.[67]

But such examples of productive use of bracero savings are exceptional. The usual pattern followed a more wasteful course. Traditionally valuing land, whether or not it could be made productive, campesinos who became braceros sought to acquire a small plot for themselves, and in the process drove up prices for relatively worthless hectares. New homes were built or old ones refurbished in imitation of American models. Clothing styles of "the North" became popular, particularly "bluejeans," as did radios and, where electricity permitted, even television sets. Alcohol consumption patterns even began to change as beer and liquor supplanted the traditional native drink, pulque, in many villages.[68]

Often his new-found ways made the returned bracero restless and uncomfortable in his village, prompting him to migrate again, this time either to an urban center in Mexico or back to the U.S.[69] For still more, experience in the U.S. meant not going home again. For the more enterprising, escape from the poverty of subsistence farming and the lack of opportunity meant a permanent move north. This was Mexico's most serious loss, the exodus of talented, ambitious people who undoubtedly would have become part of the Mexican middle class. One Mexican historian commented: "When everything is added up, it turns out that the bracero program took more than it gave."[70]

Attempts were made to slow the workers' exodus to the U.S. Governors of the states of Guanajuato, Jalisco, and Michoacán at various times protested manpower shortages caused by the bracero program. At the same time and in the same states municipal officials complained of ejidatarios abandoning their plots to go to the U.S.[71] In January 1954, a group of newspapermen issued a manifesto urging aspiring braceros not to leave Mexico without permisos. They circulated more than 20,000 copies of their manifesto in the sending states alone. All activities were to no avail.[72] "...The annual emigration of braceros to the United States," according to the pessimistic

Mexican jurist Jorge Vera Estañol, stemmed from ". . . [a] lack of an attractive
return from the cultivation of communal lands."[73]

The social consequences for the Mexican bracero have been little appreciated. Only recently has a voice been raised to describe the costs of this
migration to family and spirit. Francisco Jiménez, son of a bracero and
himself a child laborer in the fields of California, has written of his experiences
in both Spanish and English. His short story, "The Circuit," poignantly
relates the impact of migration on a child working in a Spanish-speaking
environment trying to attend school in an English-speaking milieu. "Arado
sin Buey" crystallizes an image of exploitation of braceros by the man many
hated most—the Mexican labor contractor. When writing in English, Jiménez
belongs to the tradition of John Steinbeck. In Spanish, he continues the indict-
ment of the Revolution first begun by his fellow Jaliscense, Mariano Azuela.[74]

U.S. Policy Debate and
Termination of the Program

While the bracero program ostensibly affected only one region of the
United States—the Southwest—and therefore might have been ignored by
the nation, local discrimination, working conditions, and citizen workers'
fear of job displacement brought the bracero to national attention. Ultimately
the U.S. legally terminated the program unilaterally on December 31, 1964.
The issues and interest groups involved, together with the executive action
taken, strongly foreshadowed our contemporary debate.

When the Mexican government originally entered into agreements with
the United States government, one of the stipulations was that laborers not
be used in states where there was discrimination against Mexicans. By this
standard Texas could not legally receive any braceros during the war years.
Nevertheless, legal and illegal entrants did work there. In 1947, at Mexican
government request, Texas began the process of "legalizing the illegal" or
taking the detected undocumented worker to the border and having him
recross legally. From 1947 to 1949, 142,000 undocumented workers had their
status regularized.[75] Such practices made a mockery of the normative procedures and laws.

With Texans able to do their own recruiting in Mexico after 1949, direct
solicitation of documented and undocumented workers rose.[76] In 1954, when
the INS mounted its military-style "Operation Wetback" with the assistance
of the National Guard, fear of the event preceded it. During the first 30 days
of the drive in Texas, more than 60,000 Mexicans fled through ports of entry
into Mexico to avoid harassment, and countless others crossed the Rio Grande
any way they could.[77]

While the INS considered their sweep a success, believing that the "wetback problem" had been eliminated, their self-congratulation was premature. The INS apprehension figures declined, but so did its manpower. Operation Wetback involved augmenting the Border Patrol and making apprehensions at night. After the operation was over, the old hours and low staff levels prevailed. In short, although INS apprehensions declined dramatically after 1955, so did its law enforcement efforts. (During Operation Wetback the INS removed over 20,000 illegal Mexicans from industrial jobs in Spokane, Chicago, Kansas City, and St. Louis.[78]) The operation demonstrated what dedicated law enforcement could achieve temporarily, but it seems unlikely that the 1954 exercise had any lasting effect on migration.

On the other hand, projects like Operation Wetback awakened national concern about the braceros. Church groups, civil rights activists, liberals, and concerned citizens began to examine the farm labor camps, deploring the conditions they found. Housing, sanitation, food, education, and medical care were all substandard by American definition.[79] The fact that Mexicans tolerated these conditions, and may even have found some of them an improvement over circumstances in Mexico, was dismissed as irrelevant to the issues in the U.S. Critics argued that either the camps should be upgraded or, failing that, the program terminated. Scant attention was given the question of how the bracero would then feed himself and his family.

In the late 1950s and early 1960s U.S. secretaries of labor complained that foreign labor, because of its low cost, adversely affected the wages and working conditions of citizen workers. Organized labor expressed similar views, holding that the presence of cheap labor hurt the quality of life for all laborers. Nowhere were these charges confirmed by direct evidence. But late in 1961, President John F. Kennedy signed a two-year extension of the bracero law only reluctantly, claiming:

> The adverse effect of the Mexican farm labor program as it has operated in recent years on the wage and employment conditions of domestic workers is clear and cumulative in its impact. We cannot afford to disregard it.[80]

Strong pressure from the Mexican government secured an additional year for the program, but Congress voted to let it lapse at the end of 1964.

Mounting public opinion, unconfirmed reports of negative economic impacts on the domestic labor market, and a general spirit of purging an unknown evil from the body politic, coalesced in the termination of the program.[81] But two facts stand out beyond all others in the ending of the Bracero Era. First, the U.S. tried to deal with an economic and social problem by imposing a legal solution. From January 1, 1965 onward there would be no more braceros because it was against the law. Few realized that demands for cheap labor in this country, and migration as the only alternative to impoverishment in Mexico, might override such legal strictures.

Second, removal of contract workers did not automatically mean im-proved conditions for citizen workers, mainly because the termination of the bracero program failed to reduce the supply or demand for Mexican farm-workers. Despite a rise in the minimum wage to $1.40 per hour, which might have attracted more citizen workers to the fields, California growers, farmers, and ranchers maintained their preference for Mexican hands. A farm news-paper reflected a widespread sentiment:

> That $1.40 paid to a typical young school drop-out taken from the streets of Oakland or Stockton is more like a wage of $2.80 an hour in relation to the amount of work this youth can do compared to a hardened Mexican worker used to physical labor.[82]

Thus, the demand for braceros did not end with congressional termination of the contract. Nor did the labor supply in Mexico diminish. In the 1970s, the structural weaknesses of Mexican development, compounded by per-sistently high population growth rates, caused even greater dislocations in the sending region.

4

Mass Migration
to the United States,
1965-1980

Mexico's rapid population growth and its inability to provide jobs for new workers entering the labor force continued throughout the 1960s and 1970s. Although legally terminated on January 1, 1965, the bracero program simply went underground instead of disappearing.[1] National attitudes in the U.S. had shifted to favor exclusion, but local labor demand in certain U.S. regions did not reflect the national sentiment. Agriculture, the largest employer of braceros, made some adjustments, but the overall demand remained high and the Mexican labor supply increased. In California, for example, in 1964 the total seasonal labor force consisted of around 225,000 workers, 30 percent of whom were Mexican contract laborers. After 1965 the overall seasonal workforce declined, but only by about 18 percent. At the same time, many Californians began to leave the fields for the increased educational opportunities offered by the "Great Society" or for the Vietnam conflict. Their places, as well as those of the Mexican contract laborers, were taken by Mexican citizen workers who were simply included in the employment reporting category of "hired domestic seasonal." (See Appendix 5.)

But opportunities for employment were not limited to agriculture. A changing age structure in the U.S. coupled with an increased demand for semiskilled, inexpensive labor in services and light industry attracted thousands of Mexican workers, and in the process boosted a rather controlled, regionally and agriculturally specific migration to a more broadly based, massive movement of people. The following discussion treats this process and considers the questions of migrants' destinations, changing labor demand, U.S. immigration legislation, and increased income differences between the U.S. and Mexico.

Destination Patterns and Preferences

During the Bracero Era Mexicans preferred to work in California, although many were sent to work in Texas where wages and working conditions did not compare to those in California. Unrestricted by bracero contracts after 1965, Mexican migrants began exercising their preference for California. In 1968, deportation figures for the U.S. Southwest still showed substantial numbers of illegal migrants living and working in Texas. In this year, 40 percent of the illegals apprehended in the Southwest were in Texas, while 50 percent were found in California.[2] Ten years later, in 1978, the pattern was different.

A study by the National Center for Information and Labor Statistics in Mexico (CENIET) revealed that 53 percent of migrants from the sending states went to California, but that Texas's share had dropped to 21 percent. (See Table 9.) Admittedly, the samples are not very comparable but they do clearly indicate a continued and growing preference for Mexican migrants to seek their fortunes in California over other southwestern states. Further, the CENIET data permit a sense of the distribution of interregional migration. Mexican migrants from Michoacán and Jalisco overwhelmingly favor California, while those from San Luis Potosí and Durango prefer Texas. Custom and migration networks undoubtedly help contour these interregional linkages.

Further refinements in assessing the destinations of migrants are made possible by several village surveys. These surveys bear out the general picture sketched by the national samples: interregional migration between Mexico and the U.S. is geographically specific; there is a strong preference to migrate first to the U.S., and second to the Mexican North or to a Mexican urban center. One village survey conducted in the state of Jalisco in 1975-76 particularly illustrates the pattern. (See Table 10.) Of the 822 out-migrants in the survey, 83 percent went either to the United States or to a Mexican border state. Over two-thirds of those going to the U.S. settled in California. These findings are significant because they suggest that generalizations cannot be founded upon the results of one village survey, or one regional survey. Further, specific differences in migration patterns and preferences among villages or regions are essential to understanding the dimensions of and solutions to the phenomenon.

TABLE 9

Mexican Illegal Migrants
Core Sending Region Contribution to California and Texas
1978 (by percent)

	California	Texas	Total
Durango	33.0	37.3	70.3
Guanajuato	52.3	21.7	74.0
Jalisco	67.0	2.5	69.5
Michoacán	82.9	6.9	89.8
San Luis Potosí	10.8	57.9	68.7
Zacatecas	63.1	19.9	82.0
Total	53.7%	21.4%	75.1%

Source: México, CENIET, *La Encuesta Nacional de Emigración. . . 1978,* Gráficas 1–1.16. The figures for all of Mexico in this study show that California and Texas absorb 82 percent of all Mexican out-migration. The sample size was 22,822.

TABLE 10

Destination of Out-Migrants from Villa Guerrero, Jalisco
1975–1976

	Totals	
Destination	**Number**	**Percent**
United States	564	69
North Mexico	116	14
Urban Mexico	125	15
Miscellaneous	17	2
Totals	822	100%

Source: Shadow, "Differential Out-Migration. . .," in Camara and Kemper, *Migration Across Frontiers. . .,* Table 2, p. 71, with arithmetical errors in the original table corrected.

Changing Labor Demand:
Agriculture

In the 1960s, higher education and the U.S. military removed large numbers of young men from American fields and factories. The opportunities thus opened for Mexicans to work in the U.S. contributed further to the unprecedented upsurge in Mexican migration to the United States during the late 1960s.[3] This rise in employment potential was more pronounced in the services and in light industry than in the agricultural sector of the American economy. Nevertheless, we begin by considering developments affecting agriculture, continuing to focus attention on California and Texas.

California's seasonal agricultural workforce declined approximately 11 percent in 1950 to 1977.[4] Yet there was a surplus of agricultural labor in many of these 27 years, as there is today.[5] Nevertheless, farmers rarely have considered the supply satisfactory.[6] These seemingly contradictory perceptions are explained by grower anxiety over labor sufficiency at harvest time, and by changing employment and unemployment rates caused by innovations in agricultural technology and labor management.

With the passing of the bracero program, California farmers sought new ways to ease their reliance on casual labor, defined as occasional, informal working arrangements. Mechanization increased, especially in the crops requiring hand work. The tomato canning industry is a good example. It was noted earlier how by the end of the Bracero Era only 25 percent of canning tomatoes were harvested by machine. But the nation's demand for canned tomatoes was increasing. Thus in 1952, California's tomato canning industry processed around 2 million tons of tomatoes, 35 percent of the nation's total. Between 1960 and 1975, per capita tomato consumption rose 77 percent, reflecting increased demand for catsup, chili sauce, tomato paste, puree, and sauce, and California supplied most of that demand. Thus in 1977 California processed over 7 million tons of tomatoes, 90 percent of national production. Over 90 percent of this had been machine harvested, and the 1977 labor force was radically different from that of the earlier years. By the late 1970s over two-thirds of the workers were women, 90 percent of them of Mexican descent, and the majority were local residents.[7] The labor force had also shrunk in size dramatically. A comparative study by the University of California found that harvesting processing-tomatoes by hand required 5.26 man hours per ton, while machine harvesting needed only 2.85.[8] In short, mechanization in this industry permitted nearly a 50 percent savings in labor.

Developments in the tomato-processing industry highlight two characteristics of some areas of California agriculture. First, and most obvious, is selective displacement of labor. Second, and less obvious, is the contribution to decasualization, which is the regularizing and formalizing of the employer/worker relationship. Mechanization in this industry has meant a smaller, more stable workforce than obtained under the more casual labor contractor system.

Decasualization has also been attempted with other agricultural crops without mechanization, e.g., the citrus industry. The Coastal Growers Association, Oxnard, California, comprises 300 citrus producers whose harvest workers are recruited, paid, and managed through one organization. Before 1965 nearly all the seasonal work had been performed by braceros. In 1965, with the bracero program and supply gone, Coastal Growers hired more than 8,000 workers. High turnover and uncertainty about labor availability caused management to institute changes. It wanted an orderly workforce and clearly preferred Mexican labor.

Consequently, it began to hire only Mexican workers who had proper papers. Coastal Growers offered benefits and forms of personal contact that directly catered to the workers' lifestyle. Paid vacations in Mexico, Christmas and birthday greetings in Spanish delivered to the workers' Mexican homes, in conjunction with health and accident insurance, promotion from within, and a seniority system, have produced a workforce of fewer numbers but with higher skills. In 1972 the annual number of pickers employed stood at slightly more than 3,000,[9] whereas by 1978 that figure had declined to around 1,000.[10] At the same time production increased from 4 million boxes picked in 1965, to nearly 7 million in 1972[11] and 10 million in 1978.[12] Phrased another way, the number of boxes picked per hour per worker rose steadily, from 3.4 in 1965, to 4.5 in 1972 and 9.4 in 1978.[13]

Worker productivity tripled in little more than a decade, and without mechanization. Wages more than doubled in the same period.[14] The experience of Coastal Growers demonstrates the dramatic results possible through decasualization by using modern labor management practices.

Collective bargaining and unionization have also contributed to decasualization of seasonal labor. Nonunion employers' anticipation of union activity has undoubtedly contributed as much as direct labor organizing to expanding benefits and increasing farm wages in some agricultural areas. Nonunion employers in Monterey County have developed the most extensive benefit programs for seasonal and regular workers, but is also the area where union membership is highest.[15] Both union and nonunion activity have helped regularize the county's seasonal labor employment for citrus and fresh vegetables.

Generally, decasualization has not been widespread in California seasonal agriculture, but neither is it an isolated phenomenon. This has led one agricultural economist to describe contemporary California agricultural employment as changing "...from casual to non-casual" status.[16] The implications of such a change are of great import. A casual labor market

means lack of structure, low skill levels, free substitution of laborers, acceptance of high turnover, little or no future for individual employees, casual
employer/employee relationship, and selective demand. These features
characterize a secondary labor market. In contrast, a primary labor market
implies structure, more advanced skills, low turnover, promotion and
advancement opportunities, an ongoing employer/employee relationship,
and stability in demand over time.[17] A transition like this in California
agriculture will mean continued worker displacement, as an increasingly
rationalized agribusiness employs fewer but better-skilled workers. Although
total decasualization of seasonal work seems unlikely, the trend toward
noncasual employment suggests that the displacements will mean a continuation of unemployment and underemployment, probably at current levels,
for at least the next 20 years. Such long lags in labor-market adjustment to
changes in technology and labor management are to be expected. The group
most adversely affected during the transition will be the migrant worker
from Mexico.

Texas farmers, except for cotton growers, saw little reason to mechanize
or to decasualize seasonal labor. True, there was some active recruiting of
illegals in 1965-66, especially among the farmers of the lower Rio Grande
valley,[18] but most growers found a sufficient if not abundant supply of
low-cost labor, from Mexico, already present in Texas.

The continuation of an adequate labor supply, coupled with farmer
perception of labor adequacy, discouraged rationalization of much of
Texas agriculture. Citrus growers in the lower Rio Grande valley, unlike the
Coastal Growers Association of California, do not see labor inactivity as a
significant harvest cost. Consequently the bins for fruit collection are
inefficiently placed at the ends of orchard rows, rather than in the center,
requiring longer periods of worker inactivity while the bins are removed
from the field, and work is lost because longer distances must be traveled
to fill them.[19] Such practices contribute significantly to worker inefficiency.

Texas's combination of surplus labor and farmer attitudes have contributed to the low prevailing wage rates. Approximately 86,000 migrant
and seasonal farmworker households, 95 percent of which are of Mexican
or Mexican-American origin, receive annual incomes that put the vast
majority below the officially defined poverty level.[20]

Changing Labor Demand: Services and Light Industry

What appears to have been an oversupply of low-cost Mexican labor
began entering U.S. urban areas in significant numbers in the late 1960s.
Urban-related employment opportunities began to open as the large supply

began to affect demand. For example, services expanded as illegal Mexican laborers found work in restaurants and hotels as dishwashers, kitchen helpers, busboys, and maids. Those with better education and language skills became waiters, head waiters, cooks, and even clerks. Domestic service, an old phenomenon thought to have ended with the Depression, reappeared. Families in many parts of the nation, e.g., Los Angeles, Houston, San Diego, Chicago, found that they could hire a full-time combination maid/babysitter for less than the cost of the traditional part-time babysitter. In short, the availability of cheap labor reestablished a demand that had virtually vanished.

Light industry also benefited from Mexican labor. Mexicans operated on cleanup crews in housing construction, laid floors, tiled, shingled, and tarred roofs, and did carpentry and sheet-metal work, to name only a few kinds of jobs. In manufacturing they worked on things as diverse as toy assembly, garment sewing, and electronics production. Available low-cost labor was also an incentive for the small entrepreneur to go into business, or to expand his current operation. The savings in labor costs constitute a form of subsidy for such ventures. This applies equally to the large business or agribusinessman, who because of the labor subsidy continues his operation instead of curtailing or closing it.

In short, the Mexican worker found an economic niche in the American labor market, not only in agriculture but also in the more advanced areas of manufacturing, light industry, and services. Mexican labor outside of agriculture shows some parallels with rural occupations. As seasonal farmwork has been casual, so have been many of the urban-based jobs. At the lower skill levels, busboys, dishwashers, cleanup crews, and some maids have informal work relationships with their employers, lack of a future, and experience the free substitution of one employee for another. In the modern or advanced sectors of the U.S. economy, a segmented labor market has also persisted partly due to an abundant supply of cheap labor. But this secondary labor market does change as those with more skills, primarily language, advance to more highly paid positions, with greater stability and a better future, e.g., work as roofers, waiters, and seamstresses.

Recent studies agree that since 1969 a majority of Mexican workers in the U.S. have been employed in the nonagricultural labor market.[21] From 1970 to 1975, the population of California's three southernmost counties grew 18 percent, while the labor force was expanding 32 percent. Similar labor market growth occurred in Napa valley.[22] These increasing demands significantly affected villages in the sending region whose residents already had a propensity to migrate. Wayne Cornelius found that 45 percent of his migrant sample from nine sending villages in Jalisco had worked in agriculture, 20.8 percent in industry, 14 in commerce, 10.6 in construction, and 8.6 percent in services.[23] Another study of 694 migrants found that of those not employed in agriculture, 6.7 percent were in construction,

20.2 in manufacturing, and 68 percent in services.[24] These trends will probably persist. Recognizing the continuing labor supply and the role of supply in shaping demand, we turn to the legal strategies used by the United States in the past 15 years, as well as the demographic realities those strategies have ignored.

Cues and Quotas: Legislation

The Immigration and Nationality Act Amendments of 1965 were signed into law on October 3 of that year. These amendments, representing the most thoroughgoing revision of U.S. immigration policy since the 1920s, eliminated all previous quotas and imposed a ceiling of 120,000 immigrants annually from the Western Hemisphere. There had been no previous restriction on immigration from the Americas. Beginning July 1, 1968, people born in the Western Hemisphere were eligible for immigrant visas on a first-come, first-served basis until the annual quota was filled.[25] Clearly, the purpose of these amendments was to restrict immigration to the United States from the Western Hemisphere.

In 1976, further restrictions were imposed, taking effect on January 1, 1977. The overall annual ceiling remained at 120,000, but individual country limits were set at 20,000 each. Mexico clearly came under and was affected by this act: since 1955 Mexico had sent each year more than 40,000 legal immigrants to the U.S.[26] (See Table 11.) Recognizing the special relationship of the U.S. with Mexico, Congressman Peter Rodino, Senator Edward Kennedy, and Congresswoman Elizabeth Holtzman introduced the "Refugee Act of 1979" (S 643) on March 9, 1979, seeking greater flexibility in admitting immigrants from all parts of the world.[27]

Meanwhile the U.S. has continued to treat migration—an economic and demographic phenomenon—almost exclusively in legalistic terms, as with the bracero program, overlooking important aspects of Mexican immigration. The legal entry of an immigrant into the United States is not a guarantee that the immigrant will become a citizen. It takes five years for an immigrant to be naturalized and many, especially those coming from nearby regions like Mexico, may change their minds or not be naturalized for other reasons. Table 11 presents both entry and naturalization figures for five-year periods. Comparing entry figures for one period with naturalization data for the subsequent five-year period tells us that since 1940 only about one-fifth of those who entered were actually naturalized. Further, the naturalization rate has steadily declined from 42 percent in 1955-1959 to 14 percent in 1970-1974.

Although more than 1.1 million Mexicans have legally migrated to the U.S. since 1955, relatively few have committed themselves to full citizenship.

TABLE 11

Number of Legally Admitted Mexican Migrants
1940–1974 (by five-year periods)

Years	Migrants Admitted	Migrants Naturalized	Percent Naturalized[a]
1940–1944	16,548		
1945–1949	37,742	18,945	114
1950–1954	78,723	13,226	35
1955–1959	214,746	32,845	42
1960–1964	217,227	32,021	15
1965–1969	213,269	28,046	13
1970–1974	300,339	29,119	14
Total, 35 years	1,078,594		
Total, 30 years	778,255[b]	154,202	20%

Notes: [a]Based on number admitted during previous five-year period.

[b]The 30-year total does not include the 300,339 migrants admitted during 1970 through 1974.

Sources: Cornelius, *Mexican Migration...Responses,* Table 1, pp. 4–5; U.S. Immigration and Naturalization Service, *Annual Reports* for 1952, 1960, 1969, and 1976.

Many factors may contribute to this reluctance: discrimination, preference for family and kin in Mexico, the opportunity to use funds saved in the U.S. for upward economic mobility at home. Whatever the cause, there is a clear and persistent pattern of nonpermanent involvement.

Quotas, restrictions, and ceilings deal only with the legal aspects of migration. But demographic realities in Mexico and labor demand in the U.S. suggest that legalistic quotas will be ignored. Requiring a "green card" to work in the United States, or even requiring a limited visa, is rarely an obstacle to a determined migrant. "In Villa Guerrero," said one anthropologist, "the lack of *papeles* [papers] is viewed more as a minor nuisance than as a major obstacle to migration into the U.S."[28]

Cues and Quotas: Illegal Migration

All sources agree that there has been a major influx of illegals from Mexico since the late 1960s, with 1969 usually given as the watershed. One question has been raised repeatedly, but never satisfactorily answered: How many illegal migrants are there? For estimates one needs to know the size of the stock population of illegals present in the United States and the rate of flow of that population in and out of the country. We discuss this issue and its ramifications in detail in Chapter 6 and Appendix 8. Here we must note a Mexican government survey on the subject of stock. In Mexico, the results of a nationwide household survey conducted in December-January 1978-1979, by CENIET, indicate that the stock of Mexican illegals in the U.S. may be less than the three to five millions now commonly given as an estimate in the U.S. But no doubt the merits of this survey will be debated for years and will be subject to the criticism that the Mexican government has a vested interest in demonstrating low levels of out-migration.

There is a structure whereby Mexicans can leave their country surreptitiously and powerful financial incentives for them to do so. There is an informal network of family and village ties that facilitates illegal migration. This network operates as follows. A sending village establishes a community—consisting of one or several village families—in a North Mexican border city, such as Tijuana or Juárez. When potential migrants come north, they have a known environment in which to prepare for the border crossing, as well as a refuge to which they may return in case of robbery or exhaustion of funds.

More established villages will also have a settlement community in the U.S. People in the settlement community help newly arrived migrants find work. Properly prepared, a migrant from a village that has both a Mexican border settlement and an American community can pass from one country to the other fairly easily and with little risk of apprehension.[29]

Other evidence helps illustrate the historical evolution of the informal network. In the decade of the 1970s, the sending region accounted directly for about half the illegals, and the northern tier states another quarter to one-third. (See Table 12.) The villages of the sending region that contributed during the Bracero Era also tended to have members take up residence both in the north of Mexico and in the U.S. When the program ended and people still needed to migrate, these friends and relatives helped. But individuals from villages with no border or interior settlement communities were left to their own devices and had to go it alone. In the main, however, U.S. labor shortages in the 1940s and 1950s, coupled with diminished opportunities in Mexico, meant that the bracero program laid the foundation of illegal Mexican migration to the United States. The 1970s provided the keystone, with migration spurred recently by increasing income disparities between the two countries.

TABLE 12

Estimated Illegal Migration from Core Sending Region and Northern Tier, 1969–1978

	Sources of Estimates			
Migration to U.S.	Samora 1969	North and Houstoun 1975	CENIET 1977	CENIET 1978
Percent from Core[a]	48.2	48.5	46.4	51.2
Percent from Northern Tier[b]	38.9	31.3	33.9	27.1
Total	87.1	79.8	80.3	78.3
Sample Size	(493)	(481)	(9,992)	(22,822)

Notes: [a]Core Sending Area: states of Durango, Guanajuato, Jalisco, Michoacán, San Luis Potosí, and Zacatecas.

[b]Northern Tier: states of Baja California Norte, Coahuila, Chihuahua, Nuevo León, Sonora, and Tamaulipas.

Sources: Samora, *Los Mojados...*, p. 92; North and Houstoun, *The Characteristics and Role...*, p. 53; México, CENIET, *Análisis de algunos resultados...1977*, p. 19; México, *La Encuesta Nacional de Emigración...*, cuadro 8.

Disparity in the 1970s: Growing Economic Divergence Between the U.S. and Mexico

No other two nations in the world sharing a common boundary have differences in average annual personal income that contrast as sharply as those of the United States and Mexico. Moreover, the disparities between California, the major receiving state, and Mexico are even greater than the aggregate differences between the two nations. For example, the 1970 average daily wage for hired farmworkers in California was nine times that of their Mexican counterparts. The 1975 Gross Domestic Product of Mexico, with 57 million population, was $71 billion U.S. That same year, the greater Los Angeles area, with only 10 million inhabitants, had a gross product of $81 billion U.S.[30]

The course of inflation has been quite different in Mexico and the United States, contributing significantly to the growing income disparity. A review of recent price supports for maize illustrates this. Despite annual inflation between 15 and 20 percent in 1977 to 1979, the Mexican government held the price of maize steady at 2,900 pesos.[31] In effect, this reduced the guaranteed maize price by one-quarter, also reducing the profits of the very farmers in the sending region with the highest propensity to migrate. In the urban sector, the 1976 devaluation of the Mexican peso has meant, at best, maintenance of the income disparity. Because of the heavy rural bias of migrants, undoubtedly the combination of inflation, devaluation, and preexisting economic disparity stimulated migration from the sending region.

5

The Growth of Displacement in Mexico: The 1970s

Caveat: The Meaning of Development

Since 1940, aggregate data summarizing the economic performance of Mexico have shown sustained increases in production, productivity, and technology. At times, aggregate agricultural data have even shown large surpluses. Taken together, these pictures of progress have often been interpreted as "development" and "modernization." But as demonstrated earlier, the benefits from such progress have been inequitably distributed. Because of its selective nature we do not call such progress "development." Instead we prefer the term "modernization" as more accurately describing *aggregate* increases in Mexico's agricultural productivity since 1940. Because we use aggregate data in our analysis, readers are reminded that increases in total numbers do not necessarily signify general or overall improvement in human conditions.

When the bracero program officially ended in the mid-1960s, it was assumed that Mexico would ride the wave of its development "miracle" for decades. Growth rates in all sectors of the economy for the previous 15 years promoted at least one highly respected observer to call the development "spectacular prosperity."[1] Indeed, between 1950 and 1970 Mexico's gross domestic product grew by an annual rate of over 6 percent.[2] But just

61

as we have seen structural weaknesses underlying the agricultural sector, the nation's overall economy also betrayed weaknesses. In the 1970s, a combination of long-term structural problems, short-term development decisions, and changes in world markets, curtailed Mexico's growth. The resulting stagnation was especially acute in the agricultural sector and accentuated rural displacement, greatly increasing the pool of potential migrants to the United States.

Following is a brief statistical analysis of the Mexican economy since 1965. Our emphasis on statistical data should not, however, obscure the long-term deteriorating human conditions that they reflect. As before, we focus on agriculture because most international migrants continue to come directly or indirectly from rural areas of Mexico's six sending states.

Agriculture: A Brief Respite

After growing at high rates for nearly two decades, Mexican agricultural production began leveling off in the late 1960s. Real growth, which had averaged 3.9 percent in 1960-64, declined to 2.7 percent the following five years.[3] The 1970s brought even more dismal numbers, as agricultural output (not including livestock) slowed to 0.9 percent. By 1976, agriculture saw a negative real growth rate perhaps for the first time since the Great Depression.[4] Difficulties in the maize-growing sector, which occupied a majority of Mexico's rural inhabitants, accounted for much of the loss in vitality.

In one sense, Mexico's production revolution caused some of these problems. Despite inequities in the development strategy, the policies of the period helped maize production outrun population growth, particularly after 1958. A dramatic increase in hectares under cultivation and a rise in yields were largely responsible for the new output. Part of the increase in cropland devoted to maize resulted from the government's raising the guaranteed price of the grain by 71 percent between 1958 and 1965. In the same seven-year period, the real price of maize received by farmers increased by 47 percent. (See Table 15.) In response, maize farmers increased the number of hectares under cultivation from 5.6 million in 1960 to 8.3 million in 1966. Total production was further pushed up by increases in yields, which rose by 15 percent. Thanks to the price incentive, maize production shot upwards from 5.4 million tons to 9.2 million tons in 1960-1966.[5] Wheat and bean production benefited from similar favorable policies and enjoyed similar increases.

In the early 1960s the increases in production, and area cultivated, coincided with the phasing out of the bracero program in the United States.

The growth in employment opportunities in the maize-producing sector absorbed part of the growth in Mexico's labor force and offset some of the losses of legal employment in the U.S. The favorable input/output ratio caused by the increase in the guaranteed price of grains, especially maize, gave the countryside in the six sending states temporary relief and thus reduced the pressure to migrate. The short-lived decline in migration pressure shows up clearly in the census data. As noted, Mexico's northern border states were a favorite in-country destination for the sending region's migrants. In the decade of the 1950s, the numbers of migrants from the six sending states residing in the six border states increased by 244,000 people. In the 1960s, however, the number grew by only 125,000, or about half the rate for the previous decade. (See Table 7.) This brief respite lasted five or six years, quickly disappearing as maize and wheat surpluses developed. The following pages will show how surplus agricultural production helped intensify migration pressures in the late 1960s and throughout the 1970s.

Exports in the 1960s, Stagnation in the 1970s

The oversupply engendered by Mexico's new short-term policy toward grain farmers made Mexico a wheat exporter in 1963 and a maize exporter the following year. The surplus available for export soon reached large proportions: in 1965 wheat exports accounted for nearly half of national production, while maize exports absorbed 15 percent of the total harvest. Grain production stabilized after 1965. For a time thereafter, the country continued exporting basic grains, but in 1970 importing resumed once more. Hardly noticeable at first, maize and wheat imports started to soar as the 1970s progressed, and shortfalls supplanted surpluses. (See Table 13.)

By 1975, maize output was 24 percent short of national consumption. The wheat deficiency was generally smaller, but nevertheless amounted to 19 percent of national needs in 1977.[6] The yield stagnation affected maize growers more than wheat growers, as shown by Table 14. The leveling off in the production of maize—Mexico's principal staple—between 1965 and 1975 also took on a much greater significance in the light of Mexico's 39 percent population growth during the same decade.

What caused this poor yield performance to follow on the heels of dramatic increases? Maize yields slowed their rate of growth between 1965 through 1969 and 1970 through 1974 (see Table 14, and Table 2). In fact, the decade 1965-1975 represents the lowest rate of growth in yields for any period after 1940. Inflation affected the maize-producing sector. Costs of

TABLE 13

Net Exports of Maize and Wheat
Mexico, 1964–1980

Year	Maize (Metric Tons)	Wheat (Metric Tons)
1964	282,000	576,000
1965	1,335,156	751,369
1966	847,363	51,494
1967	1,248,883	233,633
1968	891,107	(−255)[a]
1969	780,621	247,310
1970	(−740,025)[a]	29,810
1971	259,880	(−167,496)
1972	228,638	(−605,601)
1973	(−1,114,166)	(−701,899)
1974	(−1,275,861)	(−1,013,665)
1975	(−2,626,597)	(−66,346)
1976	(−901,673)	(−815)
1977	(−1,692,606)	(−425,654)
1978	(−1,351,449)	(−664,248)
1979	(−848,204)	(−1,178,148)
1980[b]	(−2,300,000)	(−1,000,000)

Notes: [a]Negative figures reflect net imports.

[b]1980 figures are estimated.

Sources: Maize and wheat for 1964, Banco Nacional de México, *Review of the Economic Situation of Mexico,* 52(605) (April 1976), p. 115; maize, 1965–1978, Appendini and Salles, "Algunas consideraciones sobre los precios de garantía," Table 3, p. 426; wheat, 1965–1971, Grindle, *Bureaucrats, Politicians, and Peasants...,* Table 10, p. 78; wheat, 1972–1978, U.S. Department of Agriculture, "U.S. Agricultural Exports, 1972–1978." Tables provided by Agricultural Economics Department; maize and wheat, 1979, ibid., "U.S. Agricultural Exports, 1979"; 1980 estimates from Foreign Agricultural Service, Department of Agriculture, March 1980. Note that 1979–1980 maize figures and 1972–1980 wheat figures are for U.S. exports to Mexico only.

TABLE 14

Average Annual Maize and Wheat Production and Yields
1965–1979

Period	Maize (tons)	Yields (kg/ha)	Wheat (tons)	Yields (kg/ha)
1965–1969	8,862,172	1,153	1,805,511	2,415
1970–1974	8,868,970	1,206	2,157,200	3,817 (1970)
1975–1979	9,491,116	1,293	3,871,000	3,575 (1975–77)

Sources: Maize, 1965–1979, Appendini and Salles, "Algunas consideraciones sobre los precios de garantía," Table 3, p. 426, with 1979 as our own estimate of 10 million tons; wheat, 1965–1970, Alcántara, *Modernizing Mexican Agriculture*, Table 38, p. 111; wheat, 1975–1977, FAO, *Production Yearbook, 1977* (Rome, 1978), p. 94.

crucial inputs rose markedly after 1965, as fertilizer price increases outstripped the general inflation rate.[7] But the most important cause of the leveling off of maize production seems to have been government pricing policy.

Governmental Pricing Policy and the Erosion of Rural Income

When Mexico began exporting grains on a large scale in 1964, it found an international market characterized by substantial supply and low prices. The high costs of Green Revolution technology in the wheat sector, the inefficiencies of technological improvement, and the inefficiencies in maize growing meant that Mexican grains cost more to produce than world markets would pay. In the late 1960s, midwestern farmers in the U.S. attained corn yields 4.5 times that of their Mexican counterparts. In short, Mexico simply could not compete.[8] The maize and wheat exported between 1964 and 1969 was sold at a loss. These losses represented subsidies the government paid to agriculture.

The government's response to these developments was conditioned by its long-term policy favoring urban/industrial growth over rural/agricultural development. The rural sector had been defined as a supplier of inexpensive foodstuffs and laborers for urban centers. Its role was not to be the over-production of grains, subsidized by urban taxpayers. Just as the government had guaranteed grain prices to stimulate production during the 1950s, it employed the same mechanism to control output in the last half of the 1960s. Thus the guaranteed price of wheat was lowered from 913 pesos per ton to 840 pesos per ton in 1965. The following year, the price of wheat was once again adjusted downward, but the new price of 800 pesos applied only to the extensively irrigated region of the Pacific North.[9] The government's action was intended to encourage farmers in highly productive areas to grow more profitable crops, such as vegetables and cotton.

The new maize pricing policy did not include a downward price adjustment, but instead left the price unchanged. From 1964 until 1973, the guaranteed price of this staple was fixed at 940 pesos per ton. The fixed price of maize and the reduced price of wheat meant that urban Mexico would continue to receive essential foodstuffs at low cost. But it also meant that unless there were significant productivity increases, the profits of grain farmers would erode. Table 15 indicates the magnitude of that erosion for maize farmers.

The real price of maize paid the farmer declined by 19 percent from 1965 to 1972. Clearly this unfavorable movement of inputs and prices prompted many maize growers to reduce their production. Numbers of hectares under cultivation dropped from the 1966 high of 8.2 million to a low of 6.7 million in 1975.[10] Despite slight increases in yields, overall output declined and Mexico has had to import a substantial portion of its maize requirements throughout the 1970s. (See Table 13.)

Many economists lament the fact that Mexican grain imports contribute to the growing imbalance of payments. While unfavorable balances of payments affect Mexico in many ways, e.g., especially by encouraging inflation, a focus on the balances overlooks the plight of the small farmer whose economic survival depends upon maize growing. In 1970, two-thirds of Mexico's maize crop came from plots of less than five hectares, and 90 percent of all maize was (and still is) grown on lands that rely on rainfall for moisture.[11] Perhaps as many as two million farm units depend almost entirely on maize production for survival, hundreds of thousands of these being concentrated in the six sending states. The 1970 census indicated that over 1.3 million people in the sending region derived their livings primarily from agriculture.[12] The bulk of these were heads of households. Consequently, the sending states had an agricultural population approaching six million souls, the majority of whom depended on maize growing.

Underemployment and Unemployment in the 1970s

The drop in the real price of maize reduced profits (for those who realized profits) and lowered living standards (for those who subsisted). Thousands

TABLE 15

Real Guaranteed Price of Maize
1958–1978

Year	Wholesale Price Index (1958 = 100)	Guaranteed Price of Maize	
		in pesos	in 1958 pesos[a]
1958	100	550	550
1959	101	800	792
1960	106	800	755
1965	116	940	810
1970	134	940	701
1971	139	940	676
1972	143	940	657
1973	166	1,225	737
1974	203	1,500	739
1975	224	1,750	781
1976	270	1,900	703
1977	381	2,900	761
1978	438	2,900	662
1979	—	2,900	—

Note: [a]For this column, the current price was expressed in 1958 pesos in order to show the true (deflated) value of the guaranteed price.

Sources: Price index, Clement and Green, "The Political Economy of Devaluation in Mexico," *Inter-American Economic Affairs,* 32(3) (Winter, 1978), adapted from Table 3, p. 50; maize prices, Grindle, *Bureaucrats, Politicians and Peasants...,* p. 87, and Banco Nacional de México, *Review of the Economic Situation of Mexico,* 52(603) (February 1976), p. 52; the year 1977 was calculated by using the consumer price index for 1977 from José Luis Reyna, "El movimiento obrero en una situación de crisis: México, 1976–1978," *Foro Internacional,* 19(3) (January-March, 1979), p. 394, and ibid., Appendini and Salles, p. 427 for the guaranteed price of maize; the 1978 price index was calculated by using the 15.0 percent inflation rate cited in *Comercio Exterior,* 29(3) (March 1979), p. 355.

chose to curtail maize production, causing higher unemployment and under-employment. The national census data for 1970 show clearly the effects of the pricing decisions of the 1960s. In number, subsistence farms dominated private holdings in Mexico. (See Table 16.)

As the data suggest, unemployment and underemployment reached astoundingly high levels in agriculture. Maize producers, traditionally the most marginal cultivators in the country, were especially hard hit. By the mid-1970s, 69 percent of those economically active in agriculture did not work at all, or worked only part-time.[13] Underemployment affected 86 percent of the small landholders, who are most reliant on maize.[14] The rural labor pool, already swollen by the population growth of the 1970s, now had more potential migrants than any time previously.

TABLE 16

Private Holdings: Mexican Agricultural Income by Farm Classification, 1970

Farm Type and Income	Percent of Farms	Percent of Value of Production
Subsistence ($0–$241)	78.6	5.4
Semicommercial ($241–$4,000)	18.5	23.3
Commercial ($4,001–$80,000+)	2.9	71.3

Note: These figures do not include ejidos; total number of farm units in survey = 997,324.
Source: México, *Quinto censo agrícola, ganadero y forestal, 1970.*

Surprisingly the Mexican government had—at least by implication—anticipated the worsening employment picture for the poorer strata in agriculture. Thus the Banco de México, in an interpretive role, stated in 1976 that the policy of price stabilization in 1965-1972 was intended to stimulate the more efficient producers to grow more remunerative crops. It continued, "Thus the traditional crops were left for technically less developed farmers to grow in rainfed zones. If these crops were affected by bad weather conditions, i.e., lack of rainfall, it would be easy to purchase cheap grain abroad with the foreign exchange earned by the export of more profitable farming commodities."[15] Rainfed croplands employed 85 percent of the total agricultural force in 1970, consequently the new government policy seems to have left the fate of the mass of farmers and laborers to the vicissitudes of the weather.[16] Once again, the subsistence and semicommercial portion of the agricultural sector financed cheap foodstuffs for urban areas, such financing representing an outright transfer of capital from agriculture to industry.

Commercial farmers with larger land units and irrigation fared much better than maize farmers. Wheat farming best illustrates the differences in the 1970s between maize growing and commercial farming. As noted, wheat farming predominates in Mexico's irrigated zones, consequently wheat growing does not depend upon uncertain rainfall. Therefore, crop production is more predictable, and economic decisions can be made with greater reliability. Reliability, economies of scale, an institutional bias towards larger producers, and a greater ability to increase yields, all enabled wheat production to continue its expansion through the decade, in contrast to maize production. The rise in productivity was a particular boon to wheat agribusiness, ensuring that even when there were crop shortfalls, profits nevertheless stayed ahead of inflation. (See Table 14.)

In 1973, when it became clear that massive maize imports would be necessary to feed Mexico, the Echeverría government raised the guaranteed maize price to 1,225 pesos. It continued to raise prices until 1977, when the price per ton reached 2,900 pesos, where it remained for the next three years. (See Table 15.) As in the late 1950s, the hope was that the increase in the guarantee would help Mexico to retain its highly valued self-sufficiency in basic grains. But conditions in the 1970s proved quite different from those of the early 1960s. Inflation rates extraordinary even for Mexico, a population explosion, and other constraints (to be discussed shortly) kept the price mechanism from significantly stimulating profits, as the increases barely kept up with inflation. Accordingly per capita maize output has fallen since 1970, and unemployment and underemployment in the maize sector have not been alleviated. (See Appendix 4.)

The picture emerging from this analysis fits into a pattern established during and after the Revolution of 1910. Brought into full relief after 1940, the principal feature of this persistent pattern is dislocation in the countryside. In the 1970s the agricultural sector has remained firmly dualistic, the masses of farmers and laborers falling on the disadvantaged side of the ledger. Not only were these rural inhabitants at a comparative disadvantage within agriculture, but also they lagged far behind the urban population in income and social benefits. For example, agricultural wage rates were only 34 percent of manufacturing wage rates in Mexico for 1974.[17] (In contrast, California farm wage rates in 1977 were 62 percent of that state's manufacturing wages.[18])

The Nonagricultural Economy:
Slowdown in the 1970s

Nonagricultural Mexico also experienced growth problems in the 1970s. While the agricultural sector began to weaken in the late 1960s, industrial growth did not begin to falter until after 1970. Per capita Gross Domestic Product (GDP), which had grown at a high 3.7 percent annually in 1965–1970, fell to 2.0 percent in 1970–1972. After a slight resurgence in 1973–1974, the per capita GDP declined to a negative 1.4 percent in the dismal year of 1976.[19] Most of this decline can be attributed to the combined effects of two austerity programs in public-sector investment imposed upon Mexico by international lending agencies, a worldwide inflationary spiral felt particularly in developing countries, and one of the world's highest population growth rates.

We will not explore in detail the nonagricultural slowdown during the middle years of the 1970s. But several major problems are noted to suggest that unemployment and underemployment were not limited to the agricultural sector. Worldwide inflation moved into high gear after 1972, meaning that Mexico had to pay more for its imports. Simultaneously, a recession in the U.S. reduced demand for Mexican products. Internal decisions allowing certain wage and price increases fueled inflation still further. These increases combined with growing imbalance of payments set off an inflationary cycle that is still not under control.

Attempts were made in 1971, 1973, and 1976 to deflate the Mexican economy by curbing government expenditures.[20] Since the economy has been increasingly dependent upon public-sector investment, these austerity programs severely reduced growth that would create new jobs. In addition to efforts to control spending, Mexico devalued its peso by some 60 percent in 1976, setting off another round of inflation. The inflation rate reached 27 percent in 1976, and only declined to 21 percent a year later.[21] Such inflation rates lowered real wages because salary increases did not keep pace with prices, consequently the internal demand for goods and services declined.[22] The net effect was further unemployment increases in urban areas, especially among the lower-income population.

In short, the relative demand for urban labor contracted in the 1970s, paralleling the decline in the agricultural labor market and small farming opportunities. Admittedly jobs were still being created in the industrial and service sectors, but not fast enough to keep pace with a growing labor supply fed by population increases and migrants from rural areas. Depending upon definition and source, unemployment in Mexico ranged between 4 and 25 percent during the 1970s. Whatever the base figure used, there is little doubt that many members of Mexico's actual or potential labor supply were going without work, and thus increasing overall unemployment.

An average of 800,000 people are expected to enter the labor market annually during the 1980s, an estimate that assumes no further "feminization" of the labor population.[23] In 1978 and 1979, the numbers of employed increased by about 450,000 annually, leaving a minimum of 200,000 new unemployed per year.[24] Even with boom rates of growth, Mexico will continue having difficulty providing employment for its population in the short run.

The agricultural sector experienced an especially unfavorable pinch in the 1970s. The trend to an absolutely declining number of persons economically active in agriculture in the 1960s apparently reversed itself in the 1970s, with substantial gains in numbers. The Banco de México has estimated that additions to the economically active population in agriculture in 1970–1976 averaged 243,000 per year.[25] Given the stagnation in agricultural production, unemployment and underemployment, already at high rates, are reaching a critical stage.

Population

Population growth plays a major role in these severe employment/ unemployment problems. Birth control programs have been initiated, although they have had limited impact on rural Mexico. It now does appear likely that Mexico is reducing its fertility rate, but the extent of the slowing of the birth rate and its future trend is unknown. What is known, however, is that a total fertility rate of 2.3 children per female of childbearing age means simple replacement of the existing population. Mexico's fertility rate now hovers between six and seven children per woman. A pessimistic view of these figures appeared recently on the pages of *The Economist:* "The very best that Mexico's too-long delayed birth control programme can achieve is to make the avalanche a little smaller than it would be."[26] We will address this issue in greater detail in Chapter 7, but the significance of these programs, only recently begun, is that Mexico will not have any relief from population/unemployment pressure for several decades at best.

The addition of some 13 million people to Mexico's population in the 1960s, and still another 20 million in the 1970s, severely exacerbated the country's employment problems, and seem likely to continue to do so in the next decades. (See Appendix 6.) This spectacular growth is a major reason why Mexico's combined unemployment and underemployment rate rose from 41 percent in 1962, to 49 percent in 1970, to 57 percent in 1977.[27] When the effects of unemployment growth are considered in the context of the national development strategies previously discussed, one is not surprised that income distribution in Mexico has not become more equitable in the past 15 years. The share of the total income received by the lower half of the nation's population fell from 18.3 percent in 1968 to 16.0 percent in 1979, intensifying the cleavage between wealth and poverty.[28] The poorer half of Mexico has experienced diminishing returns of its participation in the benefits of national economic development.

Response in the 1970s: Accelerated Migration

The Mexican people, particularly those in the sending region, have responded to the deepening crisis with a time-tested alternative to lack of opportunity: migration. To repeat a theme, disadvantaged Mexicans from the sending states sought new futures in major cities in central Mexico and along the northern border. There they joined hundreds of thousands of their countrymen who had migrated to those urban centers in previous decades. For many, the in-country migration has been a short-term solution to dire economic difficulties.

For the nation as a whole, however, migration has created long-term problems of staggering proportions. Mexico City has mushroomed into one of the world's largest megatropolises. It now numbers some 14 millions, having added seven million in only 10 years. Other cities experienced influxes of similar magnitude. Guadalajara had 736,000 inhabitants in 1960, but now approaches 2.5 million. Monterrey, with a 1960 population of slightly more than half a million, will have nearly two million in the 1980 census.[29]

Border urban areas in particular have grown at phenomenal rates in the past 20 years, as the following figures demonstrate:[30]

City	1960	1980 (estimated)
Tijuana	155,300	683,493
Mexicali	197,076	441,520
Juárez	270,279	695,445

Certainly a portion of this growth is the direct result of natural increase. But in the largest receiving cities, including those of the border, much of the increase represents migration from provincial Mexico, with the six sending states major contributors to the influx. In 1970, for example, fully a fifth of the population of Baja California, which includes Tijuana, had been born in one of the six sending states.[31]

It is common to label these phenomena as "urbanization" and, in fact, we employed such terminology in discussing migration prior to 1970. But in reality, "urbanization" is too tame a term to apply to a process that defies the concept of orderly or even semiorderly adjustment or adaptation. In short, the massive influx of migrants into Mexican cities has far outrun the capacity of the urban infrastructure to absorb them. The result is what we call "urban massing," in which rural migrants mass on the outskirts of cities, living under conditions as severely deprived as those in the countryside that previously forced them to seek new opportunities.

Consequently, many of these cities, especially border cities, have become supplementary sources of migrants to the United States. Since the sending states have traditionally been the major supplier of migrants for the northern border states, and since in the past 15 years Mexico's border cities have increased their share of migrants to the U.S., we are convinced that the six sending states are directly and indirectly responsible for at least 70 percent of all Mexican migration to the U.S.

Despite the urban nature of this secondary migration, the latest Mexican government surveys indicate that the migration phenomenon from the sending region is still overwhelmingly rural in origin. The two regional classifications that include the six sending states contributed 57 percent of all illegal migrants to the U.S., according to a 1977 study of nearly 10,000 deportees. Of the total coming from these two regions, fully two-thirds originate in villages of less than 2,500 people.[32] In short, the migration from the six sending states continues to be largely a rural phenomenon.

6

Contemporary Impact of Illegal Mexican Migration on the United States

To provide relevant information for timely policy decisions, we have chosen to summarize a large amount of disparate material. Readers may consult Appendices 7 through 9 for detailed elaboration and methodological evaluations. Information is condensed here for two reasons. First, knowledge of the contemporary migration process is necessary to consider its impact. Second, both process and impact must be understood before policy recommendations can be considered. We concentrate on the key impact questions in the United States because as the receiving country it is likely to make a policy decision sooner than Mexico. But Mexico is not omitted. As demonstrated in the preceding parts of this study, a program pursued in one country will necessarily affect the other, and the care with which alternative policies are chosen will depend upon the degree of sensitivity to the migration process and its consequence.

Profile and Status

Because legal immigrants enter the United States under sanction of law, more is known about this group than about those who are undocumented.* It is thus relatively easy to determine the age, destination, employ-

---

*"Undocumented" and "illegal" are used interchangeably in this chapter.

ment, education, and other characteristics of documented migrants.[1] No such statistics are readily available on those who enter the country surreptitiously. Recent research on Mexican illegal migrants has produced a number of studies that, taken together, give a very general profile.[2] After discussing this profile, we will indicate our reservations about it.

Illegal migrants are overwhelmingly young and male. Average age is in the mid-20s. Perhaps half of the migrants are married, and each of these is likely to support four or five dependents in Mexico. At least half come from the agricultural sector, many of them being landless laborers or *ejidatarios*. Their average length of stay in the U.S. is about six months, and their wages average between $400 and $600 per month.

Obviously such a general profile risks loss of detail and cannot show the individual realities behind the generalizations. Although a more meaningful typology is far beyond the capability of present research, the pursuit of certain categories of information should facilitate future study and make a typology possible. We believe that two broad status categories—"legal" and "illegal"—should be used for initial screening. As noted earlier, different villages have different migration patterns. For example, villages with a strong pattern of legal migration, complete with the proper green card identification, exhibit different migration styles from those relying on illegal entry. One of the most obvious differences in the case of legal entry is the absence of a *coyote* (smuggler) and his attendant costs. Another is the relative lack of need for a satellite village on the border to facilitate entry for village members. In other words, legal status at entry makes possible direct migration from Mexican village to American field or urban area, without heavy reliance on an extensive support network.

Illegal status at entry, in contrast, implies another set of conditions. In addition to the psychological strain associated with illegal migration, the unlawful entrant must sometimes garner large amounts of cash to cross the border, or enter into deferred payment agreements with smugglers. Perhaps a quarter of all illegal entrants employ the services of coyotes.[3] Those without the resources or connections to seek smugglers are forced to depend upon friends and familial ties to facilitate their movement from Mexico to the U.S. destination. The remainder simply "go it alone." For the latter, the chances for interdiction by the Border Patrol are high, and serve to exacerbate any feeling of desperation that might have stimulated illegal migration in the first place.

Their rural origins and lack of skills set illegal migrants apart from legal migrants. According to a recent study, first-time legal migrants without previous illegal experience in the United States have an educational level twice that of the illegal migrants, work at higher-skilled urban jobs, and have a history of much higher wages and earnings than their illegal or formerly illegal counterparts.[4] In contrast, the illegal migrant comes from a rural environment, has a low educational level, and is more likely to be unemployed at the time he makes the trip.

If illegality is the prevailing norm for certain villages, it would be useful to identify characteristics. A tradition of clandestine entry may suggest the presence of more elaborate border satellite communities than those that exist for legal entrants. But for both groups, legal and illegal, success in making the move across the frontier undoubtedly depends on the informal network of family, friends, and fellow village members who can facilitate the transition. Success in making the transition has significant implications.

A major problem with a general profile based on contemporary studies is that data for both groups, the apprehended and seldom- or never-apprehended, are usually lumped together, giving cloudy, distorted pictures. Sampling methods mean that community impact studies, especially in the United States, are already loaded in favor of the never-apprehended, which include those who enter legally but who later become illegal through visa abuse or for other reasons, as well as those who have entered without papers. (See Appendix 7 for further discussion of informational bias.) Undoubtedly the studies count a higher percentage of what might be termed the well-established, and sample more of the long-term migrants—those with better jobs, higher pay, and greater length of stay. The deportee interviews, on the other hand, sample more of the first-term aspirants, those who stay an average of only about three months.

These reservations about data and methodology illustrate the riskiness of generalizing about the impact of the migrants on either Mexico or the United States. Migration is a selective, highly varied, biregional, binational phenomenon. Understanding it requires a careful look at the migrants' origins, their entry processes into the United States, and their destinations and settlement patterns.

Origin

All studies agree that migrants are neither from the lowest economic class nor from the highest. They are from somewhere in between, but generally nearer the bottom. Typically they are personally determined individuals. Not all low- and middle-income Mexicans view migration to the United States as a viable alternative to their economic status. For example, the *morosos*—a proportion of village Indians of Michoacán—who view their lives as determined by forces beyond their control—do not become migrants, just as they fail to respond to agricultural extension or local grassroots agricultural improvement programs.[5]

The majority of contemporary migrants continue to come from the six principal sending states: Durango, Guanajuato, Jalisco, Michoacán, San

Luis Potosí, and Zacatecas. The majority are still overwhelmingly rural. Mexico's phenomenal population growth of recent decades, described earlier, means that towns of up to 10,000 inhabitants may still appropriately be classified as "rural" in terms of the inadequacy of health and sanitation facilities, housing, schools, transportation and roads.

Recent Mexican surveys have failed to take the process of secondary migration into account, which means that many people who leave the border towns and larger Mexican cities for the United States actually originate in the countryside. (See Table 12.) While older migrants participating in this process undoubtedly developed urban skills, they must be distinguished from the more recent arrivals to large urban centers, such as Mexico City, Guadalajara, and the twin border cities along the international boundary from Brownsville-Matamoros to San Diego-Tijuana.

The phenomenon called "urban massing" characterized the influx of hundreds of thousands of rural migrants to the border in the 1970s. Only a small proportion of these people have an opportunity to learn urban skills, so they bring their rural traditions and experiences with them when they come to the United States. But many studies do not take this into account when they report a migrant from, say, Tijuana as "urban."

We have shown that a majority of the illegal migrants originate in the rural areas of the sending states. Our study of residence places of 3,654 green card holders employed in California agriculture reveals their heavily rural origin. Using the 10,000 population figure as the threshold for urban status, a figure that is both in keeping with Mexican reality and quite conservative (i.e., many researchers argue for an even higher number), our preliminary analysis of 690 cities, towns, and villages of origin shows that more than 70 percent of these locations can be classified as rural.[6] Our data on green card holders closely parallels the patterns for illegal migrants with respect to state of origin and rural condition.

The Entry Process

Transportation plays an important role in entry into the United States. Ground conveyance is the major mode of travel, but sea and air travel are not unknown. In any event, the transportation revolution of the past three decades has influenced migration by facilitating movement. While cheap bus fares attract the majority, one study has found that some people prefer to travel to the border by train, as it is less expensive than air transport and more comfortable than a bus.[7]

Once at the border, the migrants divide according to status. The legals continue on by bus, private vehicle, or on foot, unhampered by the Border Patrol. The illegals have several options for crossing the border. Most illegals apprehended by the Border Patrol are classified as EWIs (those who entered without inspection). A proportion, however, gain entrance via a series of false claims, fraudulent papers, and other devices. For fiscal 1975, David North counted nearly 42,000 such entrants detected at the nation's land ports, the chief place of entry for Mexicans.[8]

Even possession of an INS form I-151, the green card that permits Mexican residents to live in Mexico and work in the U.S., does not necessarily mean legal entrance. There is a thriving business in the production of green cards, and no one knows how many thousands of the counterfeits are circulating. To further complicate an already confusing situation, other migrants possess valid I-186 forms, the commuter card permitting Mexican nationals to enter the U.S. to shop and visit, but not to work. The I-186 restricts travel and limits the time of stay to 72 hours. If they choose, of course, I-186 holders can forsake the terms of their cards and seek employment, overextending their stay in the process.[9] By mailing the I-186 card back to Mexico upon crossing the border, these people ensure themselves reentry into the U.S. should they be apprehended and deported back to Mexico. Despite the tens of thousands who enter the U.S. illegally by using false cards or violating the terms of legal entry, the majority of Mexicans enter this country by simply hiking across the border undetected.

At the border, the arriving illegals must decide whether to risk crossing alone, or to secure the assistance of a coyote. If a migrant has been in the United States before, and entered successfully without a coyote, he may try it again. If the village of origin has established a border community, such as Animas, the Zacatecas community in Tijuana, the new arrival will seek experienced counsel there.[10] In some cases, relatives in the United States may already have contracted with a coyote to ensure safe passage.[11] Only about 20 percent of deportees use coyotes. This means that four times as many of the people who try on their own are apprehended as contrasted with those who use smugglers. We believe this to mean that coyotes are generally effective in getting people safely into the U.S., an interpretation borne out by our field work in Chula Vista, California.

But crossing with a coyote is expensive. In the late 1970s the cost ranged from $250 to $350 per person. While a migrant usually has to borrow money to make the trip, the rewards are generally perceived as worth the risks and the high interest rates charged by local money lenders. Thus, the coyote usually is in touch with contractors who help the migrant to find work, or to reach his final destination.[12] Obviously not all experiences with coyotes are positive, and incidents of smugglers robbing, abandoning, and even accidentally killing their charges are not unknown.[13]

As noted earlier, the border passage of illegal migrants carries the threat of violence. A growing phenomenon of the 1970s has been the rising incidence of Tijuana street gangs preying on illegal migrants as they try to cross into the United States. These gangs have robbed, beaten, raped, and killed migrants. For a time, the San Diego Police Department operated in the Chula Vista corridor to protect the migrants, but stopped when the job proved too difficult and the jurisdictional boundaries too vague.

Ironically the Border Patrol now provides physical security for those whom it must also try to prevent from entering the country.[14] The job is dangerous, and over half of the officers on night watch at Chula Vista have taken to wearing bulletproof vests for protection, which they have paid for with their own funds. In such a climate it seems inevitable that charges of harassment and brutality would be leveled at members of the Border Patrol. In late 1979, four officers were indicted and tried in federal court on charges of mistreating illegals in their care. One officer admitted striking illegals with his hand and his nightstick.[15]

In addition to violence, prospective illegal migrants also risk apprehension and its attendant consequences. If a migrant is fortunate when apprehended, he will be voluntarily returned (VR) to the interior of Mexico. If he is familiar with the system, he will give a border city as his address so his return will be to a point near the site of apprehension, and he will then be free to try again, possibly even the same night.

If he is unfortunate when apprehended, he will be referred for detention. He may be detained because he has a false passport, bogus social security number, or fraudulent green card, or perhaps for some other reason. In any case, at the discretion of the apprehending officer, and later at the discretion of the judge, the illegal can be sent to a minimum security prison to serve a 179-day sentence before being deported.

John Ehrlichman, while a prisoner at Safford Federal Prison Camp in Arizona, had an opportunity to observe and interview Mexican inmates serving their 179-day sentences. "The quality of sanitation and health care at the camp usually hovered between awful and scandalous," he wrote, "except when an inspection by outsiders was anticipated."[16] Time spent at Safford apparently was not much of a deterrent, as nearly everyone interviewed by Ehrlichman intended to return to the United States when released and deported, legally if possible, but illegally if necessary.

Destination, Settlement Patterns, and Length of Stay

Mexican migrants prefer the southwestern United States. Since 1969, nearly two dozen empirical studies of illegal Mexicans sampled subjects ranging from those apprehended at the border through to those living in the United States and seldom or never apprehended. The evidence agrees on one major point: Mexican migrants much prefer the border states, although some may go to other destinations. Thus in a 1977 CENIET study, more than three-quarters of the sample apprehended in the United States were detained in either California or Texas,[17] and U.S. Census data show the vast majority of Mexican descendants residing in the Southwest.[18]

Settlement patterns depend in part on the traditions of the villages from which migrants come. We have noted that some sending communities are almost exclusively accustomed to illegal migration,[19] while others depend principally on legal entry, and some are mixed.[20] Those villages committed to illegal entry tend to establish a subcommunity at one of the large border conurbations. From there, people can cross casually into California, Arizona, New Mexico, or Texas to work in adjacent fields, recrossing at dusk.[21] Others may use the subcommunity as a waiting place for longer-range movement into the United States.

Sending communities that are predominantly committed to legal migration do not need the border community. Instead they have evolved another type of settlement, with subcommunities established directly in one or more urban areas of the United States. For example, one researcher found that half the families of an Jalisco village were actually residing in San Francisco, California at the time of her investigation. Often entire families had relocated, temporarily or indefinitely, while maintaining their old village residence in Mexico.[22]

For the mixed legal/illegal migration characterizing some sending villages, a smaller subcommunity is established on the border, and ultimately another in the United States. Legal commuters can bring their families into the U.S., often illegally, using the subcommunities to facilitate the movement. For all three sending orientations, family, friends, and village loyalty play very important roles in helping people move from Mexico to the United States and back.

The length of stay varies. Earlier we noted an average stay of six months for illegals, but there are wide variations. Thus the CENIET studies found the average time in the U.S. to be 1.5 days, while the Orange County survey found 19 percent of its sample to have been residing in the United States for more than 10 years.[23]

Presently there is no accurate way to determine the residual illegal population remaining permanently in the United States. For the legal population it is somewhat easier. Our work on green card holders in Ventura County detected a trend toward longer-term patterns of settlement. For many of the green card holders Mexico is a place to visit, but the U.S. is their place of residence, their home. Only further work will show whether our sample is unusual, or indicates a more widespread phenomenon.

What seems clear is that long-term residents, both legal and illegal, tend to put down roots in the United States. In the following sections, after discussing numbers we will examine how migrants interact with the U.S.

economy and governmental services. At this point we note only that the longer people stay, *regardless of status,* the more closely they resemble one another in their social and economic lifestyles.

Impact Issues

Numbers

How many illegals are there? This is a two-part question: (1) how many are here now or at any other *specific* time (the stock of the population), and (2) how many enter during identifiable *periods* of time (the flow)? Stock and flow are critical issues in determining the effects of migration on matters ranging from health care to political redistricting. Understandably the question of "how many" remains highly controversial because it is so important, while the evidence is ambiguous. Uncertainty about numbers is a core problem in the study of illegal immigration, affecting interpretations of all the impact issues.

The early 1970s saw increased public and governmental concern over the number of persons residing in the U.S. illegally. In trying to measure the stock of this population, the Immigration and Naturalization Service (INS) commissioned Lesko Associates to estimate the total number of illegal immigrants, as well as to estimate the Mexican undocumented population.

The Lesko estimates were derived as follows: the stock of illegal Mexican migrants was presumed to be equal to the stock of the previous year plus the net yearly inflow, minus the number of those returning to Mexico or dying in the U.S. To determine the previous year's stock, Lesko utilized a graduate seminar paper by Howard Goldberg of Georgetown University, in which the author estimated the undocumented Mexican population by using Mexican censuses to compare the expected versus the enumerated population in the year 1970. Goldberg assumed that all "missing persons" from the 1970 census had migrated to the United States. Lesko Associates took Goldberg's estimate of 1.6 million illegal Mexicans in 1970 as its base stock in 1970.[24]

To this base stock figure, they added a net yearly inflow derived by multiplying the number of Border Patrol apprehensions by a presumed "got-away-at-entry" ratio.[25] They then subtracted the expected mortality of the illegal population in the U.S., and the number of return migrants (whose size they estimated by applying the annual rate of return migration observed for European immigrants, 2 percent). The Lesko equation yielded an estimate of 5.2 million Mexicans illegally residing in the U.S. in 1976.

The Lesko report clearly illustrates the principal difficulty in estimating the illegal population. Estimated stock or flow is based upon a series of variables, some of which (such as Lesko's 2 percent return rate) must be assumed with little or no supporting evidence. But a change in a single variable geometrically alters the magnitude of the stock estimate. Recently a group of University of Texas researchers reworked the Lesko data, using different coefficients of return migration. The following table summarizes some of their calculations, and emphasizes the wide variations that may be obtained when trying to estimate stock.

TABLE 17

Final Lesko Estimate Adjusted for Differences in the Coefficient of Return Migration

Return Migration (percent)	Mexican Illegal Stock 1975 (thousands)
02 (Lesko)	5,200
10	4,234
30	2,649
50	1,811
80	1,195

Source: Roberts et al., "The Mexican Migration Numbers Game: An Analysis of the Lesko Estimate of Undocumented Migration from Mexico to the United States," Table 5, p. 22.

We lack comprehensive data on return migration flows for Mexican illegals, but samples indicate that the Lesko figure of only a 2 percent return rate grossly underestimates the real return flow. This illustrates how a single variable based on assumptions rather than observation can dramatically alter the estimates of stock. Other estimating methods have similar drawbacks. The clandestine nature of illegal migration requires estimators to make various assumptions about the characteristics of the population. In short, estimators can only provide broad ranges of estimates, indicating their "preferred" estimates.

Since the Lesko attempt in 1975, other and more sophisticated techniques have been used to estimate the illegal population in the United States. Appendix 8 examines the methods and assumptions employed. Recent studies appear to agree that the number of people residing illegally in the United States in 1975 was only *half* of Lesko's 5.2 million figure. However, the seeming agreement is itself misleading. The newer estimates are equally sensitive to slight variations in assumptions that in turn have correspondingly significant impacts on final calculations. No two estimates measure the same population, so there is little clear agreement among them. In short, the evidence does not support *any definitive* estimates of the size of illegal stock and flow.

Another point worth noting is the relationship of the INS apprehension data to the illegal population. The apprehension data set, the longest-lived and most generally consistent file on illegals, actually measures INS workload and thus *law enforcement,* rather than the number of discrete people entering the country. In other words, the total number of Mexican apprehensions per year tells how many times the INS did its job, not how many separate individuals were caught. Current INS questionnaires do not even ask how many times that year an apprehended illegal had entered or tried to enter. Fortunately, that question was included in the Mexican government's CENIET interviews of more than 25,000 deportees arriving in Mexico from the U.S. in August 1978, who accounted for 47,000 entries into the U.S. —or an average entry rate of 1.89 times each deportee. We took 1.89:1 as the ratio of gross apprehensions recorded in 1978. Applying the same ratio to the apprehension data for 1976 and 1977 gives estimates of the true number of individuals apprehended. (See Table 18.)

TABLE 18

Number of Illegal Mexican Migrants Apprehended 1976–1978

Fiscal Year	INS-Reported Apprehensions	True Number of Apprehensions[a]	% Increase Over Previous Year[b]
1976	781,474	413,478	
1977	954,763	505,165	22
1978	976,641	516,741	2

Notes: [a]The "true" number is the INS figure deflated by 1.89, which was derived from a sample of 25,138 deported Mexicans interviewed by Mexican government researchers in August 1978.

Each interviewee had been asked how many times he or she had been apprehended that year. The total number deported had accounted for 47,519 entries, or 1.89 per person in the sample. Assuming direct proportionality for the year, and applying the deflator, we extrapolated over the previous two years, when law enforcement procedures had been modified, to permit estimating the 1978 figure. (These procedures included the acquisition of two helicopters for night patrol, employment of infrared telescopes to improve night vision of patrolmen, and the use of seismic sensors to detect human movement in remote areas.)

[b]These percentages relate to the true number of apprehensions.

Sources: INS apprehension data from Cornelius, *Mexican Migration to the United States ...Responses,* p. 11; North, "Analyzing the Apprehension Statistics," p. 7. The Mexican report is CENIET, *La Encuesta Nacional de Emigración a la Frontera Norte del País y a los Estados Unidos: Descripción del Proyecto y Hallazgos de la Segunda Etapa (Agosto, 1978),* Cuadro 4.

Data like those gathered by the CENIET survey give at least part of what is needed to establish total flow. Thus, when the numbers of those actually apprehended are combined with reliable "got-away-at-entry" ratios, it will be possible to make accurate estimates of how many Mexicans enter illegally. Meanwhile our analysis and that of two Mexican researchers suggest that Mexican migration has been increasing.

Over half a million Mexicans entering the United States annually in the late 1970s were being caught by the INS. The figure is undoubtedly growing, because the proportion of children under 12 and women apprehended for the first time, increased from 1972 to 1977. At the same time, the proportion of males apprehended more than once declined, which is interpreted to mean that male repeaters are succeeding.[26] In short, more new people of different age and sex groups have begun to migrate. Our previous analysis in Chapters 4 and 5 of growing dislocation in Mexico in the 1970s, and increasing opportunities in the United States, is supported by the INS records.

Partly because we lack accurate figures on the stock and flow of the illegal Mexican population, there is great debate over the impact of that population on the U.S. economy and society. Job displacement is one aspect of the issues to which we now turn.

Job Displacement

The question of job displacement—do illegal Mexican workers take jobs away from eligible citizens—is probably the most controversial migration-related issue.It is also the most difficult to analyze. Researchers, accustomed to using aggregate data in measuring income distribution, wage levels, and a variety of labor market activities, are frustrated by a labor force that does not lend itself to the national information reporting system. The illegal worker is often outside of the formal or routine business reporting processes, and most data relating to illegal workers consequently are limited and ambiguous. Despite the elusiveness of hard data, through a combination of theory and scattered evidence it is possible to reach some tentative conclusions about the labor-market impact of illegal workers.

Differing Theories of
Labor-Market Impact

When precise data are not available to measure illegal activity, it is necessary to rely on less direct data, and on theoretical interpretation. The two most prevalent theoretical schools hold differing briefs. Michael Piore of MIT argues that advanced capitalism creates undesirable jobs at the very bottom of the industrial economy, that even poor citizens will not take. These poor-paying, dead-end, low-esteem tasks are then taken by those who are even poorer, i.e., those "outside the system." In this view, the illegal migrant therefore actually contributes to the good order of the receiving country's economy.[27] Wayne Cornelius has expanded upon this theme by arguing in various studies that illegal workers from Mexico do not take jobs from U.S. citizens (and residents) for these same theoretical reasons, and because no evidence supports the view that displacement occurs.

To Vernon Briggs, Jr., the situation looks quite different. He believes the availability of cheap labor tends to depress certain labor markets, for it is a truism that expanding the supply of a commodity (in this case labor) affects its price (in this case wages) by keeping wages constant or even lowering them over time. Since Mexican illegals tend to concentrate in border regions, they compete both with citizen-workers in general and with Chicanos in particular. Chicanos, especially those living near the border, argues Briggs, have only limited access to employment opportunities because illegal Mexican competition clusters in the same locations.[28] These two opposing positions illustrate serious theoretical differences in interpreting information about a complex phenomenon.

In the next pages we will examine some of the evidence supporting the contrasting views about whether illegal migrant workers displace U.S. workers.

Aggregate Data

One of the more widely circulated analyses of the job displacement issue is Wayne Cornelius's effort to compare the national unemployment rate with what he calls "high impact" labor areas. High-impact labor areas are those which are thought to have a high proportion of illegal workers relative to the total labor force. According to Cornelius, if Mexican illegals cause the displacement of U.S. workers, the unemployment rates in these high-impact areas would be much greater than the national average. His calculations, shown in Table 19, lead Cornelius to conclude that, "Nationwide, there seems to be virtually no correlation between numbers of illegal Mexican migrants and levels of unemployment,"[29] as the unemployment rate in the high-impact areas is less than the U.S. average.

Some well-deserved doubt has been cast upon Cornelius's analysis, because his figures are not weighted by numbers but represent simple averages of regional unemployment rates. When David North made appropriate statistical calculations with the same data set, he discovered that there was no difference between the high-impact areas selected by Cornelius and the national averages. (See Table 19.) Though North's corrected figures cannot

TABLE 19

Unemployment in the U.S. and in Major Labor Areas Highly Affected by Mexican Migration, 1969–1977

| Year | United States[a] | Unemployment Rate | |
		"High Impact" Labor Areas (per Cornelius)[b]	"High Impact" Labor Areas (corrected by North)[c]
1968	3.6%	3.0%	3.2%
1969	3.5	3.1	3.1
1970	4.9	5.2	5.3
1971	5.9	6.1	6.7
1972	5.6	5.3	5.9
1973	4.9	4.8	5.3
1974	5.6	5.2	5.7
1975	8.5	7.5	8.3
1976	7.7	7.3	7.1
1977	7.0	6.7	6.4
Average	5.7	5.4	5.7

Notes: [a]Unemployed as a percent of the total labor force. Data from U.S. Department of Labor and Department of Health, Education and Welfare, *Employment and Training Report of the President, 1977,* Table D-8, pp. 246–248; U.S. Department of Labor, *Manpower Report of the President, 1969,* Table D-8, pp. 284–286; U.S. Department of Labor, *Monthly Labor Review,* Table 1, p. 63.

[b]Unemployment rate averaged across the following labor areas (as defined by the U.S. Department of Labor): Los Angeles-Long Beach, Calif.; Anaheim-Santa Ana-Garden Grove, Calif.; San Diego, Calif.; Dallas, Texas; Fort Worth, Tex. (data combined for Dallas-Ft. Worth labor area since 1974); Houston, Tex.; San Antonio, Tex.; Oklahoma City, Okla.

[c]North's data on high impact labor areas are those identified in *Employment and Training Report of the President, 1979,* Tables D-6 and D-7.

Source: Table from David S. North in U.S., *Congressional Record, Senate,* S 19523-S 19525, 20 December 1979.

be used to dismiss Cornelius's conclusions, they do detract from Cornelius's argument that illegal workers do not take jobs from citizens.

North carries Cornelius's analysis several steps further. Since migration and destination patterns of illegal and legal Mexican workers are very similar, North decided to compare unemployment rates of U.S. cities with high ratios of legal Mexican migrants to the total population. In the same manner as Cornelius, North expected that a comparison of unemployment rates of high-impact cities with national averages would reveal indirectly the labor-market impact of illegal workers. The advantage of his method is that the results are much more geographically specific than those of Cornelius. (See Table 20.)

North's findings are striking and turn out to be opposite those of Cornelius. In the five highest-impact cities, which had a total of 2.1 million workers in 1978, the unemployment rate for the same year was 26 percent higher than the national average (7.6 percent vs. 6.0 percent). The second group of four cities, with 2.7 million workers, had an unemployment rate only slightly higher than the country average (6.2 percent vs. 6.0 percent). In this latter group, however, is Chicago, with a 7.3 percent unemployment rate among its labor force of 1.6 million. Finally, the average for the low-impact cities was a bit below the national average.

The evidence put forth by Cornelius and North is circumstantial in character. So far, there is no way other than theoretical reasoning to support the presumed relationships between unemployment and the presence of illegal migrant workers. Nevertheless, the connection between them is logical and the North method, suggesting some measure of displacement, is more persuasive.

Vernon Briggs advances a similar causal connection but expands the indicators of "sizable numbers of illegal aliens." The indications of large numbers of undocumented Mexicans in South Texas, according to him, are reflected in the following conditions:[30]

1. An unemployment rate higher than the state or national rate;

2. The two poorest Standard Metropolitan Statistical Areas (SMSAs) in the nation in per capita terms;

3. The poorest counties in Texas measured by median family and per capita income;

4. A prevailing unskilled wage rate at or below the federal minimum wage;

5. Public school dropout rates higher than elsewhere in the state or nation;

TABLE 20

Selected Data on Major U.S. Cities with High Mexican Immigration
(cities ranked in ascending order of ratios)

City of Intended Residence	Ratio of 1976 Mexican Immigrants to U.S. Population[a]	City Data for 1978		
		Unemployment Rate[b]	Labor Force (thousands)	Unemployed (thousands)
El Paso, Tex.	1:139	9.2	156.4	14.4
Santa Ana, Calif.	1:279	5.6	107.0	6.0
Stockton, Calif.	1:398	11.3	59.7	6.7
Los Angeles, Calif.	1:407	7.7	1,418.6	109.2
San Antonio, Tex.	1:496	6.5	317.0	20.8
Average (of high-impact cities)	n/a	7.6%	2,058.7	151.1

Houston, Tex.	1:567	4.2	834.5	35.0
Fort Worth, Tex.	1:672	5.2	224.6	11.6
Chicago, Ill.	1:689	7.3	1,610.5	118.3
Pasadena, Calif.	1:714	5.4	57.5	3.1
Average (of medium-impact cities)	n/a	6.2%	2,727.1	168.0
Glendale, Calif.	1:812	5.0	71.9	3.7
San Diego, Calif.	1:857	6.8	366.1	24.8
Fresno, Calif.	1:888	8.1	107.3	8.7
Torrance, Calif.	1:901	5.1	72.0	3.7
Dallas, Tex.	1:902	4.0	498.5	19.9
Anaheim, Calif.	1:916	5.3	128.6	6.8
San Jose, Calif.	1:958	5.3	264.0	17.8
Tucson, Ariz.	1:992	5.7	138.6	8.0
Average (of low-impact cities)	n/a	5.7%	1,647.0	93.4

Notes: [a]Population data are for 1973 estimates. The ratio of 1976 arriving Mexican immigrants to population is computed from the *INS Annual Report, 1976*, Table 12A (for immigrants), and *The World Almanac and Book of Facts, 1977*, pp. 234–235 (for population).

[b]Data are for annual averages. The national annual average unemployment rate for that year was 6.0 percent. The 1978 labor-market data are from a computer printout supplied by the Division of Local Area Unemployment Statistics, Bureau of Labor Statistics, U.S. Department of Labor.

Source: Table from David S. North, U.S., *Congressional Record, Senate*, S 19523–S 19525, December 20, 1979.

6. Manpower development programs that become unofficial income maintenance programs, as stipends are often higher than program graduates can obtain in the local market;

7. Scant or nonexistent union activity and frequent strikebreaking;

8. High use of food stamps and public assistance.

While there may be a link between the presence of illegal laborers and the above conditions in South Texas, we still face the fundamental question of establishing that a causal relationship exists. Briggs is the first to suggest that there may be no final proof that illegals cause high unemployment or take jobs from citizens, but some relatively simple labor theory and evidence certainly tend to support the views of Briggs and the unemployment data and conclusions of North.

Without depicting a set of complex supply and demand curves, it is possible to conceptualize wages and numbers of employed in the following way. Most studies have established that a large proportion of illegal migrants work for lower wages than those of the least-paid citizens, at the minimum wage or below. A 1977 California survey of 506 apprehended Mexicans showed that 60 percent earned the minimum wage of $2.50 or less.[31] A year earlier, North and Houstoun found that the average wage for their sample of 223 illegals in the Southwest border area was just $1.98.[32] These wage differences mean that two distinct supplies of workers are available at different wage levels. Mexicans are therefore likely to be hired before citizens, particularly in the lowest paid unskilled jobs. The significance of this can be seen by hypothetically removing the supply of illegals from the labor market. Since the wage structure for citizens is higher than that of Mexicans, wages would have to rise if only citizens were permitted to work. There also would be fewer total jobs available, but they would be filled at the higher wage rate by citizens. Consequently, this reasoning suggests that illegal Mexican workers depress wage levels (especially at the lower end of the scale) to some as yet indeterminate degree. The simple fact that numerous Mexicans work illegally at wage rates below those acceptable to citizen-workers confirms this assertion.

As Briggs suggests, one would expect to find lower wages in those areas having the highest concentration of illegal workers. Indeed, one investigation found that annual wages along the Texas border were $684 less there than in Houston, an 8 percent discrepancy. Lower wages near the border or in certain labor markets may be compensated for by various noneconomic intangibles, such as proximity to Mexico or cultural preference.[33] Because unemployment is higher, at least along the Texas border with Mexico, and because non-Mexicans and Mexican Americans may be leaving the border in favor of higher wages elsewhere, some job displacement is probably occurring. Those who most feel the impact of this competition are Mexican Americans.

Wages alone can give clues about the question of job displacement. As wages rise above the minimum, more and more citizen-workers become available for employment, while fewer illegals seek or are qualified for jobs. All things being equal in this theoretical world of supply and demand, there have to be wages for which both citizens and illegals compete. Thus, if one finds illegals working for wages for which a citizen would also work, then there is a strong case that displacement is occurring. Indeed, there are numerous examples of illegals who earn substantially more than the minimum wage. A 1977 survey in San Diego County discovered that six out of 19 apprehended Mexican construction workers were earning more than $5.00 per hour. The federal minimum hourly wage at the time was $2.30. Similarly, of the 54 illegals working in manufacturing, 12 were making more than $4.00 per hour.[34] Our investigation of apprehended workers in San Diego County for 1978 and 1979 revealed that of a sample of 1,624 workers, 231 earned over $4.50 an hour. In 1979, nearly one in 10 made more than $6.50 per hour.[35] Again, these rates of pay were double and triple that of the national minimum wage.

More revealing is the sample of long-term illegal migrants interviewed by the Van Arsdol team in Los Angeles. These interviews, conducted between 1972 and 1975, produced wage data for 1,956 workers, the majority of whom were Mexicans. The upper 40 percent of this sample (801 individuals) earned an average of $8,260 annually.[36] If we take 1974 as the base year for this average, these average wages are equal to between $13,000 and $14,000 annually in 1980 dollars. Surely these wage levels indicate some overlap in supply, and consequent competition between long-term illegals and citizens.

The combination of theory and evidence reviewed here strongly supports the hypothesis that some illegals work at jobs that could be filled by citizens. The most difficult question is not *whether* displacement occurs, but to *what extent* it occurs. If only a small number of Mexican illegal workers displace citizen workers, then Americans' fears that illegals cause high unemployment would be ill-founded. If the numbers of illegals with jobs that could be held by citizens reaches the hundreds of thousands, however, then there would be legitimate concern over potential adverse labor-market effects of illegal workers.

At this writing it is not possible to determine conclusively the real extent of displacement. To do so would virtually require an examination of each and every case of illegal employment. At a minimum, one would have to analyze specific labor markets, taking into account the factors influencing supply and demand. In addition, market influences such as discrimination, artificially fixed wages, and labor practices must be considered when seeking to measure displacement. The following section illustrates the impact of some of these influences, and points out the pitfalls of oversimplifying the displacement issue.

Other Considerations on Displacement

Illegals Create Demand

The fact that illegal labor is generally inexpensive (in many cases below the minimum wage) helps these workers create a demand for themselves. The demand for low-paid, low-skilled workers in services, manufacture, and light industry has proliferated in the past decade. For example, domestic service as an occupation has become common in such cities as El Paso, Tucson, and parts of Los Angeles and San Diego. Middleclass families in these parts have found that a live-in or commuting Mexican maid costs less than a baby sitter, and offers more in return. Illegal domestics largely spur a new demand by simply being available at a low wage.

Reported Wages
Not Always Accurate

One of the most thorough researchers currently working on illegal migration related an account of illegal Mexican employment in construction cleanup in a California area. Illegals from the village he had studied in Zacatecas were employed in the U.S., sweeping up after construction crews. They were union members and the union scale for their work was $6.80 per hour, yet their actual rate of pay was substantially less. While they worked at least full time, not all hours were reported.[37] Undoubtedly unionized jobs like these would be filled by citizens if the employees actually received full pay. But in this case and perhaps others, the benefits of unionization are greatly reduced and the undocumented employee may represent a different category of worker, more akin to the live-in maid.

Perhaps one of the most frequently cited examples of job displacement were the illegal painters apprehended while working on the Statue of Liberty. These unionized painters allegedly received more than $7.00 an hour. If the facts are accurate as presented, there would be a clear case of displacement. But if union practices and rates had been circumvented as in the case noted above, the argument for displacement would be weakened and possibly untenable. That is, lower rates mean depressing the wage market, but not outright displacement.

Employer Preference

In San Diego County, the U.S. Immigration and Naturalization Service conducted an employer education program entitled "Operation Cooperation" from November 1975 to April 1976. During this period special investigators interviewed more than 7,000 employees at several businesses, 5,000 at a single site. To ensure employer cooperation, confidentiality had to be respected. Consequently, few specific details are available. It is known that the INS did locate illegals among the 7,000 employees, and that many of these possessed counterfeit green cards. During "Operation Cooperation," 340 illegal workers were identified and citizen replacements were sought. Contrary to expectations, the jobs were not filled by unemployed San Diegans, but rather were taken largely by green card commuter workers from Baja California.[38] Since most of these were low-paid jobs in low-skilled occupations (hotel maintenance, food handling, food processing, etc.), it may be argued that these cases parallel that of the domestic servants whose presence creates a demand for their services.

But some of the 340 identified illegals worked at the largest company where the INS interviewed employees. The heavy industry that employed them is unionized, with relatively high wages and substantial benefits. The strength of this union has been ranked with that of the International Brotherhood of Teamsters. If these data are accurate, illegals employed in this industry undoubtedly displace citizen workers. Nevertheless, when INS investigators followed up to check on the fate of desirable jobs vacated by illegals, they discovered that the same employer still hired illegal workers. The causes of the failure to replace illegals with citizens may be that employers simply cannot discern counterfeit green cards, or that Mexican green card holders are preferred and will be hired with few questions asked. More likely, some employers prefer some classes of Mexican workers for reasons of work habits, productivity, culture, or friendship. In the case of a growers association in Oxnard, California, only green card holders are hired. They are much preferred by management simply because they are the most skilled at citrus picking and sorting. Thus, for reasons of either low wages or special skills, employers may seek workers in labor markets that comprise principally Mexicans.

Further substantive evidence demonstrates that employer preference plays an important role in shaping certain labor markets that attract illegal workers. In June 1975, federal and state authorities in Los Angeles cooperated in identifying and deporting 2,154 undocumented workers from positions in garment-assembly, hotel, and restaurant work. Subsequent efforts to fill the positions with citizens failed, largely because employers apparently did not want them. The *Los Angeles Times* reported the difficulties in replacing the illegal workers as follows:

> Nearly 99% of the employers contracted by the state have refused to accept help in hiring U.S. workers to replace illegal aliens. ...Fred Brenner, head of the California Employment Department here [Los Angeles] said, "Almost all employers who have lost illegals to the immigration authorities say they don't want to use our services, or give us substandard job orders to which we cannot refer American citizens because they pay less than the minimum wage laws allow or pay less than the wage rates prevailing in their industries.... We cannot be informers [against the employers who violate labor laws] because that is not our task and we would then lose the cooperation of some employers in placing workers on jobs which do pay the proper minimums....[39]

Clearly, nearly all the employers had wanted illegal labor, since they refused to seek out citizen-workers when it was removed. Accordingly, employment of illegals in these jobs would not seem to represent displacement, but involves a special labor market for illegals only. Further, since employers refused to comply with state and federal minimum wage levels for employment, it is questionable to allege, as some observers do, that citizens consider themselves "too good" for the jobs.[40] (In these cases, citizens simply did not have access to the market, and thus there is no way of telling whether or not they would have taken these jobs.) This is an example of the type of special labor market that Mexican sociologist Jorge Bustamante identified in Texas. There, certain sectors of the lumber industry routinely recruit illegals in Mexico for employment in Texas. In these instances, then, when a job opening occurs it is not an opening "at large," but rather an opening for a specific kind of person—the undocumented worker.[41]

Conclusions About Job Displacement

Because of the lack of *conclusive* evidence, we cannot presently draw firm conclusions regarding the labor-market impact of large numbers of illegal Mexican workers in the United States. On the other hand, economic theory supported by wage data strongly suggests that some citizen-workers are directly displaced by illegals from Mexico. Since most surveys show that the average wages of illegals are near the minimum wage (i.e., low), job displacement is probably not widespread, and is most likely limited to certain occupations and businesses. A national sample survey of illegals' wages would render a rough indication of the extent of displacement, if one assumes a correlation between high wages and desirable jobs. Based upon our review of available surveys, we conclude that no more than one or two of every 10 illegals directly takes a job that could be filled by an unemployed citizen. Thus, three million illegal workers would displace somewhere between 300,000 and 600,000 American workers. The figure of 300,000 displaced citizen-workers would represent about 4 percent of the total number of unemployed in the entire country in the middle of 1980, and, of course, a much higher percentage in the Southwest, where the majority of illegals seek employment.

The real proportion of Americans who find themselves directly unemployed because of illegal workers will not be known until extensive field work supported by sound methodologies is undertaken. Such knowledge may require the kind of investigative reporting instigated by the United Farm Workers in Salinas, California during March and May of 1979. The UFW kept daily logs showing date, grower, number of illegals employed by job classification, and mode of transportation to work. For May 11, 1979 the log revealed 377 illegals working at 10 locations.[42]

The greatest labor-market impact of illegal workers probably does not result from direct displacement. Consider that a large proportion of illegals, perhaps as high as 80 percent according to some surveys, work at wages that are below or at the minimum wage. Most illegals, therefore, would fall into the lowest quarter of U.S. wage-earner incomes. Any impact they have on the wage structure would most affect those in this country who also earn the lowest wages.

If two, three, or four million illegal workers are earning $2.50 to $2.75 per hour, they have to exert a downward pressure on wages at the lower end of the scale. If one doubts the impact of these workers, one need only construct a simple counterfactual model wherein the supply of illegal labor would be restricted from the market. This would drive up the wages of the lowest-paying jobs in the country. Not only would the living standards rise for those citizens working for low wages, but perhaps many of those who would refuse to work for the minimum wage would be brought into the market at higher wage levels. But against this apparent benefit from removing illegal labor is a real cost, borne by businesses and consumers, of paying the higher prices that increased wages would bring. Many companies forced to pay more for their labor would pass costs on to the consumer in the form of higher prices for goods and services. Moreover, increased labor costs would force some of the more inefficient operations to close, and would add to unemployment. At some point, then, the process of upgrading wages could also lead to unemployment and higher costs.

Again, we are prevented from precisely measuring the indirect impact

of illegal workers on the labor market due to lack of data, but the fact that
all studies show a majority of illegals working for very low wages confirms
that their presence in U.S. labor markets tends to depress the general wage
scale, especially at the lower end. The results are lower wages for citizens
who work in those markets, and a lack of jobs for those who would be
willing to work in those markets for somewhat higher wages.

Tax Contributions and
Use of Social Services

Tax and Social Security
Contributions

In considering the use of social services by undocumented Mexican
migrants, it is best to begin by asking to what extent they *support* the public
system. With few exceptions, employers are required by law to withhold
federal and state taxes, as well as social security contributions. Recent research has developed primary data showing that at least some undocumented
migrants do contribute regularly to the U.S. tax and social security systems.
A study by North and Houstoun (1976), one of the earliest to address com-
prehensively the issue of social services utilization, found that 74.5 percent
of their sample (including 481 Mexicans) had been paying into the Social
Security system while working in the U.S.[43] Nearly the same percentage had
income taxes deducted.

It has been conceded even at the highest government levels that illegal
migrants are frequent taxpayers and contributors to the Social Security
system.[44] Belief in the "illegal migrant as taxpayer" also prevails in scholarly
and political circles. But a closer look at the data presented in Appendix 9,
Table 9-1, suggests a variety of interpretations. The range for undocumented
workers paying taxes and social security falls between 88 and 27 percent.
The largest sampling, that of CENIET with 2,176 interviews, shows about
half of all workers paying income taxes while in the U.S., while 46 percent
had social security deducted. The smallest sample (Cardenas, 79 workers)
indicates that about 60 percent paid income taxes. When the samples are
aggregated, slightly more than half of those surveyed (55.2 percent) paid
federal and/or state income taxes while working.[45] In short, these figures
suggest that the tax payment rate may not be as high as is commonly supposed.

Differences by Region

Evidence suggests that along the border, wages are paid in different ways than elsewhere. Most illegal migrants securing employment in border counties obtain work in the agricultural sector, especially in Texas and in Imperial County, California, where agriculture dominates the local economies.[46] Because of the seasonal nature of labor requirements, agricultural wages are often paid in cash. North discovered, for example, that 63.3 percent of his border sample received wages in cash, contrasting with 24.2 percent for the national sample.[47] As one might expect, the low rate of payroll tax deductions (24.6 percent) in the border counties approximated the proportion of those receiving wages by check (36.7 percent). Thus there is some correlation between agricultural employment along the border and limited payments of income taxes by undocumented workers.

The data also suggest that Texas employers make fewer deductions than their California counterparts. Avante Systems discovered that in El Paso and McAllen/Edinburgh, in a sample comprising less than 600, only 17.0 percent paid income taxes. In San Antonio, further from the border, Cardenas used an admittedly small sample (79) in finding an income tax payment rate of 59.5 percent. By contrast, in Los Angeles, 84.4 percent of North and Houstoun's sample contributed to the Social Security system while working.[48] A similar high proportion paid this contribution in Chicago. The Orange County Task Force report of 1978 indicated equally high rates of income tax and social security payments, as did the Van Arsdol, et al. study of Los Angeles conducted in 1972–1975.

The probable reason for the difference between Texas and the other states is that in the latter, agriculture is not the principal employer of illegal migrants. In short, Texas employers are more likely to pay undocumented workers in cash. Regional differences thus play an important role in determining the extent to which undocumented migrants pay into the public system in the form of payroll deductions. Generalizations based on the samples (Appendix 9) must take these regional differences into account.

Differences by Apprehension Status

Another factor helps explain differences in income tax and social security payment rates: differences between the apprehended and the never- or infrequently apprehended in the samples. In general, the apprehended are caught near the border after a relatively short stay in the United States. A CENIET study based upon its 1978 survey showed an average preapprehension residence of 83 days.[49] The nonapprehended in the same survey indicated an average residence of more than a year. Other research suggests even longer stays for the never-apprehended.

The implication is that apprehended persons engage in work of shorter duration, under conditions of greater exposure to the INS, and are situated close to the border (i.e., they work mainly in agriculture). Those never or infrequently apprehended, with their longer-term residence and experience in the U.S., tend to have established jobs that are more permanent, under conditions of limited risk, and farther removed from the border. Thus one would expect the kinds of differences found between the apprehended and nonapprehended samples. The Orange County study (1978) found 19 percent of its sample of 177 nonapprehended to have resided in the U.S. since before 1967, the average length of residence being about five years.[50] Nearly 90 percent of the workers in this survey contributed to the Social Security system. The Van Arsdol survey of over 2,500 nonapprehended illegal Mexican migrants showed a similar high tax-paying percentage.[51]

In contrast, CENIET's interviews of only those apprehended (most of whom were detained in California), found less than half of its sample (2,176) to have been making social security contributions.[52] This fragmentary evidence suggests that, in addition to regional variations, the individual status and security of the undocumented worker—i.e., the long-term migrant established in the system vs. the short-term, not established—plays a key role in determining the proportion of migrants who pay taxes and social security.

It has been argued that while most illegal workers pay taxes, a majority of them do not file for their entitled income tax refunds. Certainly this is true for many of the apprehended, although it is of course possible for a repatriated migrant to return to the U.S. to collect the previous year's refund. Moreover, as we have indicated, the apprehended are less likely to have had income tax deductions.

We find a very different pattern for those who are apprehended infrequently or not at all. Since they have been in the U.S. longer and are more familiar with the system, the majority pay taxes and file for refunds. Illegal migrants no doubt have a higher rate of refund than the national average, since their wages are lower than the general population and they also tend to have more dependents. Both factors mean that their proportional taxes are less than average.

Data in the Van Arsdol team's report provide evidence that the tax contribution rate is substantial. Their information pertains to a population that was nonapprehended at the time of the interview (during 1972 to 1975). A total of 2,905 undocumented persons (92.5 percent Mexican) were asked: If you have ever filed income tax, for what years? The answers tabulated as follows:[53]

Years	Filed Income Tax
Filed in 1901–1970	108
Filed in 1971–1975	1,544
No response	224
Not earning wages at time of survey	1,029
Total	2,905

The percentage of those filing income tax forms during the interview period varies according to interpretation. Assuming that the "not earning wages" category comprised those who at one time in fact worked in the U.S., and deleting those who did not respond, the percentage of those who filed in 1971–1975 is 57.6. If we delete housewives (166), retired (8), private household workers (76), and those with no occupation (321) from the "not applicable" category, the rate of those filing income tax returns rises to 73.2 percent.[54]

A similar finding was made by the Texas study of Avante Systems (sample less than 600). According to their research, "...slightly over 27.0% [sic] in both samples had income tax deducted. Almost 20% filed income tax returns."[55] Thus, about three-quarters of those paying income taxes in this sample filed for refunds. Clearly, in this mixed sample from Texas and in the large sample from Los Angeles, there is a strong tendency for non-apprehended or infrequently apprehended undocumented workers to act in the U.S. tax system much as citizen-workers do.

Contrary to the above data on income tax payments and filing, limited information suggests that undocumented workers have little access to social security benefits, although illegal status does not necessarily preclude a person from rightfully claiming such benefits.[56] In the Avante survey in Texas, none of the sample reported receiving social security benefits, but in the Los Angeles survey (Van Arsdol, et al.), 30 individuals—9.6 percent of those receiving any kind of public payments—were receiving income from the Social Security system.[57] In short, longer residence in the U.S. appears to mean better integration into society, and greater opportunity to receive social security benefits.

Welfare and Unemployment Benefits

It is often alleged that undocumented Mexican migrants do not constitute a "burden" on U.S. social services because they pay their fair share in
taxes and receive little, if anything, in return. Even President Carter's Task
Force on Undocumented Aliens (1977) and its chairman, Secretary of Labor
F. Ray Marshall, concluded that undocumented workers do not "...place
any substantial burden on State or local social services."[58] These observations were based on the results of some of the initial research efforts aimed
at determining the impact of illegal migrants. The often-cited North and
Houstoun study, for example, found that less than 1 percent of its Mexican
sample had ever received welfare payments. This and other estimates of
welfare and unemployment utilization are tabulated in Table 21.

It is difficult to make generalizations because of the wide variation in
the data resulting from sampling disparate populations. However, a trend is
revealed in the data: the more time and familiarity that illegal workers gain
in the U.S. system, the more they will interact with it in the same manner
as citizens.

Some surveys have been used to demonstrate that illegals do not utilize
welfare and unemployment programs. But these studies often sample populations that are unlikely to make use of these benefits. For example, the
North and Houstoun data are commonly cited to show minimal use of benefits, which should not be surprising because only employed illegals were
sought.[59] Similarly, the Orange County sample had a high percentage of
employed; nearly all of the families represented by the 177 interviewees had
at least one member employed at the time of the interviews. Many had lived
in the U.S. for five years or longer, and some owned their own homes.
Accordingly, only 2.8 percent of this population had collected welfare payments at some time.[60]

More diverse samples were undertaken by Mexico's CENIET and Van-
Arsdol. The 1977 CENIET survey of 3,689 apprehended Mexicans reported
only 2.5 percent as having collected welfare or unemployment payments
while in the U.S. It also reported that over half the sample had been caught
and returned to Mexico within 48 hours of crossing the border.[61] If the
CENIET data are recomputed to include only those who resided in the U.S.
long enough to initiate public assistance payments (at least one month), the
proportion collecting benefits rises to 7.6 percent, approximating U.S.
national averages for the total population. This finding suggests that longer-
term illegal migrants who are not as settled or secure as those enumerated in
the Orange County study make substantial use of social services.

The Los Angeles survey (Van Arsdol) certainly supports this finding.
This sample included a large number of females (35.4 percent), as well as a

TABLE 21

Percent of Undocumented Mexicans Who Have Received Welfare and Unemployment Benefits, by Sample

Social Service	Van Arsdol 1972-75	North and Houstoun 1975	Bustamante 1975	CENIET 1977	Orange County 1977-78	Avante Systems 1978
Welfare (mainly AFDC)	12.4[a]	0.2	3.2[b]	2.5	2.8	2.3[c]
Unemployment Benefits		3.6				>10.0[c]

Notes: [a]Includes 210 "other Latin American" clients in a sample of 2,800+.
[b]A significant number in the "welfare recipient" category refused to answer the inquiry. When these refusals-to-answer are included with the known percentage of welfare recipients, the figure is raised to 5.5 percent.
[c]Applications only.

Sources: Van Arsdol, et al., *Non-Apprehended and Apprehended...*, p. 89; North and Houstoun, *The Characteristics and Role...*, pp. 145-149; Bustamante, "Undocumented Immigration...," in *International Migration Review*, p. 170; México, CENIET, *Primera Encuesta a Trabajadores Mexicanos...*, pp. 32-33; Orange County, Task Force..., *The Economic Impact...*, p. 18; Avante Systems..., *A Survey of the Undocumented Population:*..., pp. 41-42.

high percentage of married or never-married persons (74.6), most of whom had children. Unlike the surveys of apprehended migrants, the majority of the Van Arsdol interviewees had children residing with them in Los Angeles, which in turn meant high rates of economic dependency because of the ratio of dependents to wage earners in a family. Altogether, the 2,905 migrants (7.5 percent of whom came from other Latin American countries), had some 5,817 children, three-quarters of whom lived in the U.S.[62] Clearly, this is a settled population of long-term U.S. residents. Indeed, the average length of residence for Van Arsdol's 2,314 Mexicans who responded was 3.7 years for men and 4.9 for women.[63] These figures contrast with the CENIET average length of stay of under three months for the apprehended, and a year for the nonapprehended. Greater use of social services would be expected of a long-term, settled population with a high degree of economic dependency.

When the Van Arsdol interviews were conducted in 1972–1975, 8.1 percent of the 2,621 illegal Mexicans responding reported they were currently receiving welfare support, and an additional 2.4 percent got benefit payments from social security or other sources. In short, over 10 percent of the sample was receiving income from public sources. Females were the heaviest users of public assistance programs, with 15.6 percent receiving some kind of financial aid.[64] According to these data, undocumented Mexicans had a higher proportion of welfare recipients than the California or U.S. populations: an 8.1 percent AFDC* rate as compared to 6.6 percent for California and 5.9 percent for the nation in 1976.[65] Given these general results, it is not surprising that 12.4 percent of the sample indicated they previously had received or were presently receiving welfare. (See Table 21.) Of the 1,015 women in the survey, 18.5 percent indicated that they previously had collected or were collecting AFDC benefits.[66]

In sum, all evidence points towards the substantial use of welfare and unemployment benefits by illegal Mexicans. But there is a wide variation in the rates of use, depending on population sampled. Length of stay is perhaps the key variable. New migrants who are intercepted and deported within days or weeks of arrival, or those who work for several months and return to Mexico, do not have the time or knowledge to take advantage of public assistance programs. On the other hand, illegals who have resided in the U.S. for years at a time have more opportunity to receive benefits. But as the Orange County survey suggests, long-term stay does not necessarily mean that there will be substantial use of benefits. The Van Arsdol study also indicates that the numbers of women and children in the sample are two

---

*Aid to Families with Dependent Children

other important variables. Only when longevity of stay is combined with high rates of economic dependency do illegals rely more on public assistance than citizens.

Use of Health and Education Facilities

Illegals' use of health and education facilities is closely linked to their use of welfare and unemployment benefits and length of stay. Table 22 shows six rates of health and education service usage by samples of illegal Mexicans.

The samples agree that health care is the social service most freely rendered to undocumented Mexican migrants. North and Houstoun found the lowest rate of hospital or clinic usage, i.e., only 3.7 percent of their Mexican sample had received free medical services. Their population had been workers, and either had insurance or were able to pay for services out of their own pockets.[67] Thus a low use of free medical services is to be expected of this group.

The much larger 1977 CENIET sample found that 324 (8.8 percent) of 3,689 undocumented migrants availed themselves of free medical services. But this percentage is seriously deflated by the sample's inclusion of those who were apprehended immediately after crossing the border (25.1 percent), as well as those who stayed less than 24 hours (22.5 percent).[68] Obviously these short-term border-crossers were highly unlikely to make use of public medical facilities.[69] Adjusting the CENIET data to exclude the immediately apprehended, 16.8 percent of those who stayed in the U.S. more than 24 hours utilized some kind of publicly financed health service. This finding, corroborated by Van Arsdol's Los Angeles study, suggests a correlation between duration of U.S. residence and use of free medical services.

The Van Arsdol study did not determine how many received free medical care from public facilities, but did ask respondents whether they currently owed bills to a Los Angeles county hospital; more than a third answered "yes." (See Table 22.) This is only a clue, however, as we do not know how many paid their bills or received free care at noncounty facilities. Nevertheless it indicates a significant rate of public health-care utilization, fulfilling the expectation that a settled undocumented population, with high percentages of women and children, is more likely to make substantial use of public services.[70]

The samples suggest that 10 to 20 percent of the illegal migrant population probably receive free medical care at some time while they are in the U.S. This range is consistent with rates for the general population. In California, for example, those holding Medi-Cal cards (state-financed medical

TABLE 22

Percent of Undocumented Mexicans Who Have Used
Health and Education Services, by Sample

Social Service	Van Arsdol 1972–75	North and Houstoun 1975	Bustamante 1975	CENIET 1977	Orange County 1977–78	Avante Systems 1978
Free Hospital or Clinic Care	7.3[a]	3.7[b]	7.8[c]	8.8	9.0	6.3
Children in School	21.1	2.7	0.9	1.2	—	—

Notes: [a]Signifies those who owed bills to the Los Angeles County Hospital at the time of survey.

[b]Percentage calculated by taking the percent of Mexicans utilizing medical facilities (22.0 percent), and adjusting it to those (83 percent) who paid their own bills or had them paid by insurance or employer.

[c]The categories "free medical care" and "children in school" included a significant number who refused to answer. Subtracting these refusals-to-answer from the total sample gives the following figures: free medical care, 9.7 percent; children in school, 3.4 percent.

Sources: See Table 21.

care) average between 12 and 15 percent of the total population. In some counties, more than one-fifth of the population are Medi-Cal recipients.[71]

In economic terms, it is more cost-efficient to furnish immediate medical care to undocumented Mexicans in need, regardless of their legal status. The economic argument has been advanced by the Orange County Task Force on Medical Care for Illegal Aliens, and by others, with respect to the long-term costs/benefits of prenatal child care.[72] Moreover, for a number of reasons, it is in the interest of U.S. citizens to support reasonable use of medical facilities by Mexican migrants. It is important to the physical wellbeing of U.S. citizens that illegal residents receive proper medical treatment when necessary. Many undocumented workers and their families (if they have families here) live in crowded conditions in low-income neighborhoods. Some of these neighborhoods have substandard sanitation and thus increase the opportunity for spreading contagious diseases such as tuberculosis and gastrointestinal disorders. Consequently, low-income Americans have been exposed to strains of drug-resistant tuberculosis peculiar to Mexico. As Dr. Joseph Brooks succinctly analyzed the problem, "It is important to understand that undocumented workers live in communities mixed with native poor, Blacks and Chicano people, and a communicable disease doesn't check your immigration papers before it spreads."[73]

Nevertheless, providing medical care rendered for indigents is an expensive proposition. Los Angeles County, for example, has estimated that its Department of Health Services spent a minimum of $31 million on medical care for illegals in 1977.[74] While this estimate has received much criticism, other data tend to support the figure. In 1971 Orange County determined that its contract hospital provided inpatient care for 1,361 confirmed illegal persons at a cost of $1.4 million. This figure represented services over a seven-month period and did not include those with fraudulent green cards.[75] University Hospital in San Diego provided medical care for 44 nonpaying illegals in a four-month period in 1976, at a total cost of $81,730.[76] These figures and others show that small percentages of undocumented migrants can incur substantial medical bills, with a considerable financial impact on receiving communities.[77] Given the great increases in medical costs in the 1970s, far outstripping the general inflation rate, and the fact that migrants are entering the U.S. in increasing numbers, costs of providing adequate medical services will be a key issue in the 1980s.

Assessing the cost of educating children of illegal entrants has proven as difficult as evaluating other aspects of migratory phenomena. Two sampling techniques have been employed: individual interviews, and disparate surveys conducted by school officials. The Van Arsdol and Bustamante investigations again illustrate the wide variations among samples. The Van Arsdol population, rather well-settled in Los Angeles and with 2.00 children per interviewee, had a large proportion with children in school; the opposite was true of Bustamante's relatively transient population, with only 0.9 percent having children in school. In short, once again the data show marked differences between the apprehended and the nonapprehended.

School district data have yielded other results. In 1978, the Orange County Task Force used Orange County Board of Education figures for the number of undocumented children in school (7,672). Based on information gathered in classrooms, many teachers apparently classified a child as undocumented if the parents could not produce citizenship documents or did not know the legal status of their child.[78] This method means that many citizen school children are likely to be categorized as undocumented, just as many AFDC applicants are judged to be "illegal aliens" by social workers and thus referred to the INS. In the first quarter of 1979, for example, the Los Angeles County Department of Public Services referred 380 persons to the INS; well over half (53.4 percent) were confirmed to be legal residents.[79] If the same rate of "real legality" applies to the Orange County school children, then one must consider the Board of Education calculation to be overestimated.

Focusing on the schooling costs of Mexican migrants obscures the benefits that accrue to both countries when the individual receives an education. The case of Francisco Jiménez is an excellent illustration. Born in Jalisco, Mexico, Francisco Jiménez came to California with his father in the late 1940s. He worked in the fields alongside his bracero father and attended school intermittently. But over time he acquired an education in English and studied Spanish formally. Jiménez earned his PhD at Columbia in Spanish literature. He has published extensively in both languages and is regarded as a significant new writer. His short story, "The Circuit," which recounts some experiences of his youth, won the *Arizona Quarterly* Annual Award in 1973.[80] Francisco Jiménez exemplifies the best of the possibilities of Mexican migration to the United States.

The very education Jiménez received, albeit erratically, was denied even legal or green card migrants in California due to the controversy and confusion following in the wake of Proposition 13. For example, in Monterey County during the summer of 1979, migrant farmworkers' children were denied the use of the Spreckles School for badly needed supplemental instruction, because the local school board determined that since Proposition 13 had removed funds for summer school "regular" students it would be unfair to let the dependents of migrants use the facility. As a result, teachers had to go to the children in the camps. Garages became classrooms, trailer hitches served as tables. Pieces of cardboard placed on the lap functioned as desks.[81] Long-term problems of adjustment and adaptation cannot be solved in such fashion. Increased sensitivity to the human problems and concerns involved in the migration of Mexicans to the United States is thus essential to sound policy formulation.

Some Social, Cultural, and Economic Considerations

At this point it seems advisable to consider the larger context of illegal Mexican migration to the U.S. While we can only touch on some of the broader issues that affect the United States and Mexico separately, as well as some mutual issues, we stress that the to-and-fro interchange of population necessarily has major long-term social, cultural, and economic effects. This is a complicated and often contradictory phenomenon, and the contradiction between perception and reality is perhaps most evident in the discrepancy between the *attitudes* of most Mexican immigrants toward the length of their stay in the U.S., and the actual period of residence.

Length of Stay Reconsidered

We have referred to Mexican nationals working and living illegally in the U.S. as migrants, because some but not all of the available evidence suggests that a majority of those crossing into this country do not come intending to stay permanently. Wayne Cornelius concludes that they are mainly "sojourners" and not "settlers."[82] Many studies of *apprehended* illegals also show relatively short lengths of stay. Thus the 1977 CENIET survey found an average sojourn in the U.S. of under three months, and Cornelius's own research in Jalisco reported an average length of stay for illegal visitors of 5.5 months.[83]

Legal Mexican immigrants, whose settlement patterns often closely parallel those of illegal migrants, for the most part do not see themselves as permanent residents of the United States. (See Table 11.) Beginning in the mid-1950s a clear pattern and preference emerged in the naturalization process. The percentage of naturalization as a proportion of total immigration fell sharply to 15 percent of entering cohorts, where it has remained through the 1970s. These data support the contention that the Mexican population in the U.S., both legal and illegal, do not see themselves as permanent settlers. But their perceptions often do not correspond with fact. Although holding attitudes favoring a short stay, they may become long-term and even permanent residents.

Despite the naturalization figures noted above and studies that indicate relatively abbreviated stay in the U.S., there is ample evidence that segments of migrating populations reside here for periods longer than can be considered "temporary." Table 23 is an attempt to sort from existing data sets the number of migrants whose length of stay is longer than that commonly cited in the literature. Studies of populations that include apprehended

TABLE 23

Examples of Length of U.S. Residence
by Undocumented Mexicans

	Avante Systems	Flores and Cardenas	Van Arsdol et al.	Orange County	CENIET	Villalpando
Period in U.S.	6 yrs +	1 yr +	3 yrs +	2 yrs + (10 yrs +)	1 yr +	1 yr +
Percent of Sample	50.0	20.0	51.9	70.0 (19.0)	30.7	44.4
Location and Sample Size	El Paso (300)	San Antonio (976)	Los Angeles (2,314)	Orange County (177)	Mexican border cities (1,444)	San Diego (160)

Sources: Avante Systems. . . , *A Survey of the Undocumented Population.* . . ; Roy Flores and Gilbert Cardenas, *A Study of the Demographic and Employment Characteristics of Undocumented Aliens in San Antonio, El Paso and McAllen*, report submitted to the Southwestern Regional Office of the United States Commission on Civil Rights (August 1978), p. 19; Van Arsdol et al., *Non-Apprehended and Apprehended.* . . , Table 10, p. 47; Orange County, Task Force. . . , *The Economic Impact.* . . , p. 17; Mexico, CENIET, *Tabla de estancia en Los Estados Unidos para trabajadores Mexicanos indocumentados* (México: 1979), Table 2.4, p. 16; Villalpando, *Illegal Aliens.* . . , p. 36, calculated from length of time workers were employed in the U.S.

migrants (Flores and Cardenas, Villalpando) report shorter residence durations than those surveying the nonapprehended. But even with the apprehended samples, significant percentages stay longer than one year. In the Villalpando survey, more than 40 percent of 160 workers had been employed in the U.S. for more than a year. Once we move into the non-apprehended samples, the length of stay rises dramatically.

Most impressive are the Avante Systems findings for their El Paso sample of 300 individuals, 200 of whom were nonapprehended at the time of survey. Half of these undocumented Mexicans had resided in El Paso for more than six years. Similar results were found by the Van Arsdol and Orange County investigations. One in five of the Orange County study had resided in California for more than 10 years.[84] Further, there are many examples of illegal residencies lasting decades.[85]

Length-of-stay data are essential to help evaluate the impact of illegal Mexican migrants upon the United States. A migrant who stays only three months to harvest citrus in Arizona is unlikely to apply for and receive welfare, or to have children in school. An established family with seven children in a Los Angeles barrio, however, is very likely to use educational and health facilities and to compete in a labor market with low-income citizens. The question is not one of semantic designation (temporary vs. permanent), but of functional interaction in the U.S. social and economic system. At this point, then, we can conclude that while the majority of people sampled are migrants, to date this majority has consisted of appre-hended individuals. When the nonapprehended minority are examined, we find a substantial percentage who for all practical purposes do become settlers. Whether or not they intend to be lifelong residents, those who are here for many months or years at a time have inevitable impacts, which increase with their length of stay. Certainly they and their children augment the population of Mexican ancestry in the United States, whether they choose to or not.

Changing Mexican-Descent Population

Not even the very size of the population of Mexican ancestry in the United States is well established. Despite an expressed goal of counting everyone in the country every 10 years, the U.S. census-takers have tended to overlook many minorities, including those of Mexican origin. Table 24 gives estimates of the 1950-1978 population of Mexican descent in the principal states of residence and in the nation. No attempt has been made to include estimates of the illegal Mexican population, or to correct for undercounts in census enumerations. In short, these figures are useful to indicate order-of-magnitude, but should be regarded as minimums, since they include only a portion of the legal residents.

Notably, while the U.S. population of Mexican descent doubled between 1950 and 1970, it nearly tripled in California. Approximately 80 percent of the people in the United States with Mexican antecedents legally reside in California and Texas. Moreover, these two states are also the chief recipients of illegal migrants.

Legal and illegal migration is a continuous, long-term process that feeds into an already large and growing population of Mexicans and their descendants in the United States. Many of these—perhaps most—have reasonably direct connections with Mexico through kinship networks, friendships, and

TABLE 24

Estimated Mexican-Descent Population
California and Texas, and U.S. Total
1950–1978

	1950[a]	1960[a]	1970[a]	1978[b]
California	758,400	1,426,538	2,222,185	—
Texas	1,027,455	1,417,810	1,663,567	—
Subtotal	1,785,855	2,844,348	3,885,752	—
U.S. Total	2,351,710	3,558,536	4,939,597	7,151,000
California and Texas Totals as % of U.S. Total	75.9%	79.9%	78.7%	

Notes: [a]Includes unknown percentages of 60,000 (1950), 131,397 (1960), and 322,179 (1970) Spanish-surnamed of non-Mexican ancestry in the southwestern states of California, Texas, Arizona, New Mexico, and Colorado. Does not include estimates of illegals, or of legal residents not counted by census-takers.

[b]1978 figures are for total U.S. population of Mexican descent, the only such figure available.

Sources: Arthur F. Corwin, ed., *Immigrants—and Immigrants: Perspective on Mexican Labor Migration to the United States* (Westport, Conn.: Greenwood Press, 1978), Table 7, p. 124; U.S. total from U.S. Bureau of the Census, *Current Population Survey: March 1978*, report P-20, no. 339 (Washington, D.C.: June 1979).

village or regional ties. The consequences of these relationships, especially in the context of continued migration, are truly imponderable.

In any event, the movement of undocumented Mexicans and their residence in the U.S. will have far-reaching consequences. As with past migrations of Mexicans to the U.S., the entrants will affect—and in many ways enrich—social and cultural life. The demand for Mexican foodstuffs has already proliferated throughout the Southwest and beyond. The economic ramifications of increased demand for cornflour, tomatoes, and chiles have already begun to be felt. Intermarriage between citizens and illegals has occurred and will continue to occur at an unknown rate. The children of these unions will be U.S. citizens. Since the Mexican-Americans' birth rate is greater than that of the U.S. as a whole, the proportion of Americans of Mexican ancestry will increase.[86] In fact, this population joins with other Hispanics in being the fastest-growing minority in the nation, particularly in the Southwest. They are gaining significant access to political power and their potential for future influence is growing. Culturally and socially, the presence of this population manifests itself in increased Spanish-language media coverage by and for Hispanics. Radio and television programming, exclusively in Spanish, have become standard features of major urban areas such as Los Angeles, San Jose, San Francisco, Houston, San Antonio, and even Washington, D.C., and other areas. Spanish-language street signs, ballots, motor vehicle examinations, and highway codes all testify to the increasing importance of people of Mexican ancestry in local life in the Southwest. The proximity to Mexico and the ease of travel back and forth, reinforced by family and village ties, have combined to provide cultural reinforcement and continuity in a new environment. But it would be a mistake to think there is a unified world-view among people of Mexican descent in the United States, or that there are smooth relationships between Mexicans and their countrymen who have lived for a prolonged period in the U.S. and have become part of the U.S. economic system.

Intra- and Inter-Cultural Contact

Citizens of Mexican descent in the U.S. are divided in their response to continued Mexican migration. Privately, many long-term residents and second- and third-generation offspring who struggled in the 1960s and 1970s to seek more equitable treatment for all Hispanics, express fears that the Anglo response to the "silent invasion" may mean a loss of hard-won political and other gains. Others see no threat in the ongoing migration and instead urge an open border. Still others decry the treatment of Mexican migrants but find the problem too intricate to justify taking a political position on the issues.[87]

A further complication is found in the very use of descriptive language. Not all people of Mexican ancestry wish to be called "Chicano" or "Mexican-American." Some prefer "Mexicano" to denote their ultimate origins. Others prefer terms such as "Latino" or "Hispanic," as including both those of distinctive Mexican origin and the other Spanish-surnamed populations of the United States. These differences over terminology signify a growing political awareness, and a search for ethnic identity.

Manuel Gamio, father of Mexican anthropology, observed in the 1920s that relations were often strained between what he termed American-Mexicans and recent Mexican immigrants. The attitude of the former was sometimes slighting and disparaging toward the newcomer, while the Mexican immigrant regarded his precursor as a man without a culture, a *pocho*.[88] Moreover, Gamio noted that Anglo America discriminated against both American-Mexicans and the more recent Mexican arrivals, a discrimination characterized by indifference.[89]

While much has changed in both Mexico and the United States since Gamio wrote, his observations still have contemporary relevance. Sound policy must take into account social relations between the settled population of Mexican descent and Mexican immigrants, as well as Anglo attitudes toward both. As the migration issue becomes more important to the relationship between the United States and Mexico, both countries will be forced into much closer dealings than they have had in the past. There will be great risks as well as great opportunities in developing binational and biregional strategies to cope with the excruciatingly difficult problems both nations confront. One increasingly volatile policy issue is the treatment illegals receive while in the United States.

Treatment of Illegals in the United States

The presence of large numbers of illegal migrants in the United States raises questions regarding their treatment. Kenneth Johnson recently called to our attention the plight of the "stranded" Mexican illegals around St. Louis, Missouri.[90] By that term Johnson means those who for a variety of reasons cannot readily return to Mexico. Sickness, debt accumulation, detention by the authorities, and the social disorientation caused by partial acculturation, coupled with family separation, have combined to leave these people stranded in powerlessness and often hopelessness. A cursory examination of the legal entanglements and due-process problems an illegal can encounter supports Johnson's concern. One of the country's more celebrated recent inmates mentioned earlier, John Ehrlichman, served his sentence at a minimum-security prison in Arizona that also housed illegals sentenced to detention. Personal observation and extensive interviewing revealed that very few of the detainees knew why they had been incarcerated. Ehrlichman attributed their ignorance to the wide discretionary powers of local prosecutors. But whatever the cause or process, once they were in prison the exploitation hardly stopped. At Safford, Mexicans worked in light manufacture, specifically the assembly of work gloves. The product was made for the General Services Administration to sell, and inmates each received approximately $2.00 a day. Health and sanitation facilities and housing were substandard by Bureau of Prison criteria. When inspections of the facility were conducted, Mexicans were kept out of sight. This practice was even followed on the day of Ehrlichman's release, lest the press notice.[91]

Ehrlichman's story touches on larger issues than the treatment of illegal Mexicans in detention facilities. For his future employment, the illegal's work while in detention has given him a useful skill that should enable him to enter the garment and apparel industry anywhere in the Southwest. Since nearly all of those interviewed intended to return to the U.S. upon release, this on-the-job training has implications for the labor market. Moreover, from the standpoint of due process, we know that the illegal, or suspected illegal, is frequently denied the opportunity to understand the charges against him, let alone to respond effectively. Even an interpreter, when present, may not be able to translate English-based legal concepts into Spanish.[92]

These specific instances relating to the undocumented Mexican are part of a larger pattern of law enforcement pertaining to immigration and naturalization. Important changes in national quotas and individual police procedures have taken place in the past five years. There is a climate of confusion and apprehension among many citizens respecting the consequences of such changes. The Mexican-American Legal Defense and Educational Fund (MALDEF) has expressed concern that regulations designed to restrict the activity of undocumented Mexicans might be translated into discriminatory actions against all Hispanic people regardless of status or citizenship.[93] To MALDEF, the proposal to impose an employer sanction for knowingly hiring an illegal could lead to discrimination against other Mexican-Americans and Latinos. In short, law enforcement policies must be carefully devised with an eye to their probable impact on the Hispanic community in the United States.

While the discussion has concentrated on issues affecting the United States, we have not forgotten the impact of migration on Mexico. We turn to that subject next.

Mexico: Remittances and
Other Considerations

The money remitted by its nationals is by far the most important short-run economic consequence for Mexico of migration to the United States. Manuel Gamio first noted its importance when he examined the phenomenon, using information on postal money orders processed by the national post office in Mexico. Only aggregate monthly amounts were reported according to state of origin in the United States, reflecting seasonal variations in employment.[94] Consequently, the data were incomplete. The important missing element which would have permitted measurement of regional impact was the identification of the Mexican states to which the postal money orders were sent. Moreover, the post office was only one remittance vehicle, as bank drafts also were used, and much cash was taken back during visits or upon final return to Mexico. But Gamio's work called attention to this important source of economic impact on Mexico and suggested further research.

Wayne Cornelius's review of earlier remittance studies, including Gamio's, confirmed his own field-work findings that the illegal typically sends more than one-third of his earnings back to Mexico. In some areas this contribution is an essential addition to a family's disposable income, and can mean the difference between starvation and survival. One researcher recently compiled an incomplete run of money orders for the Banco Nacional de México, which is responsible for one-fourth of all international banking transactions in Mexico.[95] The most nearly complete series had data for all but one month in 12 respecting the State of Guanajuato, June 1975-May 1976. According to this study, Mexicans in the United States sent $7.6 million to Guanajuato that year. This figure represented one-fourth of total estimated remittances to Guanajuato from the U.S. that year of $30.2 million, a per-family annual contribution to the rural sector of 1,424 pesos, or the equivalent of 6 to 8 percent of rural per capita income. Recalling that mailed remittances are not the sole means of getting funds to Mexico, one concludes that the total for Guanajuato is probably higher. Perhaps 10 percent of that state's entire rural per capita income comes from the United States. In certain villages, where there is thorough documentation, the percent of total income derived from U.S. earnings exceeds 50 percent.[96]

Whether the actual total of remittances is in hundreds of millions or several billions of dollars,[97] the crucial point is that remittances have great regional significance for Mexico, providing essential support for large numbers of the population in some areas. Further research on remittances, combining the techniques of Gamio and others, should yield better insights into the magnitude of the impact on the region sending migrants. As with every other aspect of the phenomenon, it is the *regional* impact that helps to explain the power of the migratory impulse.

Unfortunately for the migrants and their families, remittance funds can be used for little beyond subsistence and perhaps the purchase of a small plot or house. While some instances of investment in machinery and renewable resources have been found,[98] the overall pattern reminds us of the problems that plagued returnees during the Bracero Era and even earlier in the 1920s.[99] There is little infrastructure in the sending region to facilitate conversion of new capital into productive enterprises. Moreover, the sending region—which lost the Revolution and the Rebellion, and failed to benefit from the Green Revolution—must use the bulk of income earned in the United States just to survive. Remittance money for the most part simply augments the meager incomes of those who continue to survive in Durango, Jalisco, Guanajuato, Michoacán, San Luis Potosí, and Zacatecas.

Throughout this study we have tried to demonstrate that the phenomenon of migration from Mexico to the United States has been a long-term, fairly continuous, makeshift response to the problems of poverty and lack of opportunity in rural Mexico. But it is only a temporary solution, subject to alterations of governmental policy in both nations, to economic cycles, and to other influences. The question raised by our work reiterates that of Manuel Gamio more than 50 years ago: Do the short-term benefits of employment in the United States outweigh the costs of continued lack of economic development in the sending region? Gamio lamented the loss to Mexico of many of its most enterprising citizens who, having learned skills and acquired possessions in the U.S., could not use them in their local villages.

Individuals and families brought back automobiles, tractors, and home appliances into areas of Mexico that lacked the roads, the gasoline stations, and the electrification needed to make them usable. Mexicans' new-found skills in sowing and harvesting, transportation and marketing, proved equally inapplicable in their native environment. Gamio called for time and governmental investment in rural development to help save and use a natural resource which he saw being wasted—people. He also worried about the cultural change that prolonged contact with the United States might cause in Mexico.[100]

Gamio's comments are as relevant now, at the beginning of the 1980s, as they were when originally made in 1930. Money earned in the United States by migrants from the sending region is still being spent either for survival, or on luxury goods that do not and cannot promote local capital development. In Michoacán, for example, both patterns have been observed. Study of several Tarascan Indian villages and communities has demonstrated that migration to and work in the U.S. has become an essential component of household budgeting and survival. Little in the way of consumer durables, such as appliances, is purchased. Indeed the villages lack the infrastructure— paved roads, petrochemical services, and electricity—to use them.[101] In another, more modern village, where an electrification project followed paved roads, and where gasoline and diesel fuels are readily available, most of the U.S. migrants have acquired color television sets and pick-up trucks. Obviously this village has more exposure to both American and mainstream Mexican culture than do the Tarascan settlements, but it still lacks the facilities for economic development.[102] At this stage the observable impact on Mexico of migration to the United States strongly suggests that the opportunity to convert earnings abroad into development at home is a challenge that still awaits a Mexican solution.

Conclusions

We have touched on many topics in this chapter, and a summary of findings is essential before policy recommendations can be considered.

1. Questions regarding the number of immigrants and their length of residence influence all other policy considerations related to Mexican migration to the United States. The available data are inadequate, but all studies indicate some proportion of long-term residency. Determining the extent of this residual population is essential to assessing the magnitude of illegal Mexican migration, and its long-term social and cultural implications for Mexican descendants in the United States as well as for other citizens.

2. At first glance, estimates of the illegal population in the United States seem to show some concurrence. But in fact no two estimates are based on measures of the same population. When appropriate adjustments are made, little real agreement is found among estimators except on a very broad range, i.e., two to five million Mexicans in the mid-1970s.

Estimators have focused on stock and flow, both being key determinants of the impact of undocumented Mexicans. But *net flow* is also important, as it represents the number of illegal Mexican migrants who decide to reside permanently in the United States each year or each decade. These permanent migrants interact in the job market and use social services much as do U.S. citizens. Consequently their impact is felt more than that of the shorter-term shuttle migrant. So far, no methodology has convincingly estimated the net flow of undocumented Mexican migrants, although most observers agree that it is increasing.

3. Illegal Mexican migrants seeking work in the United States affect the labor market in two major ways. In general, the temporary or shuttle migrant who works at or below the minimum wage level contributes indirectly to displacement by depressing wage rates in specific areas, such as South Texas. Long-term or permanent residents who work well above minimum wage levels tend to directly displace citizen or legal migrant workers. The magnitude of these impacts—contributing to lowered wage levels at the bottom of the wage continuum, and displacing citizen-workers at the upper end—cannot be ascertained accurately in part because other factors influence employment patterns. In some urban labor markets, the availability of illegal labor creates its own new demand and thus does not displace citizen-workers. Also, in some areas employer preference *excludes* U.S. citizens and legal migrants from the domestic workforce. Therefore, employer preferences for workers at all wage levels must be determined before the extent of displacement can be measured accurately.

Any sudden attempt to remove illegals from the labor market would have profound negative consequences for citizens. The increased labor costs employers would face would drive the inefficient or marginal operators out of business, thereby adding to unemployment rates, and those businesses continuing to operate would pass on at least some of their increased labor costs to consumers in higher prices.

4. Sampling techniques are the principal method for determining the impact of undocumented Mexicans on public services. This methodology's validity is limited by the lack of samples representative of Mexicans who are in the United States illegally. As samples have described only subsets of the undocumented population, they are not adequate for making broad generalizations about illegals.

5. All primary studies agree that undocumented Mexican workers pay income taxes and make social security and other contributions, but the estimated extent of such participation varies widely, depending on the sample, ranging from 27 to 88 percent. Seasonal rural laborers who are paid in cash make the lowest proportional payroll contributions. Long-term, established urban workers tend to pay taxes and social security, and also file returns with the Internal Revenue Service.

6. Short-term Mexican migrants tend to maintain low profiles and are unlikely to apply for or receive welfare benefits and/or unemployment compensation, but long-term illegal residents use social services in much the same way as legal residents. The recently adopted procedure in California of referring suspected illegals to the INS for verification of status has significantly reduced AFDC payments to undocumented Mexicans in that state.

7. Migrants' use of education and health facilities is also correlated with duration of residence. While accurate aggregate estimates of the costs of medical services for illegal migrants are not available, some data suggest that small numbers of undocumented Mexicans incur substantial medical bills in U.S. hospitals and clinics. In any event, the medical bills of indigent illegals will become a major aspect of the migration issue in the 1980s, partly due to the rapid inflation of health-care costs. It is clearly in the nation's interest to provide reasonable medical treatment for undocumented migrants, so cost-sharing programs will need to be devised to relieve the burden on local communities.

8. U.S. law-enforcement agencies have often been deficient in their treatment of illegals. Growing concern among the Hispanic population over law-enforcement methods and procedures will continue until acceptable policies have been formulated and implemented.

9. Money dispatched to Mexico by migrants and long-term residents may provide up to 10 percent or more of rural per capita income in the sending states. As in the past, it is used largely for individual and family survival. The regions' local economies are not equipped to use the capital as funds to create renewable resources.

10. Although Mexican migration to the United States has persisted for more than a century, it is nevertheless only a stop-gap response to poverty and lack of opportunity in Mexico, or to varying labor demand in the U.S., or both. Long-term solution to the interchange of people between the two countries in ways that confer more constructive benefits to all concerned will require careful policy development in both nations. This is the subject of our next and final chapter.

7

Conclusions
and Recommendations:
The United States
and Mexico

The foregoing interpretation and analysis help demonstrate the complexity of the issues relating to Mexican migration to the United States. The nature and magnitude of the migration in this century has produced a unique de facto relationship between the two countries. The interpersonal, intercultural, and historical connections associated with the migration earns Mexico a special place and priority in the international relations and policy of the United States. Further, sensitivity to the biregional and binational characteristics of the migration should be fundamental to decisions on both sides of the international border. The following recommendations are based on two assumptions: (1) decisions and implementing actions in one country will affect the other, calling for appropriate responses, and (2) implementation strategies will need to differ according to region and nation, reflecting differences in education, culture, and economic condition.

The migratory process has persisted since the turn of the century, assuming unparalleled proportions in the 1970s. The recent acceleration has identifiable causes that will persist, at least in the near future. There has been an increasingly unequal distribution of income in Mexico, with strong regional and sectoral biases. As late as 1970, more than 63 percent of all communal farmers in Mexico still depended on animals as their primary source of power.[1] At the same time, population growth reached massive proportions. (See Appendix 6.) Even if human reproduction could be curtailed immediately, the beneficial results in terms of easing pressures on the Mexican labor force would lag at least 15 years. In short, regardless of current or future population policies, most of the Mexicans who will be potential migrants to the U.S. for the next 15 to 20 years, have already been born. Added to growing income inequality and rising population pressures is the fact that until very recently the long-term development strategy of the Mexican government did not alleviate these problems, but actually intensified them. To cope effectively with the phenomena, a new development strategy must be devised and pursued, aimed at a more equitable distribution of income, and coupled with programs of population planning.

Before outlining recommendations, we present the underlying assumptions based on our research and experience.

Assumptions Underlying
Policy Recommendations

1. Long-term resolution of the conditions in Mexico, which are largely responsible for sending massive numbers of migrants to the United States, will have to take place in Mexico. Under appropriate circumstances, however, the United States can help.

2. The border between Mexico and the United States cannot be closed at currently acceptable human, economic, or political costs. The only certain way to seal the border is with violence. No matter what human or physical barriers are established along the border, Mexican citizens seeking opportunities to work will continue to attempt entry. Acts or threats of physical violence will discourage some individuals, but will not dissuade all. Economically, closing the border would have a substantial negative impact of undetermined magnitude on both countries. Closing of the migration—the safety valve for Mexican economic discontent—would have serious political consequences for Mexico, and could also pose grave security problems for the United States.

3. Despite a growing number of studies, we still do not have empirical evidence that demonstrates clearly the impact of migration on U.S. communities. The ambiguous issue of job displacement illustrates our lack of the data and analysis needed for informed decisions.

4. Answers to the major questions posed by migration are not immediately forthcoming. The kinds of information needed for well-conceived policies require time-consuming methodologies, demanding patience in awaiting results.[2]

Five Needs for Coping with Migration

Mindful of the assumptions noted above, we identify five major needs that a successful strategy for coping with Mexican migration will have to address.

1. A highly developed information base is needed on both sides of the border.

2. Policymaking should take mutual concerns into account, and commitments should be made to long-term, cooperative decisions in matters that affect both nations.

3. Time and persistence will also be needed, as it will take several more decades to deal effectively with migration phenomena.

4. Mexico needs long-term development strategies to foster employment opportunities, with special emphasis on the sending regions and the border cities.

5. Certain sectors of the U.S. economy will need the continued availability of Mexican labor.

Policy Recommendations: United States

A Five-Year Program to Admit Migrants

We propose a five-year program to admit qualified migrants from Mexico without quota, on one-year temporary work visas. The one-year visas would be renewable annually for up to five years. These temporary migrants would be free to travel and work anywhere in the United States, with rights and responsibilities comparable to those of citizen workers. Qualifications for admission under this program would include:

1. The migrant, male or female, must be 18 years of age or older, and be able to demonstrate proof of age at the border.

2. Potential migrants must then satisfy a basic Spanish literacy test, to assure their ability to function in U.S. society at a minimum level of effectiveness.*

3. Migrants must pass a basic health inspection, to ensure the absence of contagious disease.

---

*Basic literacy in some language is essential for successful adaptation to an advanced industrial society, and Hispanic immigrants who cannot read Spanish effectively are handicapped in functioning, even when they operate largely within Spanish-language communities in the United States. Moreover if they are not literate in Spanish it will be much harder for them to achieve basic literacy in English.

Program Administration

The program would be administered under these procedures:

1. Migrants would pay a deposit of $300 upon entry, to be reclaimed with interest upon departure. (This amount is roughly equal to what is paid to smugglers by illegal migrants.) In addition, each successful migrant would be assessed an entry fee of $30, to cover the cost of screening and processing. The $300 deposit would be forfeited if not reclaimed within one year of entry. At the time of entry migrants would receive identification cards permitting temporary residence and work in the U.S. Notice of entry would be duly recorded by the Border Patrol.

2. U.S. employers of the temporary workers would observe normal payroll practices, as they would with citizen workers. The only added requirement for employers hiring Mexican migrants would be that these employees be paid only by checks, not in cash.

3. U.S. employers would make only standard deductions, including federal and state taxes, and FICA deductions. The latter, after the payment of suitable processing fees to the Social Security system, would go into a fund to help meet unpaid bills of migrants at hospitals and clinics. This fund would also provide transportation expenses back to Mexico for unemployed and indigent migrants.

4. Migrants would be eligible for disability payments, but ineligible for unemployment benefits or public assistance payments.

5. Employers would extend to migrant workers the same health-care benefit plans available to citizen workers.

6. Migrants would have the same rights as citizen workers to petition, organize, and lobby for equitable working conditions.

7. The U.S. government would make appropriate guarantees to the Mexican government to ensure the fair treatment of Mexican citizens while in the United States.

To implement this program, the role and effectiveness of the U.S. Border Patrol would have to be improved. At present the Border Patrol is understaffed, and operates under an ambiguous U.S. government policy. With clarity of policy, sufficient manpower (perhaps twice the current force), and an adequate budget, the Border Patrol could effectively control illegal migration, and channel potential qualified migrants into the legal system.

Improving the Border Patrol

In conjunction with these proposals, we recommend the following changes in the interest of improved Border Patrol efficiency.

1. The U.S. Immigration and Naturalization Service should be given sufficient funding to computerize its operations in a sophisticated manner. Computer assistance would permit the keeping of accurate records on working Mexican migrants, and also greatly assist all INS functions.

2. The program's cornerstone would be a "tamperproof" worker identification card, containing a unique number selected at random by the computer system, making counterfeit numbers and visas exceedingly difficult to obtain. These "tamperproof" identification cards could easily be modeled on the counterfeit-proof green cards now being instituted by the INS.

3. Border Patrol manpower must be increased to a level consistent with the demand for migrant entry from Mexico. The same high standards that now apply to line officers (college education and bilingualism) should apply to the new staff.

Rationale

We foresee no change either in Mexico or the U.S. that would, in the short term, alter the northward flow of Mexican nationals. The proposals that are to have a real chance of dealing successfully with the migratory phenomenon must recognize the persistence of the current state of affairs at least for the short term—barring, of course, drastic measures such as construction of a "Tortilla Curtain." Our recommendations acknowledge current reality, attempting to rationalize and humanize the processes for dealing with migration.

We believe the recommendations have a good chance of being effective, as the measures would greatly increase Border Patrol capability and performance, while strongly encouraging entry into the U.S. through legal channels. The migrants' informal communications network should quickly disseminate the intelligence that it has become more difficult to cross the border illegally, and that entry with a legal visa is preferable. In addition, information about the qualification requirements should help dissuade many of those who would fare poorly if they reached the U.S. The chief reason for the three-part migrant qualification procedure is to ensure the entry of persons with the best chance of finding employment to support themselves, and in many cases their families who remain in Mexico.

The program would have the added benefit of removing from the migrant the stigma of illegality, with its attendant adverse effects. There would be an end to discretionary detention of illegal entrants at federal prison camps like that at Safford, Arizona. Meanwhile, however, until this plan or one like it is adopted, we recommend two steps to ensure the human rights of undocumented Mexican workers who are detained. First, the Federal Bureau of Prisons should make frequent unannounced inspections of its detention camps to ensure that Mexicans in them are given the same standards of housing, sanitation, work, and recreation opportunities now required for citizen inmates. Second, to ensure due process, and with it the right to be informed of charges and to offer a defense, the courts should make mandatory the use of bilingual interpreters. The legal guide of Francisco Zazueta should be uniformly adopted to achieve this end.[3]

The recommended program for qualified Mexican migrants ensures the collection of vital, reliable data on migrants, both at the border and during a five-year period of residence in the U.S. We believe this study has demonstrated that such a body of information is essential for well-informed, long-term U.S. policy decisions on migration from Mexico. We recommend implementing two additional five-year option periods in the event that impact data are not fully developed in the first five years.

Although illegal migrants come to the United States from some 60 other nations, we believe this nation has a special relation to Mexico based on geographic proximity, historical development, and cultural, political, and economic realities. If Mexico accounts for most of the illegal migration to the U.S., then the justification for close cooperation between the two is even more compelling.

In addition to a U.S. immigration policy formulated specifically for Mexican migrants, the United States should consider an economic policy designed to help Mexico meet some of its employment goals. We suggest that the leadership of both nations pursue cooperative economic planning through a joint commission, similar to the one that now exists, but strengthened. Cooperation would not necessarily involve "mixing" the two countries' economies any more than they already are, but would be aimed at developing measures to stimulate the rural Mexican economy. Possible avenues for exploration by a joint commission include encouraging the importation of capital equipment, and protecting certain labor-intensive industries in Mexico.

California is the primary receiving state for Mexican migrants, so this state's role in meeting the needs of its ethnically diverse population, a substantial portion of which is Hispanic, could become a model for the nation in the 1980s and 1990s. People of Mexican ancestry in California have many and varied needs ranging from education and health care to employment opportunities. Obviously, before sound policy can be formulated more must be known about the community impact of Mexican migration, and the county impact studies undertaken in California point the way to responsible assessment. The report to the San Diego County Board of Supervisors of April 1980, shows how sensitive these studies can be to short-term and long-term resident migrants, and legal immigrants. Similar studies, embracing the entire community of Mexican-antecedent residents, could provide new insight for thoughtful public policy. Studies that address whole communities or counties, rather than just isolated portions, are essential to develop effective coping strategies.

Policy Recommendations: Mexico

As demonstrated earlier, certain regions in Mexico have persistent and growing traditions of migration to the United States. For nearly 40 consecutive years some villages have sent members *al Norte,* a pattern that has persisted for so long that history and tradition now strongly reinforce the migration process. Neither the traditions nor contemporary economic reality in the rural countryside will be altered significantly in the short term. Our proposals acknowledge these realities and take them into account.

Mexico must simultaneously seek effective solutions to four major problems: (1) increasing local employment opportunities for low-income people in both rural and urban environments; (2) establishing a more equitable income distribution; (3) controlling population; and (4) alleviating urban massing. We suggest the following proposals as ways of dealing with the four major problems just noted.*

Increased Rural Employment Opportunities

Rural development programs must reach the working families that send members to the United States. A balanced approach is necessary, utilizing grassroots support, coupled with effective delivery of credit, technology, and leadership. Mexico's small farmers should be the beneficiaries of any such programs.

The small farmers of Mexico have the same needs as farmers anywhere: (1) advice on how to make their farming more productive and profitable; (2) demonstrations of new techniques of growing crops and caring for farm animals; (3) reliable, locally available sources of farm supplies, and credit obtainable at reasonable interest rates; and (4) help in marketing crops.

---

*In developing sound action plans, the Mexican government needs to examine the regions of Mexico in a new light. The way data are presently collected and reported, information on the primary sending states is scattered among two, three, or four different geographic groupings. For these purposes, the states of Durango, Guanajuato, Jalisco, Michoacán, San Luis Potosí, and Zacatecas should be regarded as a single, distinct statistical reporting area. Only in this way can primary data be readily accumulated that will be adequate to measure program effectiveness.

Since 1965 an organization called Farm Centers International has been at work in the State of Michoacán, helping to supply these necessities to small farmers. At first the project's emphasis was on opening small farm-supply stores in villages, and training the storekeepers to be farm advisors to their communities. Demonstrations of farm projects were made. Farmers were organized into groups to get credit from banks. A trucker supplied the stores with their stock, and hauled farm products to market. This project was successful in producing change, but because its leadership came from outside, it was difficult to keep staffed.

In 1977 a new project was started in Patzcuaro, Michoacán. Its leader, a former schoolteacher, selected men from the villages to serve as farm advisors in their home communities. There are now five of these "tecnicos" serving 50 villages. Each Saturday the tecnicos meet to receive instructions from their leader or from guest speakers.

At first the tecnicos spent much of their time helping the farmers to control the *tuza* (pocket gopher), a large burrowing rodent that each year destroys about one-third of the farmers' corn. In the first three months of 1979 alone, farmers made a calculated 65,380 applications of rodenticide bait, eliminating 45,766 tuzas, saving corn valued at $31,106. The cost of the bait to the average farmer was 22 cents. Since the beginning of the project, over a half a million dollars worth of corn has been saved, at a cost of only a few thousand dollars.

The success of the tecnicos in controlling tuzas made the farmers much more receptive than they might have been when the tecnicos offered other help, such as rat control, fertilization, control of plant diseases, and care of farm animals. Farmers feel a close relationship to a man who is "one of them," who arrives in their village on foot, on a bicycle, or on a horse. As one of the tecnicos told Howard Twining of Farm Centers International, "If you want me to advise my neighbors on how to make a change, you will have to help me to make the change myself. Farmers here will listen politely to the government extensionist, but they will only follow the advice of a farmer who has made the change himself."

The success of Farm Centers International in making change happen suggests the need for a reappraisal of Mexican extension efforts. A more humble and earthy approach may be the only one the campesinos will accept.[4]

Careful study of the experiences of Farm Centers International is in order, to guide development of similar programs capable of taking root and effecting change. Also, the subtle but important roles of governmental price supports and local corruption must be acknowledged. The government has directed Banco de Crédito Rural to sell fertilizer in Michoacán at a fixed price per load, but local sellers charge from 92 to 157 pesos more per load. Clearly such practices discourage fertilizer use. Similarly, the "guaranteed" maize price that has remained constant for three harvests in a period of severe inflation means income losses for farmers. Moreover farmers rarely get even the nominal price. Upon presentation for payment, their maize is almost invariably found "deficient"—too mealy, undersized, off color, etc. The farmers thus get less than the government guarantees, the difference going to the middleman. At the very least, the price of maize should reflect the cost of maize farming, and strong measures are needed to limit and discourage graft. Without such an approach there is little reason to believe that rural economic activity will increase sufficiently to slow the pace of out-migration. We have already seen the results, including increased employment, when the Mexican government makes maize farming profitable, as it did from 1960 to 1966.

In examining Mexico's rural development since 1940, we noted how public and private supplies of agricultural credit were channeled into modern rather than traditional farming. On a relative scale, the availability of credit for small farmers has declined, and for some has even disappeared. A crucial lack is the inadequacy of credit, due largely to an inefficient delivery system. For small farmers, credit is the greatest single stimulus to adoption of agricultural innovations.[5] If they are to increase productivity, diversify crops, develop water resources, or even combat spreading erosion by planting trees, Mexican farmers in the sending region need access to credit, dispensed by banking administrators who are sensitive to local requirements. They also need the kind of locally generated technical assistance and financial guidance that has been so successful in the Farm Centers International program.

In the early 1970s the Mexican government initiated a program designed to integrate the activities of national agencies charged with promoting rural development. This program, called PIDER (Programa de Inversiones para el Desarrollo Rural), coordinates, directs, and monitors the efforts of some 15 domestic assistance agencies. PIDER focuses on poverty areas and currently operates in 130 Mexican microregions containing some six million of the nation's rural poor. The budget is enormous by any standards, the $500 million spent in 1979 representing about a fifth of total national investment in agriculture, and perhaps 0.6 percent of the gross domestic product (GDP).[6]

Because of PIDER's design and implementation it has been judged one of the world's more effective rural development programs. It is limited to community activities in villages of between 300 and 3,000 population. Directly productive investments comprise about 70 percent of total allocations. Project investments are limited to a maximum of $100,000 each, and so far approximately 5,000 projects have been funded. A determined and partially successful effort has been made to minimize paperwork, while the organization has maintained a careful monitoring and evaluation system. With the advent of the Lopez Portillo presidency in 1976, an effort was initiated to make the program more effective by decentralizing its operations. Consequently more decisions now originate at the regional or local level, helping foster projects that respond to village needs.

PIDER's successes are well documented. For example, in certain areas small-scale irrigation projects have increased employment opportunities and improved productivity. The program's irrigation projects in one Guanajuato ejido (in Mexico's North Center) increased the average number of person-days worked per hectare by 218 percent. Similarly, in the State of Morelos, another ejido created additional employment equal to 350 new permanent jobs by bringing 2,000 hectares under irrigation with a PIDER investment. Notwithstanding such successes, PIDER has also had difficulties. Not surprisingly, many of the constraints are merely different versions of past problems. There have been substantial problems in monitoring results and it is not always apparent to what extent a given report or inventory is accurate. Evidence is unclear respecting aggregate benefits or their distribution. Helping the farmers who rely entirely upon rainfed cultivation—the majority of Mexican farmers—has been a 1970s priority for the government, yet according to PIDER studies soil and water conservation efforts in dry areas have not increased farmers' incomes.

Income Distribution

The Mexican government has a responsibility to rural and urban people whose real incomes have decreased since 1940. It has tried to halt the downward trend by tying the national minimum wage to the cost-of-living index.[7] But more can be done, especially for the people who do not benefit from national minimum wage laws, i.e., small farmers and the majority of landless agricultural laborers. Accordingly, subsistence and semicommercial farmers should be the principal target of the country's agricultural development efforts.

The future of public investment in the rural infrastructure will depend largely on national revenues, and on Mexico's ability to obtain funds from international agencies. So far, Mexico has been highly successful in getting substantial agricultural development loans from the World Bank and the Inter-American Development Bank. Oil-revenue surpluses have already been allocated to the country's National Plan for Industrial Development, aimed at creating employment through massive capital investments and decentralization. Only the future will tell whether these efforts can improve the equitability of income distribution, or for that matter whether they will even reduce the current trend toward greater inequities. One way of achieving more equitable income distribution would be reform of Mexico's tax system, which now has one of the lowest personal income tax rates in Latin America.[8]

Urban Massing and
Urban Employment

Migratory phenomena have brought hundreds of thousands of rural Mexicans into the cities, in the process causing urban crowding and the spread of infectious disease. Conurbations along the international boundary with the United States have grown so fast that anything resembling urban planning has been nearly impossible.

While the oil spill that reached the Texas coast in 1979 attracted much media notice, another form of pollution that affects many border cities— sewage from Mexico that washes into the United States—went relatively unattended. New River originates in Calexico, Mexico, opposite Mexicali, flowing from south to north through California's Imperial valley. "The river [New River] carried with it tons of human waste, the discharge of a string of slaughterhouses, dead dogs and cats, an occasional human body and a wide range of communicable diseases."[9] It is one of many open sewage lines running into the U.S., a direct result of the urban massing that has accompanied Mexican migration toward and into this country. Tijuana's decades-old sewer system discharged waste into the Pacific Ocean, where ocean currents took it up to San Diego. The sewer was discontinued after San Diego complained, and the U.S. city offered to connect its sewage system with that of Tijuana's on an "emergency" basis until a new facility could be built. The offer was accepted, but the "emergency" has persisted on a continuing basis, contributing to the overload of San Diego's system. Clearly, Mexico needs to begin solving the sewage problems of its border cities, an effort that should be made in cooperation with the sister cities to the north.

The migration of the past 10 years has overwhelmed the infrastructure and service capabilities of Mexican urban centers in all spheres of activity. In addition to problems of sanitation and health, Mexico has to cope with housing scarcity and unemployment in the Mexican portions of the border conurbations. But this needs to be done in a way and at a pace that does not make the areas even greater magnets than they are now. Therefore we recommend prudent urban planning, in conjunction with efforts to better the quality of rural life, seeking a balanced approach. Reforms must be planned and introduced carefully so that temporary improvements in one area are not immediately overwhelmed and offset by influxes of poor, desperate people.

Improved urban employment opportunities will be crucial to successful urban planning in Mexico. Again, such planning must take into account the transferability of skills, giving priority to job-related skills that are particularly suited to Mexico, otherwise the programs may unwittingly provide training principally for those seeking to migrate. The related need to develop urban-based industries that rely on renewable resources such as steel foundries is addressed by the new development plan of the Mexican government.

Such internal programs are essential, and can serve as a counterpoise to the Border Industrialization Program (BIP), which sites U.S. factories in Mexico, utilizing Mexican labor. While the effectiveness of the BIP is still not yet known, present evidence suggests very mixed results. Although individual workers have benefited, the total numbers of jobs created have been small compared to the large number of unemployed and underemployed in northern Mexico. Moreover, women comprise nearly 80 percent of the workers. Instead of providing the primary income source for the head of a household, the BIP may well be supplying supplementary income for families whose nominal head works in the United States. In any event, it is clear that employment in the urban sector, especially in the north of Mexico, is a critical need that must receive priority attention in the coming decade.

Population

To the surprise of many observers, Mexico abruptly reversed its long-standing pronatalist population policy in 1972. In the same year, President Luis Echeverría created a National Population Council charged with articulating the new national policy. Within two years, Mexico had amended Article IV of its constitution to include the following words: "All persons have the right to decide in a free, responsible, and informed manner on the number and spacing of their children."[10] Thus, Mexico is one of only four countries including China, Ecuador, and Yugoslavia that have made family planning a constitutional right. The long-overdue legalization of family planning allowed government agencies to begin the arduous processes of supplying an already existing demand for contraceptives, and even more important, to begin encouraging new demand.

Initial services came from the Ministry of Health and Welfare, which began family planning activities in early 1973. By mid-1976 their family planning programs operated in 50 hospitals, 157 urban health centers, 500 semiurban centers, and 1,564 rural centers. During the same period, the Mexican Social Security Institute began to offer similar services to its members. These programs and others like them were supplemented by an educational campaign through television, radio, and the classroom.[11]

The results of these efforts are indeed encouraging: in June of 1976, some 1.8 million women of childbearing age, married or living in union, practiced some form of contraception; this number amounted to 21 percent of the total population of childbearing-age women in Mexico (15 to 44 years).[12] The fertility decline is reflected in a drop in the crude birth rate (numbers of live births per 1,000 population) from about 45 in 1973 to 38 in 1978.[13] Mexico's coordinating agency for family planning, the Coordinación del Programa Nacional de Planificación Familiar, has recently projected a further crude birth-rate decline to 33 by the end of 1982.[14]

Unquestionably Mexico's natural rate of population increase is lower than it was in the 1960s and early 1970s, and the government's initial efforts have been laudable. But we do not know precisely how much the pace of growth has slowed, and of course the trends of the 1980s remain to be charted. While the 15 percent decline in the crude birth rate between 1973 and 1978 is certainly impressive, one can note for comparison that India currently has a crude birth rate of 34, or about 10 percentage points less than Mexico.[15]

Besides the crude birth rate, other indicators can help point out the magnitude of the change. One of these is the numbers of "acceptors," i.e., those who have accepted and presumably are currently using contraceptives. Various studies since 1973 have attempted to use sampling techniques to estimate the percentage of women and men utilizing some method of contraception. A 1978-79 survey of over 2,000 people conducted by PROFAM, Mexico's subsidized commercial retail distributor, found 56 percent currently using contraceptives.[16] In perhaps the largest such survey ever undertaken, PROFAM canvassed 122,368 women in late 1979 in a low-income suburb of Mexico City, and found that 53 percent were using contraceptives.[17]

On the other hand, contraception usage declines markedly outside of Mexico City and in the other large urban centers. Thus another PROFAM study in 1979 in the City of Queretaro, approximately 150 miles to the northwest of Mexico City, showed that 32 percent of the sample utilized contraceptives.[18] Perhaps the most comprehensive and complete survey in terms of methodology was carried out by Coordinación in 1978. Their study, a well-distributed sampling accurately reflecting urban/rural proportions, found that only 26 percent of *all* women were using a birth control method.[19] In the rural areas, the contraception rate was only about half the levels in the metropolitan centers.

The available data support these two observations: the rate of acceptors is much higher in the larger cities than in the rural areas, and there is great variation in estimates of the number of current "users." These observations have major implications for the sending region. As noted earlier, the sending region is highly rural, and most Mexican migrants, both those moving internally and those crossing international borders, originate in the rural sending region. In any event, at this writing it seems highly likely that contraception usage in the rural sending region is still minimal. Government agencies and PROFAM are now taking steps to remedy this deficiency. PROFAM has mounted a concerted effort to place its products in semi-rural towns of between 2,500 and 15,000 inhabitants.[20] Mexico is clearly recognizing that service delivery, along with educational and media promotion, must be extended to the countryside.

But the expansion of services into the rural sector will be much more difficult than the initial effort, which concentrated on the urban population. Mexico's socioeconomic structure, especially in the larger cities and in the North, has changed dramatically in the past 40 years, with rapid urbanization, industrialization, and expanded educational opportunities. Several factors that tend to reduce fertility, e.g., higher educational level and increased women's labor-force participation—more prevalent in the urban sector—combined in the 1960s to create a demand for family planning services. Thus when the government began sponsoring birth control programs in the mid-1970s, it largely was fulfilling an urban demand that already existed. In short, the initial advances in slowing the pace of population growth are likely to prove the easiest, and in the case of Mexico, have been concentrated in the urban sector. Further advances are likely to become more difficult, as people must be reached whose level of acceptance is more limited, particularly in rural areas, where custom, attitudes, knowledge, and patterns of machismo behavior are considerably more resistant to change than in Mexico City and other urban centers.

Complicating Mexico's future population growth is the fact that the high birth rates through the 1960s and 1970s have produced some relatively large population cohorts. In 1970, for example, the cohort aged 0 to 4 years comprised nearly a fifth of Mexico's total population.[21] As these cohorts move through childbearing years they will produce a second wave of the current "baby boom," *even if* the crude birth rates have been reduced. Thus, the childbearing cohort in the 15- to 44-year age range, numbering some 11 million women in 1970, will have increased to 19 million in 1985.[22] This shifting age structure means that the absolute numbers of births in Mexico will continue to grow each year for the next several decades. Accordingly Mexico must expect to add some 45 to 50 million people to its population in the 20 years between 1980 and 2000.

Mexico's efforts in the 1970s to expand its family planning activities will no doubt have a highly favorable impact on the country's long-term prospects. Thus if Mexico's rate of population growth were to continue at its current rate of about 3 percent per annum, by the year 2075 the country would have the staggering total of over a billion people. Instead, current projections suggest that Mexico will reach a stable population of about 254 million people in 2075.[23] For these projections to be met, however, Mexico will have to redouble its efforts to educate, change attitudes, and provide services for its citizens, especially those in rural areas. We have already noted why fertility declines in the 1980s will not come as easily as those of the 1970s.

Even if Mexico does achieve the predicted birth-rate reductions in the next two decades, the country will still face enormous development problems. Not the least of these is simply feeding the population. Currently,

Mexico must feed 70 million people from a supply of arable land that approximates what the State of Iowa has. It must also try to provide employment opportunities for a rapidly growing labor force. To repeat a much-used but still apt phrase, the people in Mexico who will be added to the workforce over the next 15 years have already been born. In short, despite encouraging declines in the rate of increase, Mexico's surging population and growing labor force will remain a critical factor in the migration-related phenomena for at least the short term, because many of these people will continue to seek employment in the United States.

APPENDIX 1

Results of Mexican Government Survey
of Illegal Migration to the United States
1978

State of Origin	Percent of Sample (N = 22,822)	Per Capita per 1,000 Persons
San Luis Potosí	3.68	.655
Zacatecas	5.25	1.259
Guanajuato	10.14	1.020
Jalisco	13.86	.959
Michoacán	14.74	1.448
Durango	3.48	.846
Total	51.15%	10.55
Rest of Mexico	48.85%	4.73

Source: México, Secretaría del Trabajo y Prevision Social, Centro Nacional de Información y Estadísticas del Trabajo (CENIET), *La Encuesta Nacional de Emigración a la Frontera Norte del País y a los Estados Unidos* (México, D.F.: 1979), see Statistical Appendix, Table B.

APPENDIX 2

Ejido Creation in Mexico, 1920–1940

State	Area National-ized, Hectares 12/1920–2/1930	Number of Recipients	Rural per Capita per 100 Persons	Area Nation-ized, Hectares 2/1930–11/1940	Number of Recipients	Rural per Capita per 100 Persons
San Luis Potosí	617,201	34,755	8.26	1,985,640	46,069	9.09
Zacatecas	360,297	18,085	5.18	1,186,061	37,074	8.71
Guanajuato	101,379	17,236	2.65	689,544	65,202	9.60
Jalisco	238,891	39,252	5.16	884,564	72,866	8.74
Michoacán	159,691	30,818	3.99	1,220,583	88,698	10.55
Durango	296,946	16,270	5.25	1,812,784	40,973	11.16
Mexico	5,232,818	550,859	5.00	20,157,519	991,805	7.78

Presidential Terms, 1920–1940:

1 December 1920 – 30 November 1924	Alvaro Obregón
1 December 1924 – 30 November 1928	Plutarco Elías Calles
1 December 1928 – 4 February 1930	Pascual Ortíz Rubio
5 February 1930 – 4 September 1932	Emilio Portes Gil
5 September 1932 – 30 November 1934	Abelardo L. Rodríguez
1 December 1934 – 30 November 1940	Lázaro Cárdenas

Source: México, Departamento Agrario, *Memoria* (México: D.F., 1945–1946), statistics section, unpaginated.

APPENDIX 3

Irrigated Land Newly Created by the Mexican Government
1926–1970

Region	Hectares	Area (%)	% of Total Government Investment (1941–70)
North:			
Baja California	127,408		
Sinaloa	345,057		
Sonora	212,926		
Tamaulipas	267,105		
	952,496	51.7	47.3
Sending States:			
Durango	11,400		
Guanajuato	55,925		
Jalisco	24,129		
Michoacán	104,674		
San Luis Potosí	500		
Zacatecas	11,400		
	208,028	11.3	15.0
Rest of Mexico:	680,506	37.0	37.7
Totals	1,841,030	100%	100%

Sources: México, Secretaría de Recursos Hidráulicos, *Informe de Labores, l de Septiembre de 1974 al 31 de Agosto de 1975* (México, 1975); Appendix 5–1, 5–2; investment from Alcántara, *Modernizing Mexican Agriculture...,* Table 7, p. 18.

APPENDIX 4

Per Capita Maize and Wheat Production
in Mexico, 1940–1969
(kilograms)

Period	Per Capita Maize Production	Per Capita Wheat Production
1940–44	101.8	21.1
1945–49	110.8	18.1
1950–54	135.9	24.2
1955–59	158.8	39.4
1960–64	185.1	40.4
1965–69	206.9	42.2
1970–74	179.9	44.7
1975	157.2	47.8
1980	147.1 (est.)	

Sources and methods: Maize, wheat, and population figures, 1940–69 from Alcántara, *Modernizing Mexican Agriculture...*, tables 38 and 39, pp. 110–113, and Clark Reynolds, *The Mexican Economy...*, Appendix E, p. 384. Population figures are for quinquennial years beginning in 1940. The 1965 population figure is extrapolated from Reynolds's last year of 1963. Reynolds's other population data have been adjusted slightly to reflect undercounting in the official censuses. Years 1970–75 from Banco Nacional de México, *Review of the Economic Situation of Mexico,* 49(566) (January 1973), p. 16; ibid., 51(603) (February 1976), p. 52; México, *IX censo general...1970.*

APPENDIX 5

Agricultural Peak Employment of Seasonal Workers in California, Month of September, 1950–1977

Year	Hired Domestic Seasonal	Contract Foreign	Total Seasonal
1950	172,200	7,700	179,900
1951	177,300	25,200	202,500
1952	175,600	34,200	209,800
1953	188,700	31,900	220,600
1954	158,800	47,000	205,800
1955	176,000	66,500	242,500
1956	164,700	91,300	256,000
1957	158,100	84,600	242,700
1958	142,100	89,600	231,700
1959	161,300	83,500	244,800
1960	141,300	71,600	212,900
1961	165,600	60,900	226,500
1962	158,000	72,900	230,900
1963	158,900	54,000	212,900
1964	161,200	63,900	225,100
1965	167,000	11,400	178,400
1966	173,000	7,800	180,800
1967	190,900	0	190,900
1968	176,900	0	176,900
1969	187,600	0	187,600
1970	180,600	0	180,600
1971	182,900	0	182,900
1972	151,500	0	151,500
1973	183,000	0	183,000
1974	188,200	0	188,200
1975	204,200	0	204,200
1976	191,600	0	191,600
1977	195,600	0	195,600

Source: State of California, Employment Development Department, Report 881M, various years, cited in Mamer and Fuller, "Employment on California Farms," in University of California, *Technological Change...*, Table 4, p. 16.

APPENDIX 6

Mexican Population, 1900–1980

Year	Population
1900	13,607,272
1910	15,160,369
1921	14,334,780
1930	16,552,722
1940	19,653,552
1950	25,791,017
1960	34,923,129
1970	48,225,238
1980	68,000,000e
1990	87,000,000e
2000	106,000,000e

e = estimate

Sources and methods: México, *Censos generales. . .1900–1970.* Estimated figures derived by applying the following intercensal growth rates: 1970–1979, 3.5 percent; 1980–1989, 2.5 percent; 1990–1999, 2.0 percent.

APPENDIX 7

The Contemporary Information Dilemma

The lack of reliable information makes it difficult to evaluate the contemporary impact of migration on both countries. Information on legal migrants is relatively good,[1] but for illegals it is sparse, uneven, and often questionable. The major reason for this is obvious: clandestine activity by definition precludes accurate monitoring. However, despite the difficulties in securing primary information, certain techniques make estimates and generalizations possible.

A glance at Table 7-1 might suggest a surfeit rather than a scarcity of data. But the quality of the information and estimates leaves much to be desired. The following discussion of the major data sources will help the reader judge their reliability and usefulness.

1. INS Data. These internally collected statistics are generated for several purposes, most of which have little to do with illegal migration. The data are collected and used in connection with compliance with country quota, naturalization procedures, legitimation of status, and various law enforcement functions, e.g., checking visas or apprehending illegal entrants. Data on apprehensions count the number of times the INS makes apprehensions, not the number of individuals it apprehends. While there are known to be repeaters, no one yet has developed a reliable method or ratio for adjusting the apprehension total. But despite such limitations, INS apprehension data are the statistics cited most frequently in the literature.

The reasons for widespread use of apprehension data are easy to understand, if hard to defend. The figures are readily available, and when information is scarce, virtually any figures will be used. Moreover, there is an intuitive sense of affinity, even of correlation, between the figure for those caught and the estimates of how many got away. It is tempting to use a known figure for apprehensions as a basis for guessing the number of evaders. The data we have developed on net apprehensions, presented in Table 18 (Chapter 6), show that half a million illegals tried and failed to enter the U.S. in 1977. If this technique is applied consistently over a substantial period of time to the gross INS figures, we can obtain reasonably reliable data on the flow of those who were ever apprehended. Perhaps that will provide a basis for determining the relationship of the flow of "ever apprehended" to the population stock of migrants in the U.S., and to the flow of those never apprehended.

But INS data are not limited simply to apprehensions. Reports of the investigative section of the INS San Diego office contain data on occupation

TABLE 7-1

Select Sources of Primary Information:
Recent Research on Mexican Migration

Data Source	Data Description	Examples
INS immigration data	Legal entries (l)	INS Annual Reports
INS border-crossing data	Green card commuters (l); bad-faith entries (l)	North, 1976 North, 1976
INS apprehensions	Number of illegal entries (i)	INS Annual Reports
INS forms and question-naires	Demographic information, employment (i)	Flores and Cardenas, 1978 Merrill, 1978 Dagodag, 1976
Deportee interviews: United States	Profile, origins, economic activities, social services utilization, frequency of migration (i)	North and Houstoun, 1976 Avante Systems, 1978 Samora, 1971
Deportee interviews: Mexico	Comprehensive profile, origins, destinations, employment data, remittances, FOM (i)	CENIET, 1978, 1979 Bustamante, 1977
Community impact: U.S. interviews and surveys	Social services utilization, education, labor, taxation, housing and spending patterns, the legal system, residual population (i)	Mines, 1979 Van Arsdol et al., 1979 Avante Systems, 1978 Orange County Task Force, 1978 Cardenas, 1977

Community impact: Mexico, interviews and surveys	Social change, economic change, styles of migrancy, FOM, remittance of effects, traditional sending regions (i)	Mines, 1979 Reichert and Massey, 1979 Shadow, 1979 Dinerman, 1978 Cornelius, 1976 Zarrugh, 1974
Census analysis	Aggregate migration data and estimates (i)	Robinson, 1979 Briggs, 1978 Stoddard, 1978 Urquidi and Méndez, 1978 Downing and Weaver, 1976
Analyses and estimates from aggregate data	Stock and flow of migrants, cost/benefit analysis, sector analysis (i)	Robinson, 1979 Cornelius, 1978 Jenkins, 1978 Lancaster and Scheuren, 1977
Other	Remittances through banks and post, address files; destinations, origins (i)	Cornelius, 1976 Gamio, 1930 Díez-Canedo, 1977
Overview	Summary, explanation, and interpretation (m)	Cornelius, 1978 North and Houstoun, 1976 CENIET, all studies

Key:
l = legal
i = illegal
m = mixed, legal and illegal
FOM = frequency of migration

and utilization of social services by apprehended illegals. These data are not based on apprehensions made at the border, but on forms completed when illegals come to the INS for information. Our fieldwork has indicated that the subjects appear to have been in the United States longer than those detained at the border, and thus may represent a more settled population. This information from San Diego and elsewhere may yet reveal insights into the population remaining in the United States indefinitely.

2. Deportee Interviews. Deportee interviews are valuable information sources because the interviewers are not limited by the relatively few questions included on INS forms. Thus it has been possible to obtain comprehensive profiles of large samples, e.g., the CENIET study of over 25,000 deportees, and to collect data on migrant origins, work histories, and social services utilization in the United States. But as with the INS data, this information-collecting technique necessarily emphasizes those who are detected by U.S. authorities—the "ever apprehended." As a result, data on frequency of migration, length of stay in the U.S., and even the means and methods of migration may be quite distinct from the group never apprehended. Thus caution should be used in working with and evaluating primary data gathered from border interviews of deportees.

3. Community Impact Studies. Of major interest in analyzing Mexican migration is the movement's impact on individual communities in both countries. Fortunately the number of these studies is growing. However, most of them focus on Mexico, and there is a general lack of well-founded research on the effects of illegal migration on U.S. communities. Mexican surveys usually have a village orientation, the household-sampling technique comprising the most common form of information gathering. Much useful material on the local social and economic impact of migration on the Mexican population is made possible by these inquiries. But migrant data are biased toward those who have returned to Mexico, and we are left with little knowledge about the migrant population remaining in the United States.

A second limitation of the household-survey technique in Mexico is simply the magnitude of the task. It can take years to complete full investigations even in a village with only a few thousand inhabitants. Thus the samples employed by these studies tend to be limited in number and in the degree to which they can support generalizations. This problem is compounded in regions where different investigations have found conflicting evidence. A massive survey recently completed by CENIET which sampled some 60,000 households may significantly improve the use of this important technique for collecting migration impact data in Mexico.

Community studies are less numerous and less comprehensive in the United States mainly because it is hard to find illegal residents who are willing to be interviewed. While this has been done in a few cases, the samples are small. Moreover, the interviewees tend to be persons residing in the U.S. on a more permanent basis,[2] and thus are not necessarily representative. Further, because it is not easy to find willing interviewees, the sampling technique is not random but relies on networks of trusted communication. This snowball-sampling method is less valid than random selection, but may be the only one available given the problems of data collection in the U.S.

An especially useful binational, bicommunity approach has been adopted by a few researchers. Richard Mines, for example, has studied extensively a high-percentage sending community in Mexico, along with its receiving counterpart in California.[3] Ultimately, the greatest use of such comprehensive approaches should provide the data and perspective needed for sound decisions. The investigative process is lengthy and painstaking; results of research come only years after a study begins.

4. Aggregate Data. Mexican migration cannot be understood without reference to macroeconomic and demographic developments, e.g., unemployment, labor demand, and population growth. Studies of such trends are only as good as the skill and judgment employed in data handling. Downing and Weaver, for example, have given researchers a valuable reference aid in summary migration data. But they failed to note that the 1960 and the 1970 censuses were taken in June and January respectively.[4] Given highly seasonal migratory patterns, these differences in time of data collection undoubtedly influenced the final enumerations.

Other types of aggregate data, such as those presented by Clement and Green, make possible analysis of the effects of economic change upon political decisions.[5] This kind of analysis, like that of James and Evans, facilitates understanding of the interrelation of national and international forces in migration.[6] For estimating total numbers of illegal Mexicans in the U.S., several new methodological approaches of varying persuasiveness used macrodata for new estimates. They are discussed in detail in Appendix 8.

Distribution of Primary Data Research

Much of the research founded upon the kinds of primary data enumerated above is scattered in a variety of disparate publications or, to a lesser extent, still remains as unpublished papers and work in progress. To conclude our discussion, and for a better understanding of the nature of completed primary research, we provide the following tables, 7-2 through 7-4. These include, among other information, location of research both in Mexico and in the United States, sample size, and nature of the population. The reader should consult the bibliography under the name of the principal investigator for full citations.

TABLE 7-2

Primary Biographical Data: Survey Information on Undocumented Mexican Migrants in the U.S., 1969–1979 U.S. Locations

Investigators	Data Source	Sample Size[a] (Migrants Only)	Location of Survey	Year	Nature of Information
Avante Systems	Questionnaire	600	Border Patrol centers, social service agencies, streets of El Paso and McAllen, Texas	1978	Socioeconomic profile; social services utilization, civil rights abuse
Gilbert Cardenas	Interviews	100	San Antonio, Texas	1975	Employment data
Wayne A. Cornelius	Not available	N/A	N/A	1977–79	
W. Tim Dagodag	INS forms	3,204[b]	Border Patrol stations, Chula Vista sector	1973	Place of birth, residence, some selected characteristics
Kenneth F. Johnson Nina M. Ogle	INS forms (I–213, I–274)	1,101[b]	St. Louis, Missouri	1975–78	Origins, migration patterns, employment
Philip L. Kelly	INS forms (I–213), interviews	1,662	San Luis County, Colorado	1974–78	Origins, employment

Source	Method	Sample size	Location	Year	Data
Jay Merrill	INS forms	3,417[b]	Border Patrol stations, San Diego, Riverside, and Imperial counties	1976–77	Employment in U.S., basic migrant profile
Richard Mines	Questionnaires, interviews informants	318[b]	South San Francisco and other California locations	1977–79	Socioeconomic profile, patterns and types of migration, work histories
David S. North Marion F. Houstoun	Questionnaires, interviews	481[b]	19 sites (mainly INS district offices), 1975 Border Patrol stations	1975	Employment, social services use, origins, socioeconomic characteristics
Orange County	Questionnaires, interviews	177	Orange County, Calif. (homes and places of work)	1977–78	Socioeconomic data
Julian Samora	Questionnaire	493	3 Border Patrol detention centers, California and Texas	1969	Employment data; type of migration; origins and destinations
Ellwyn Stoddard	Undetermined	71	Rural border community	1975	Employment data
Maurice Van Arsdol et al.	Interviews	2,687[b]	Los Angeles, Calif.	1972–75	Socioeconomic profile
Victor Villalpando et al.	Questionnaire	217	Border Patrol station, Chula Vista, Calif.	1976	Socioeconomic data

Notes: [a] For some analyses, sample size may be smaller, due to incompleteness in gathering information.
[b] Computerized.

TABLE 7-3

Primary Biographical Data: Survey Information
on Undocumented Mexican Migrants to the U.S., 1975–1979
Mexico Locations

Investigators	Data Source	Sample Size[a] (Migrants Only)	Location of Survey	Year	Nature of Information
Wayne A. Cornelius	Questionnaire, interviews	230	9 villages, Jalisco	1975	Socioeconomic profiles; employment in U.S.
Juan Díez-Canedo	Interviews	132	Jalisco, Aguascalientes, Guanajuato, Mexico City	1976	Selected employment and migration data
Michael Kearney James Stuart	Informal interviews	50 +[b]	San Gerónimo del Progreso, Oaxaca	1978–79	Migratory patterns, village conditions
Richard Mines	Questionnaire, interviews, informants	339[b]	Las Animas, Zacatecas	1977–79	Socioeconomic profile; types and patterns of migration
Josh Reichert Douglas Massey	Household census, school census	919[b]	Guadalupe, Michoacán (pseudonym)	1977–78	Migratory patterns, types of migration
Robert D. Shadow	Household census	822	Municipality of Villa Guerrero, Jalisco	1975–76	Socioeconomic conditions, out-migration patterns

Notes: [a] Sample size: for some analyses, sample size may be smaller, due to incompleteness in gathering information.
[b] Computerized.

TABLE 7-4

Primary Biographical Data:
Surveys on Undocumented Mexican Migrants to the U.S.
Mexican and Other Researchers, 1972–1979

Investigator	Data Source	Sample Size[a]	Location of Survey	Year	Nature of Information
Jorge A. Bustamante	Questionnaires, interviews	919	8 border cities, Mexico	1975	Socioeconomic profile
Comisión Intersecretarial	Questionnaires	2,794[b] 1,316[b] 1,618[b]	9 border cities, Mexico	1972 1974 1975	Socioeconomic profile
CENIET	Questionnaires, interviews	9,992[b]	Various border cities, Mexico	1977	Migration patterns, socioeconomic profile
CENIET	Questionnaires, interviews	25,138[b]	Various border cities, Mexico	1978	Migration patterns, socioeconomic profile
CENIET	Questionnaires	60,000[b] households	Cities and villages in Mexico	1978–79	Northward migration patterns, socioeconomic profiles
Hélène Rivière d'Arc	Informal interviews	420	Tepatitlan, Jalisco	1972	Migration patterns

Notes: [a]Sample size includes immigrants only.
[b]Computerized.

APPENDIX 8

Estimates of the Illegal Population
in the United States, Circa 1975

Table 8-1 presents information from the Lesko report of 1975, and from three other reports: Robinson (1979), Lancaster and Scheuren (1977), and Heer (1979). Note that researchers have applied various methods in estimating the number of illegal residents in the U.S. See Chapter 6 for a discussion of the Lesko method.

Gregory Robinson, of the U.S. Census Bureau, utilized a demographic technique that involved a comparative analysis of trends in age-specific death rates in the U.S. to determine the illegal male population aged 20-44 in a select 10-state area. He first assumed that deaths of illegal residents are officially recorded and that illegal immigrants tend to concentrate in a 10-state area including the Southwest (see Chapter 4, Table 9). Robinson then compared expected death rates and actual death rates and found that for the 10-state area, actual mortality rates were significantly higher than anticipated. He attributed the excess to the presence of illegal residents. Assuming that few if any undocumented persons were counted in the 1960 and 1970 censuses or in the 1975 current population estimate, Robinson "adjusted" the censuses and found after introducing numerous variants that the illegal white male population 20-44 years old in 1975 amounted to "on the order of 3 to 4 million or less" for the 10-state area.[1]

The most sophisticated study to date, that of Lancaster and Scheuren, used two population estimates to arrive at the total number of undocumented persons aged 18-44 who were residing in the United States in April 1973. The first population estimate came from an exact match study on data provided by the Current Population Survey (CPS), the Social Security Administration (SSA), and the Internal Revenue Service (IRS). The results provided an estimate of the total population of the U.S., including illegals. Since in this match the IRS and SSA payroll data corroborated the CPS findings, Lancaster and Scheuren concluded that the April 1973 CPS population count included illegals. This estimate was then compared to the U.S. Bureau of the Census total population estimate, calculated independently of the CPS, which presumably excluded illegals. After introducing several controls onto the data sets, such as the incidence of return migration, Lancaster and Scheuren concluded that the differences between the estimates represented the illegal population aged 18-44. Their preferred estimate of 3.9 million is based on a 68 percent level of confidence in a range from 2.9 to 5.7 million. Of their preferred estimate, 2.6 million were determined to be white and to include undocumented Mexicans.[2]

The most recent published estimate pertains not to stock but to flow. David Heer began his calculations by adjusting and correcting CPS data on the Mexican-origin population for the period 1969-1976. He then assumed that illegal Mexicans have been counted by the CPS and are part of the Mexican-origin population numbers. Subtracting the total Mexican population estimate in 1969-71 from the same estimate in 1975-76, Heer calculated the increase in Mexican-origin population over a five-year period. From the increase, he subtracted the estimated natural increase during the quinquennium and the numbers of legal Mexican immigrants. The remainder of the increase, according to Heer, consisted of the net flow of undocumented Mexicans residing in the U.S. After introducing several variants, including a control for legal immigrants returning to Mexico, Heer concluded that a net annual flow (preferred) of 116,000 undocumented Mexicans entered the U.S. each year from 1970 to 1975.[3]

These three recent techniques illustrate the range of data and methodologies which can be brought to bear on the difficult problems of stock and flow. All these researchers have made use of data other than those provided by the INS, and have employed a series of variants designed to make the calculations sensitive to such unknowns as completeness of data and return flows to country of origin. As a group, they appear to agree with one another in that they report figures on the order of half the Lesko estimate of 5.2 million undocumented Mexicans in 1975 (see Table 8-1). A closer examination of assumptions and results yields a somewhat different image.

Robinson's estimated three to four million undocumented white males aged 20-44 in a 10-state area in 1975, as with Lancaster and Scheuren's range of 1.96 to 3.72 million undocumented whites aged 18-44 in April 1973, are calculations that say something about the size of the Mexican illegal population. The size of the Mexican component in their respective white populations is not identified, but it is implicit that Mexicans comprise somewhat less than the total white estimate. Heer, on the other hand, attempts to be ethnically precise in his calculations by relying mainly on the Current Population Survey.

Ethnic specificity and sex are crucial questions in aggregate estimations. But unfortunately two of the estimates do not include such distinctions. Robinson's approach excludes all women, and men outside the 20- to 44-year age group. Yet most samples of Mexican illegal migrants reveal that women constitute 10 to 20 percent of the total, while youths under age 20 comprise another 20 percent.[4] The population over age 44 could easily run another 5 or 10 percent. Accommodating such upward adjustments and assuming that the 10-state region includes 80 to 90 percent of the total illegal population, we find that Robinson's calculations suggest the presence of between four and five million Mexicans in the U.S. illegally in 1975. The figure is far closer to Lesko's estimate than that of Lancaster and Scheuren.

TABLE 8-1

Recent Estimates of the Undocumented Population in the United States

Investigator	Methodology	Data Source	Estimated Size of Undocumented Population	Definition of Population	Flow Findings
Robinson (1979)	Comparative analysis of trends in age-specific death rates in selected U.S. states, 1950-1975	U.S. census data revised for undercount, male population, age 20-44	3.0 to 4.0 million in 1975	Undocumented white males, 20-44 years old, 1960-1975, in New York, New Jersey, Illinois, Michigan, Florida, Texas, Colorado, New Mexico, Arizona, California	103,300 to 114,500 annual average (into 10-state area only)
Lancaster and Scheuren (1977)	Multiple systems, or capture-recapture technique	CPS, IRS, and SSA data with adjusted U.S. census	3.89 million (range of 2.9 to 5.7 million) in April of 1973	Undocumented population 18-44 years old	Not attempted
Heer (1979)	Analysis of Mexican-origin population using CPS, 1969-1977, and the U.S. census, 1970	U.S. census, adjusted, 1970; CPS adjusted; legal Mexican immigration	Not attempted	Mexican undocumented migrants residing permanently in U.S., net additions by year, 1969-1977	115,900 annual net flow, preferred estimate; higher in late 1960s, lower in early 1970s
Lesko Associates (1975)	Combination of base-year estimate, estimates of illegals escaping apprehension each year, and border apprehensions	Goldberg seminar paper, 1974; INS data, U.S. census	5.2 million	All Mexican undocumented population	Increasing dramatically 1970-1975

Sources: Robinson, "Estimating the Approximate Size of the Illegal Alien Population..."; Lancaster and Scheuren, "Counting the Uncountable Illegals..."; Heer, "The Annual Net Flow of Undocumented Mexican Immigrants to the United States," in Van Arsdol et al., *Non-Apprehended and Apprehended...*; Lesko Associates, "Final Report: Basic Data and Guidance...."

Lancaster and Scheuren's approach yielded an estimate of the white undocumented population aged 18-44, including women. Their technique identified one out of three illegal whites as women, a figure that probably would be too high for Mexican migrants. Moreover, they abbreviated the known Mexican illegal population (assuming that it is some unknown percentage of the total estimate) only slightly less than Robinson by omitting the group 17 years of age and under. Consequently their figures would need an upward revision of considerably more than the 10 percent they accept.[5] Therefore, the range of estimates derived by Lancaster and Scheuren, if adjusted for imbalances, would show a higher stock of population than that intimated by Heer and a lower stock than that of Robinson.

Heer's series of statistical manipulations are based on the CPS and the assumptions he makes about it. The Current Population Survey of 47,000 households asks its respondents to indicate their ethnic identity in the annual March interview. Heer assumes two things about the question and the CPS coverage: (1) people answer the questions truthfully; they will answer rather than refuse to answer, fearing that the latter course will bring suspicion upon themselves; and (2) that therefore the CPS records the illegals in the population.[6] These assumptions form a highly debatable basis for estimation. Even Lancaster and Scheuren used the CPS in their exact match study for March 1973, the only example that corresponded with data from other sources and the least debated of the controversial surveys on ethnic identity.[7] The problem with ethnic identity in the CPS is that it is a self-selective choice for the interviewee. As long as it is in the interest of the interviewee to be identified as Mexican, Chicano, or Mexican-American, no control for veracity can be established. To further confound the issue, it is questionable that an illegal Mexican would answer questions rather than simply refuse to come to the door. As a result of these reservations, doubt is raised concerning Heer's estimate. Moreover, his final figure of the illegal Mexican population in 1975 tells us about net flow of the illegal population, not its stock (the number present at any given time). He correctly assumes that net flow has consequences for the domestic labor market, but he tells us little about gross flow, which could well be competitive, if only temporarily.

Thus, Heer's estimates are actually totally different from those of Lancaster and Scheuren in that he tries to determine annual net flow, and they try to determine stock as of April 1973. Heer is also different from Robinson. While their annual estimates of flow are numerically very close, Heer is speaking of all Mexican illegals and Robinson only of part of the illegal population—including Mexicans—in a 10-state area. Thus rather than agreeing, these three recent estimates are diverse and measure different things. Robinson tries to calculate stock and flow with results that place him close to Lesko Associates; Lancaster and Scheuren attempt to calculate stock for one specific period and derive a low estimate; and Heer calculates net flow only on the basis of the CPS method of counting illegals, the validity of which is highly suspect.

The Immigration and Naturalization Service has the longest series of information on one aspect of migration to the United States—the number of people apprehended for being in the country illegally.[8] It is a promising and yet frustrating data set. Each time the INS or Border Patrol detects someone in the country illegally and requires that he voluntarily leave, a form I-213 is completed. The I-213 records the event of apprehension and not the discrete numbers of people apprehended, since during any given period single individuals may account for more than one I-213 form. Multiple apprehensions of the same person are frequent occurrences. The INS annually publishes an enumeration of the total number of I-213 forms completed and identifies Mexicans specifically. For social scientists seeking to calculate the illegal population, the temptation to use its figures have proven irresistible.

There are no difficulties with INS determinations of ethnic origin. The data are age- and sex-specific, among other features, and are fairly consistent. By its nature, however, the enumeration does not indicate how many individuals are involved. Some investigators, namely Lesko Associates, have advanced "got-away" ratios in order to estimate the total number of entrants. As indicated, however, the figures derived in such a manner are only slightly better than a guess, since there is not yet a firm basis for devising an accurate "got-away" ratio.

One day the I-213 form may yield the kinds of data necessary for making reliable estimates of flow and perhaps stock. At present, the INS and researchers such as David North are investigating the possibility of modifying the apprehension form to include data amenable to estimating the total numbers.[9]

APPENDIX 9

Income Tax and Social Security Payments
by Illegals in the 1970s

The eight samples in Table 9-1 total only slightly more than 4,000, and they offer a wide regional variation. This kind of regional variation is fast becoming a common characteristic of sampling research on Mexican undocumented migrants. The San Diego study (Villalpando et al.) revealed that eight out of 10 workers paid income taxes, yet along the Texas border less than one in three Mexican workers paid into the U.S. Treasury according to the Avante survey. While North and Houstoun found that three-quarters of their Mexican sample paid taxes, only 24.6 percent of their border counties sample did likewise. The available data, then, suggest two hypotheses: that employers in border counties do not usually make payroll deductions for undocumented workers, and that employers in Texas make fewer deductions than employers in California. These hypotheses are discussed in Chapter 6.

Table 9-1 may be seen on the following page.

TABLE 9-1

Percent of Undocumented Mexican Workers Paying Income Tax and Social Security by Sample

Deduction	North and Houstoun 1975	Cardenas 1975	Bustamante[a] 1975	Cornelius 1976	Villalpando 1976	CENIET[b] 1977	Orange County 1977-78	Avante Systems 1978
Income Tax	73.2	59.5	61.8	64.0	81.0	51.3	70.0	27.0
Social Security	74.5		55.5	65.2		46.0	88.0	30.0

Notes: [a] These figures have been adjusted to include all of those who worked and received wages in the U.S., whether paid by check or by cash. Studies of Bustamante and CENIET present only the deduction percentages for those workers paid by check. A substantial portion of illegal migrants (31.1 percent in the CENIET example) either received their wages in cash or did not receive any wages at all, so that in all likelihood they did not "pay into the system." We have made adjustments to the data to reflect these variations, which have resulted in lowering the original figures.

[b] In this study, 2,176 individuals of the total sample (3,689) worked during the period prior to apprehension. Of these, 1,501 (69 percent) received their wages by check. No information was provided as to the numbers of those paid by check who had taxes and social security deducted. To estimate this percentage, we assumed that wages paid in cash did not have taxes and social security deducted. We then applied to this data the proportions found by Bustamante in a similar study in 1975 (i.e., similar locations, types of migrants, wages, occupations, etc.). Bustamante discovered that 74.4 percent of those receiving income by check had taxes deducted and that 66.7 percent paid social security. By applying the same proportions to the 1,501 of the CENIET survey, the overall percentages of those paying income tax and social security amount to 51.3 and 46.0 respectively.

Sources: North and Houstoun, *The Characteristics and Role...*; Cardenas, "Manpower Impact and Problems...."; Bustamante, "Undocumented Immigration from Mexico...," in *International Migration Review*; Cornelius, *Mexican Migration...Responses*; Villalpando, *Illegal Aliens...*; México, CENIET, *Análisis de algunos resultados de la primera encuesta...*; Orange County, Task Force..., *The Economic Impact...*; Avante Systems..., *A Survey of the Undocumented....*

APPENDIX 10

Additional Information on Social Services Data
in the Van Arsdol et al. Study

Several qualifiers should be appended to any discussion of the Van Arsdol et al. data. The interviews took place in Los Angeles during 1972-1975. In 1976, the Los Angeles Department of Public Social Services initiated a program whereby immigrants suspected of being in the U.S. illegally (i.e., those who could not produce residency papers) were automatically referred to the INS for a verification of status. According to the department director, Keith Comrie, this practice has significantly reduced the number of undocumentable migrants applying for AFDC.[1] In the first quarter of 1979, 4,083 immigrants applied for welfare without presenting acceptable identification. Of this number, 3,417 either did not appear for interviews or "refused to cooperate." The INS confirmed that only 36 of the referred cases were illegal migrants, and it is obvious that illegals constituted many of the 3,417 who dropped out of the process.[2] This rather effective referral system, therefore, appears on the surface to have discouraged many would-be illegal welfare recipients from completing the necessary steps for obtaining public assistance. No doubt, the same Van Arsdol sample would presently report a lower rate of AFDC usage. But it is also important to note that 2,712 of the 5,817 children of the Van Arsdol population were *legal*. That is, they were probably born in the U.S. of undocumented parents.[3] Despite the fact that their parents might reside in this country illegally, these citizen children are nevertheless eligible to receive AFDC payments. The high rate of dependency in the sample makes it likely that welfare usage would not have declined substantially after the initiation of the INS referral program.

Another not-so-minor factor complicates an assessment of the impact of the INS referral program now widely utilized in California. When noncitizens apply for welfare they are asked to produce evidence of legal status (usually an INS I-151 card, a green card). The social services technician then visually checks the card and, if satisfied, continues the application procedure with no further investigation. In recent years, the practice of falsifying green cards has proliferated both in the United States and Mexico. The INS estimated in 1977 that 140,000 illegal migrants, a goodly portion of whom are Mexican, enter the country each year using counterfeit versions of the I-151.[4] Recent studies of Mexican sending villages report the same phenomenon. Richard Mines, for example, estimates that only 30 percent of his sample of several hundred green card holders possessed valid I-151s.[5] As a result, with perhaps the exception of the Van Arsdol study, fraudulent green card holders who utilize welfare programs are hidden in the statistics on legal aliens, and there is no way to determine their impact on this key social service.

Notes

Preface Notes

1. Manuel Gamio, *Mexican Immigration to the United States: A Study of Human Migration and Adjustment* (Chicago: University of Chicago Press, 1930; reprinted by Dover, 1971), p. 13; Paul S. Taylor, "Mexican Labor in the United States: Chicago and the Calumet Region" [vol. II of *Mexican Labor in the United States*], *University of California Publications in Economics,* 7(2): 25-284 (Berkeley: University of California Press, March 31, 1932), see p. 49 (hereafter, "Mexican Labor...Chicago").

2. See Appendix 1 and México, Secretaría del Trabajo y Prevision Social, Centro Nacional de Información y Estadísticas del Trabajo (CENIET), *La Encuesta Nacional de Emigración a la Frontera Norte del País y a los Estados Unidos* (México, D.F.: 1979), statistical appendix, Table 8.

Chapter 1 Notes

1. See Appendix 1.

2. Archivo Gordoa, Hacienda del Maguey (hereafter, AGHM), Private Archive, Zacatecas, México. All laborer and general account books.

3. Octaviano Cabrera Ipiña, "Fincas rústicas de los Cabrera Ipiña" (manuscript, author's copy, San Luis Potosí, 1960), pp. 1-40.

4. Ibid., pp. 149-172.

5. General descriptions of North Central haciendas are based upon extensive research in the following private archives: AGHM; Archivo López, Hacienda de Trancoso, Private Archive, Trancoso, Zacatecas, México (hereafter, ALHT); Archivo Gerardo Badillo, Private Archive, Guadalupe, Zacatecas, México (hereafter, AGB); Archivo Salvador Tello, Private Archive, Zacatecas, Zacatecas, México (hereafter, AST); Archivo Cabrera Ipiña, Private Archive, San Luis Potosí, San Luis Potosí, México (hereafter, ACI). See also Jan Bazant, *Cinco haciendas mexicanos: Tres siglos de vida rural en San Luis Potosí* (México: Colegio de México, 1975); Octaviano Cabrera Ipiña and Matilde Cabrera Ipiña, *Una Hacienda Potosina: San, Francisco Javier de la Parada* (México: Editorial Universitaria Potosina, 1978); Octaviano Cabrera Ipiña, "Las antiguas haciendas mexicanas" (author's manuscript, 6 vols., San Luis Potosí, 1978); David A. Brading, *Haciendas and Ranchos in the Mexican Bajío, León, 1700-1860* (Cambridge and Great Britain: Cambridge University Press, 1978).

6. Eduardo Pontones, "La Migración en México," *Contemporary Mexico: Papers of the Fourth International Congress of Mexican History,* eds. James W. Wilkie et al. (Los Angeles: University of California Press, 1976), p. 156, part 10; México, Dirección General de Estadísticas, *Censo general de República Mexicana, verificado el 20 de octubre de 1895,* Dr. Antonio Peñafiel (México: Oficina de la Secretaría de Fomento, 1897); México, Dirección General de Estadísticas, *Censo general: Resumen general del censo de la República Mexicana, verificado el 28 de octubre de 1900* (México: Oficina de la Secretaría de Fomento, 1901-1907). See states of San Luis Potosí, Zacatecas, Jalisco, and Guanajuato along with the *resumenes* for each census.

7. Harry E. Cross, "Debt Peonage Reconsidered: A Case Study in Nineteenth Century Zacatecas, Mexico," *Business History Review,* 53(4): 473-495 (Winter, 1979).

8. AST, Rancho Grande, Estado de sirvientes acomodados en enero de 1910; Estado de sirvientes acomodados en enero de 1914; Distribución de sirvientes alquilados en enero de 1914.

9. Harry E. Cross, "Rural Labor in North Central Mexico, 1880-1940" (manuscript in preparation based upon archival sources listed in note 5).

10. ACI, Pozo del Carmen, various memorias, saldos and libros de raya, 1912-1914. For other examples of multiple employment see Oscar Lewis, *Pedro Martínez: A Mexican Peasant and his Family* (New York: Vintage, 1964), p. 116 and passim; Carlos P. Gil, "Rosendo Peña, Hacienda Laborer," from *The Age of Porfirio Díaz,* ed. Carlos P. Gil (Albuquerque: University of New Mexico Press, 1977), p. 161.

11. The latest textbook on Mexico still adheres to the notion that debt peonage was pervasive and pernicious. See Michael C. Meyer and William L. Sherman, *The Course of Mexican History* (New York: Oxford University Press, 1979), p. 461, which states that "The peon found himself in a state of perpetual debt. . . ."

12. AGHM, Libro de sirvientes, 1882-1884; Memoria para el pago de acomodados y alquilados en el mes de noviembre de 1913; Medieros en el año de 1913.

13. ACI, Bledos, Libros mayores de cuenta, 1883-1890, 1897-1904, 1905-1911. For methodology see Harry E. Cross, "Debt Peonage in Northern Mexico During the Nineteenth and Early Twentieth Centuries" (manuscript, Stanford University, 1978), p. 19.

14. Harry E. Cross, "Living Standards in Rural Nineteenth Century Mexico: Zacatecas, 1820-1880," *Journal of Latin American Studies,* 10(1) (May 1978), pp. 16-17. For other examples see ACI, San Diego, Extracto provisional de pérdidas y ganancias, 30 abril 1903, where the tienda lost 1,035 pesos for the year; Jan Bazant, "Peones, arrendatarios y aparceros en México, 1851-1853," *Historia Mexicana,* 23(2) (1973), p. 345; and José E. Ipiña, "Reglamento para la administración de la Hacienda de _____," typescript of regulations used on the estates owned by José E. Ipiña, ca. 1900. Reglamento 16: "The prices of tienda goods shall be set according to the instructions of the administrator. Prices shall not exceed those in the markets of the county seat or of nearby locations," p. 2 in ACI.

15. José E. Ipiña, Instrucciones sobre el manejo de intereses y instrucciones á mis hijos para el manejo de intereses (handwritten manuscript, ca. 1905, unbound in ACI).

16. México, Dirección General de Estadística, *Anuario estadístico de los Estados Unidos de México, 1939* (México, D.F.: 1941), pp. 28, 403; and also see price and wage data in Cross, "Rural Labor . . ."

17. Cross, "Rural Labor . . . ," see table entitled "Index of Real Wages, 1878-1939," based upon commodity prices and rural wages extracted from all haciendas and ranchos in AGHM, ALHT, AGB, AST, and ACI. Some wage data for the 1930s comes from informants. Field research in Zacatecas and San Luis Potosí, June–July, 1978.

18. John Reed, *Insurgent Mexico* (New York: International Publishers, 1969), p. 40 ff.

19. Robert E. Quirk, *The Mexican Revolution, 1914–1915: The Convention of Aguascalientes* (reprinted, New York: W. W. Norton, 1970), passim; Charles C. Cumberland, *Mexican Revolution: The Constitutionalist Years* (Austin: University of Texas Press, 1972), pp. 23-211; James D. Cockcroft, *Intellectual Precursors of the Mexican Revolution, 1900–1913* (Austin:

University of Texas Press, Institute of Latin American Studies, Monograph no. 14, 1968), pp. 173-207.

20. All archives cited in note 5; also ACI, various, Borrador de caja, Verástigui Hermanas, 1911-1921. The multiple hacienda accounts of this family ceased by 1915 and did not resume until 1919.

21. See note 17; Cabrera Ipiña and Cabrera Ipiña, *Una Hacienda Potosina...*, p. 122. Herd size declined precipitously. The Hacienda de Rancho Grande had 30,000 sheep in 1914; in 1917 the herd amounted to but 2,000 head. AST, Resumen de la liquidación de cuentas de sirvientes en enero 1914; Inventario de las existencias pertenecientes á la Hacienda de Rancho Grande, 1917. The case of Rancho Grande was typical.

22. Raymond Vernon, *The Dilemma of Mexico's Development: The Roles of the Private and Public Sectors* (Cambridge, Mass.: Harvard University Press, 1963), pp. 80-81; see the biographical notes of Mexican informants made by Taylor, "Mexican Labor... Chicago," p. 266; Antimaco Sax, *Los mexicanos en el destierro* (San Antonio, Tex.: International Printing Co., 1916), passim.

23. Cumberland, *Mexican Revolution... Years,* pp. 193-194; Quirk, *The Mexican Revolution... Aguascalientes,* pp. 170-171, passim; Edwin W. Kemmerer, *Inflation and Revolution: Mexico's Experience of 1912-1917* (Princeton University Press, 1940), passim.

24. Julio Riquelme Inda, "Las cosechas de maíz en el año de 1916," *Boletín de la sociedad mexicana de geografía y estadística,* Quinta Época, 9 (1919), pp. 131-137; Cabrera Ipiña and Cabrera Ipiña, *Una Hacienda Potosina...,* pp. 121-127. For a detailed review of the literature on the economic upheaval caused by the Revolution see John Womack, Jr., "The Mexican Economy During the Revolution, 1910-1920: Historiography and Analysis," *Marxist Perspectives,* 1(4) (Winter, 1978), pp. 80-123.

25. From all account books in archives cited in note 5. As an example, in the 1890s the Hacienda de Guascamá had 200 employees and more than 100 renters. By the 1920s there were only 15-20 employees and the hacienda was almost entirely cultivated by sharecroppers. ACI, Guascamá, Inventarios, 1889-1898; Balanza de comprobación, 30 abril 1923, Hacienda de Guascamá, nd. [late 1920s].

26. ACI, Santa Teresa, Diario número 6, 1906-1910; Raya de sirvientes y contratistas, 1927.

27. Brading, *Haciendas and Ranchos...,* pp. 102, 206.

28. ACI, Santa Teresa, Diario número 6, 1906-1910; Raya de sirvientes y contratistas, 1927; ACI, Bledos, Libro mayor de cuentas, 1905-1911; Balanza de comprobación practicada en el 31 de enero de 1928; ACI, Pozo del Carmen, Inventarios de Pozo del Carmen, 1917-1918; copia del inventario de la Hacienda Pozo del Carmen, 31 mayo 1928.

29. Nathan L. Whetten, *Rural Mexico* (Chicago: University of Chicago Press, 1948), p. 255; México, Nacional Financiera, SA, Subgerencia de Investigaciónes Económicas, *50 Años de Revolución Mexicana en Cifras* (México, D.F.: March 1963), pp. 32, 34, 52, 54-55; México, Dirección General de Estadísticas, *Tercer censo de población de los Estados Unidos de México ...1910* (México, D.F.: 1918-1920), 3 vols.; México, Dirección General de Estadísticas, *Censo general de los inhabitantes, 30 noviembre 1921* (México, D.F.: 1925-1928), 30 parts; México, Dirección General de Estadísticas, *Quinto censo de población, 15 mayo 1930* (México, D.F.: 1932-1936), 34 parts. See population data for North Central states.

30. James A. Sandos, "The United States and the Mexican Revolution, 1915-1917: The Impact of Culture Conflict in the Texas-Tamaulipas Frontier upon the Emergence of Revolutionary Government in Mexico" (PhD dissertation: University of California, Berkeley, 1978), pp. 232-257, 336-394, 442-446; Robert F. Smith, *The United States and Revolutionary Nationalism in Mexico, 1916-1932* (Chicago: University of Chicago Press, 1972), pp. 33-91; U.S., Congress, Senate, Judiciary Committee, *Hearings on Brewing and Liquor Interests and German and Bolshevik Propaganda,* Senate Document 62, 66th Cong., 1st sess., May 19-Nov. 19, 1919,

3 vols., passim; Wallace Thompson, *Trading with Mexico* (New York: Dodd, Mead, 1921), pp. 128-158.

31. On the Russian Revolution and the consolidation of power see William H. Chamberlin, *The Russian Revolution 1917-1921* (New York: Macmillan, 1960), 2 vols.; Edward H. Carr, *A History of Soviet Russia: The Bolshevik Revolution 1917-1923* (New York: Macmillan, 1950-1971), 9 volumes in 11 and continuing; Naum Jasny, *The Socialized Agriculture of the USSR—Plans and Performance* (Stanford, Calif.: Stanford University Press, 1949); A. Nove, *An Economic History of the U.S.S.R.* (London: Penguin, 1969); M. Lewin, *Russian Peasants and Soviet Power—A Study of Collectivization,* trans. Irene Nove (Evanston, Ill.: Northwestern University Press, 1968).

32. By far the best study of the Cristero movement is that of Jean Meyer, *La Cristiada,* trans. Aurelio Garzón del Camino (México, D.F.: Siglo Veintiuno Editores, 1973-1974), 3 vols. A condensed English-language version is his *The Cristero Rebellion: The Mexican People Between Church and State 1926-1929,* trans. Richard Southern (Cambridge and Great Britain: Cambridge University Press, 1976).

33. James W. Wilkie, "The Meaning of the Cristero Religious War against the Mexican Revolution," *A Journal of Church and State,* 8(1) (Spring, 1966), pp. 214-233. David C. Bailey, "The Cristero Rebellion and the Religious Conflict in Mexico, 1926-1929" (PhD dissertation: Michigan State University, 1969), pp. 118-131.

34. Meyer, *The Cristero Rebellion...,* 178 ff.

35. Paul S. Taylor, "A Spanish-Mexican Peasant Community: Arandas in Jalisco, Mexico," *Ibero-Americana,* 4 (Berkeley: University of California Press, 1933), pp. 38-39 (hereafter, "...Arandas"). David C. Bailey, "The Cristero Rebellion and the Religious Conflict in Mexico, 1926-1929," p. 268, discusses the impact of the Mexican government's reconcentration program in the Los Altos region of Jalisco where 76,000 destitute families were herded into towns. Tepatitlán, normally accommodating 10,000 people, received 30,000 of these *reconcentrados.* As a result, smallpox and typhoid fever became epidemic and valuable cropland lay untilled. In West Central Mexico the inhabitants of one village were reconcentrated for two consecutive years during the Cristero uprising; see Laura Hoffman Zarrugh, "Gente de mi Tierra: Mexican Village Migrants in a California Community" (PhD dissertation: University of California, Berkeley, 1974), p. 14.

36. Meyer, *The Cristero Rebellion...,* pp. 201-202.

37. Based upon population data for San Luis Potosí and Zacatecas from the censuses of 1910, 1921, and 1930. During 1910-1921, 166,910 people migrated from San Luis Potosí and Zacatecas. This number represented 16.6 percent of the total population born in those states and 20.2 percent of those actually living in the region in 1921. Given that an untold but large number migrated to the United States during this time and that the bulk of migrants would have been over the age of 12 (the year of adulthood in Mexico), we estimate that at least 20 percent of all adults in the North Center migrated in the two decades before 1930.

38. México, *Censo general... 1910;* México, *Quinto censo... 1930.*

39. México, *Quinto censo... 1930,* Coahuila.

40. Carlos Martínez Cerda, *El Algodón en la Región de Matamoros, Tamaulipas* (México, D.F.: Banco Nacional de Crédito Ejidal, 1954), pp. 11-14, 39 ff; México, *Quinto censo... 1930,* Tamaulipas.

41. Sandos, "The United States and the Mexican Revolution...," pp. 94-144; Edwin C. Pendleton, "History of Labor in Arizona Irrigated Agriculture" (PhD dissertation: University of California, Berkeley, 1950), pp. 13, 76-79. "Okies," people from the south central states of Oklahoma, Texas, Missouri, and Arkansas, replaced Mexicans in the fields in California; see Walter J. Stein, *California and the Dust Bowl Migration* (Westport, Conn.: Greenwood Press, 1973), pp. vii-ix, and 36-38.

42. Sandos, "The United States and the Mexican Revolution...," p. 115.

43. Paul S. Taylor, "Mexican Labor in the United States: Valley of the South Platte-Colorado" [vol. I of *Mexican Labor in the United States*], *University of California Publications in Economics*, 6(2): 95-235 (Berkeley: University of California Press, June 12, 1929), see p. 107 (hereafter, "Mexican Labor... Valley").

44. Taylor, "Mexican Labor... Chicago," p. 51.

45. Mark Reisler, *By the Sweat of Their Brow: Mexican Immigrant Labor in the United States, 1900-1940* (Westport, Conn.: Greenwood Press, 1976), p. ix. The Border Patrol was not given official sanction until 1924, and its initial task was to prevent illegal entry of Europeans and Asians into the United States through Mexico; see Julian Samora et al., *Los Mojados: The Wetback Story* (Notre Dame, Ind.: University of Notre Dame Press, 1971), pp. 34-38. The chapter was originally written by Gilbert Cardenas.

46. For the early debate on agriculture see Cumberland, *Mexican Revolution... Years,* pp. 381-385; for the later period see Frank Brandenburg, *The Making of Modern Mexico* (Englewood Cliffs, N.J.: Prentice Hall, 1964), p. 85.

47. See Appendix 2: México, Departamento Agrario, *Memoria* (México, D.F.: 1945-1946), statistics section, unpaginated.

48. México, Dirección General de Estadísticas, *Segundo censo agrícola ganadero de los Estados Unidos Mexicanos, 1940, Resumen general* (México, D.F.: 1951), pp. 13, 22. For hacendados' fears see STC, Memorandum, basado en pláticas con prominentes políticos y otros sectores, que en tono "confidencial" han extado, varios datos, Mexico City, nd (1937). For examples of partitioning see Brading, *Haciendas and Ranchos...,* pp. 205-217; ACI, general account books reveal that the following haciendas were divided in whole or in part and sold in the 1930s: Guascamá, Pozo del Carmen and Bledos Bajos; Octaviano Cabrera Ipiña, *Las antiguas haciendas mexicanas,* 6 vols. (San Luis Potosí, 1978), reports that the haciendas of Agua de Enmedio and Gallinas were also partitioned and sold; the Hacienda de Rancho Grande was divided and sold in 1933, according to informant Salvador Tello (former owner), October 12, 1977, in Zacatecas, Zacatecas. In the highlands of Jalisco, many haciendas around San Miguel el Alto were divided to avoid nationalization; see Maria Antonieta Gallart Nocetti, "El cambio en la orientación de la producción ganadera en San Miguel el Alto, Jalisco" (Licenciado Thesis: Universidad Iberoamericana, México, 1975), p. 30. For the same in the area of Valparaíso, Zacatecas, see informant Aurelio R. Acevedo (Mexico City: June 2, 1964), James W. Wilkie and Edna Monzón de Wilkie, Oral History Interviews (University of California, Berkeley, Bancroft Library), p. 29 (hereafter, WOHI).

49. Michael Belshaw, *A Village Economy: Land and People of Huecorio* (New York and London: Columbia University Press, 1967), p. 333.; Gil, *The Age of Porfirio Díaz,* p. 162, observes "Ironically, the fever of agrarian reform which spread throughout Western Jalisco in 1937, forced Rosendo off what was once hacienda property in order to make way for the land-hungry residents of the nearby mining village in Navidad." Lewis, *Pedro Martínez...,* pp. 444, 456, records the following from his subject: "... [nowadays] I can't pay my debts and that is why I am behind. We weren't rich in Don Porfirio Díaz times, but at least we got by. Since the Revolution we have more freedom but life is more difficult."

50. Eyler N. Simpson, *The Ejido: Mexico's Way Out* (Chapel Hill: University of North Carolina Press, 1937), p. 701; Reisler, *By the Sweat...,* p. 233.

51. Cynthia Nelson, *The Waiting Village: Social Change in Rural Mexico* (Boston: Little, Brown, 1971), pp. 17-19. Resentment of change found expression in other villages, and many peasants objected to taking property which they felt did not belong to them; see Taylor, "... Arandas," pp. 30-32; May N. Díaz, "Tonalá: A Mexican Peasant Town in Transition" (PhD dissertation: University of California, Berkeley, 1963), p. 114; Cabrera Ipiña, *Una Hacienda Potosina...,* p. 124.

52. ACI, untitled document, loose, December 29, 1935, begins with, Los vecinos originarios de la Hacienda de Santa Teresa, perteneciente al municipio de Ahualulco, Estado de San Luis

Potosí...and ends with the certification and offical seals of the three judges of the municipio.

53. Brading, *Haciendas and Ranchos...*, p. 215; Vernon, *The Dilemma of Mexico's Development...*, pp. 80, 83-84; John M. Ingham, "Culture and Personality in a Mexican Village" (PhD dissertation: University of California, Berkeley, 1968), p. 57; Charles C. Cumberland, *Mexico: The Struggle for Modernity,* (New York: Oxford University Press, 1968), p. 296; Simpson, *The Ejido...*, pp. 410-411; México, Partido Nacional Revolucionario, *La cuestión agraria mexicana* (México, D.F.: 1934), pp. 109-110, shows no ejidal credit facilities for Zacatecas, San Luis Potosí, or Durango, and only three for Jalisco. Guanajuato proved an exception with 10 branches, but these served the Bajío, traditionally one of the richest agricultural areas of Mexico. The upland reaches of our study did not receive adequate service.

54. Díaz, "Tonalá...," p. 115.

55. The best example of this process is the Hacienda de Bledos which possessed 1,000 hectares of irrigated cropland supported by a waterworks system (including a 25 million cubic meter dam/reservoir and aqueduct network) valued at 3 million pesos in 1935. The ejido abandoned the waterworks system and the prime irrigated land reverted to seasonal cropland. See Octaviano Cabrera Ipiña, "Datos sobre las Haciendas de la Familia Ipiña en el Estado de San Luis Potosí" (typescript, San Luis Potosí, nd). Another good example of the failure of ejidos to maintain extensive waterworks after expropriation is found in Billie R. DeWalt, *Modernization in a Mexican Ejido: A Study in Economic Adaptation* (Cambridge and Great Britain: Cambridge University Press, 1979), p. 39.

56. George M. Foster, *Tzintzuntzan: Mexican Peasants in a Changing World* (Boston: Little, Brown, 1967), pp. 261-262.

57. See note 53. For water see México, Secretaría de Recursos Hidráulicos, *El riego en México* (México, D.F.: 1975), foldpaper following p. 12, which shows that until 1940 the North Center received only two dams with a storage capacity of not less than 5 million cubic meters.

58. México, *50 Años de Revolucion...*, p. 32; México, Dirección General de Estadísticas, *Anuario estadístico de los Estados Unidos Méxicanos, 1939* (México: Tallares Gráficos de la Nación, 1941), pp. 403, 405, where the price of maize fell 30 percent between 1928 and 1931, and the price of beans dropped by more than 50 percent from 1929 to 1933.

59. Reisler, *By the Sweat...*, pp. 228, 233.

60. Many others were repatriated both before 1929 and after 1933. For a good discussion of the statistics see Abraham Hoffman, *Unwanted Mexican Americans in the Great Depression: Repatriation Pressures, 1929-1939* (Tuscon: University of Arizona Press, 1974), pp. 126-127, and 174-175; Taylor, "Mexican Labor...Chicago," p. 37; Taylor, "...Arandas," pp. 47-63.

61. Cynthia Hewitt de Alcántara, *Modernizing Mexican Agriculture: Socioeconomic Implications of Technological Change, 1940-1970,* United Nations Research Institute for Social Development, Report no. 765 (Geneva, Switzerland: 1976), p. 9; México, *Quinto censo...1930;* México, *6º censo de población, 1940* (Mexico City: 1943-1948); repatriates from Taylor, "Mexican Labor...Chicago," p. 37.

62. México, *Anuario Estadístico...1939,* pp. 29, 398-399, 564-565, 604-621, and 698-699; for North Center maize prices see Cross, "Rural Labor...," table on maize prices.

63. See note 17.

64. México, *Quinto censo...1930;* México, *6º censo...1940.*

65. Clark Reynolds, unpublished manuscript cited in James W. Wilkie, *The Mexican Revolution: Federal Expenditures and Social Change Since 1910,* 2nd ed. (Berkeley: University of California Press, 1970), pp. 256-257.

66. Those entering the job market were estimated by calculating the number of males coming of working age (12 years) during 1930-1939. From this figure we derived the rural population and subtracted from it the number of deaths by cohort using mortality rates from 1930. We then subtracted another 20 percent for outmigration, an estimate which is probably

too high given the near-termination of migration to the U.S. in the decade. "New jobs created" is derived from the difference between the numbers of those economically active in agriculture in 1930 and 1940. México, *Quinto censo... 1930;* México, *6° censo... 1940.*

67. Pontones, "La Migración en México," *Contemporary Mexico...,* pp. 135-163, cuadro 10, p. 156; México, *Anuario estadístico... 1941,* pp. 633-635.

68. The number of ranchos in San Luis Potosí and Zacatecas grew from 2,977 in 1910 to 4,455 in 1940, even though the population increased by only 11.1 percent. By 1939, 1,221 ejidos had been created with a total population of over 350,000; México, *Tercer censo... 1910;* México, *6° censo... 1940;* México, *Anuario estadístico... 1941,* p. 617. For loss of security and rising unemployment see Taylor, "...Arandas," p. 24; and informant Aurelio R. Acevedo in WOHI, pp. 30-31.

Chapter 2 Notes

1. Centro de Investigaciones Agrarias (hereafter, CDIA), *Estructura Agraria y Desarrollo Agrícola en México,* ed. Sergio Reyes Osorio et al. (México: Fondo de Cultura Económica, 1974); Cumberland, *Mexico: The Struggle...,* p. 229.

2. Howard F. Cline, *The United States and Mexico,* revised ed. (New York: Atheneum, 1963), p. 378.

3. Edwin J. Wellhausen, "The Agriculture of Mexico," *Scientific American,* 253(3): 128-150 (September 1976); Cline, *The United States and Mexico,* pp. 70, 378, and 380.

4. Howard F. Cline, *Mexico: Revolution to Evolution* (New York: Oxford University Press, 1963), passim.

5. Alcántara, *Modernizing Mexican Agriculture...,* pp. 19-23.

6. Morris Singer, *Growth, Equality, and the Mexican Experience,* University of Texas, Institute of Latin American Studies, Monograph no. 16 (Austin: University of Texas Press, 1969), p. 41.

7. Clark W. Reynolds, *The Mexican Economy: Twentieth Century Structure and Growth* (New Haven and London: Yale University Press, 1970), p. 96.

8. Wilkie, *The Mexican Revolution...,* Table 6-3, pp. 134-135, adjusted to pesos of 1954.

9. Cumberland, *Mexico: The Struggle...,* Table IV, p. 369.

10. Alcántara, *Modernizing Mexican Agriculture...,* Table 4, p. 14.

11. Ibid., Table 16, p. 56 and p. 69; Wilkie, *The Mexican Revolution...,* Table 6-4, p. 139.

12. Cumberland, *Mexico: The Struggle...,* Table VIII, p. 374.

13. Alcántara, *Modernizing Mexican Agriculture...,* Table 39, pp. 112-113.

14. See Appendix 4.

15. Richmond K. Anderson et al., "Nutrition Appraisals in Mexico," *American Journal of Public Health and the Nation's Health,* 38(8): 1128-1135 (August 1948); Whetten, *Rural Mexico,* p. 305; Salvador Zubiran and Adolfo Chávez, "Algunos datos sobre la situación nutricional en México," *Boletín de la Oficina Sanitaria Panamericana,* 54(2) (February 1963), calculated from Table 1, p. 103.

16. Alcántara, *Modernizing Mexican Agriculture...,* Table 38, pp. 110-111.

17. Wellhausen, "The Agriculture of Mexico," *Scientific American,* p. 129.

18. Agricultural productivity figures are available from various *Anuarios Estadísticos* published during these years under the auspices of several different secretaries.

19. See Table 2, wheat yields.

20. Sherburne F. Cook and Woodrow Borah, *Essays in Population History: Mexico and California,* vol. III (Berkeley: University of California Press, 1979), pp. 165-167.

21. See Table 2, maize yields.

22. Kirsten A. de Appendini and Vania Almeida Salles, "Algunas consideraciones sobre los precios de garantía y la crisis de producción de los alimentos básicos," *Foro Internacional,* 19(3) (January-March, 1979), p. 403.

23. See Table 13, net exports, in Chapter 5.

24. Merilee Serrill Grindle, *Bureaucrats, Politicians, and Peasants in Mexico: A Case Study in Public Policy* (Berkeley and Los Angeles: University of California Press, 1977), p. 88.

25. Alcántara, *Modernizing Mexican Agriculture...,* Table 9, p. 25.

26. Ibid., Table 10, pp. 32-33, and Table 38, pp. 110-111.

27. México, *Memoria...,* see statistical part 4, unpaginated.

28. CDIA, *Estructura Agraria...,* Table XII-6, p. 880.

29. Loc. cit.

30. Alcántara, *Modernizing Mexican Agriculture...,* pp. 174-175.

31. Calculated from Alcántara, *Modernizing Mexican Agriculture...,* Table 7, p. 18; and México, *VIII censo general de población, 1960* (Mexico City: 1962-1964).

32. México, Secretaría de Recursos Hidráulicos, *Informe de Labores, 1974-1975* (México, D.F.: 1975), appendices 5-1 and 5-2, unpaginated at the end of the book.

33. Alcántara, *Modernizing Mexican Agriculture...,* p. 13.

34. Wellhausen, "The Agriculture of Mexico," *Scientific American,* p. 130.

35. In 1940, 83.6 percent of all cropland of small Mexican farms (under 5 hectares) was devoted to maize cultivation. See Whetten, *Rural Mexico,* Table 39, p. 244; for recent figures see Alcántara, *Modernizing Mexican Agriculture...,* p. 39.

36. Appendini and Salles, "Algunas consideraciones...," *Foro Internacional,* p. 415.

37. Ibid. In Guanajuato, for example, the high maize yields on certain irrigated farms substantially raised overall productivity figures for the state.

38. Alcántara, *Modernizing Mexican Agriculture...,* pp. 37-41.

39. Ibid., p. 40.

40. Wilkie, *The Mexican Revolution...,* pp. 133-135.

41. Calculated from Alcántara, *Modernizing Mexican Agriculture...,* Table 27, p. 87; and Mexico, *VIII censo...1960.*

42. CDIA, *Estructura Agraria...,* p. 135, current pesos converted to constant pesos; Grindle, *Bureaucrats, Politicans...,* p. 88.

43. Alcántara, *Modernizing Mexican Agriculture...,* pp. 55-59.

44. Ibid., pp. 60-64.

45. Womack, "The Mexican Economy During the Revolution, 1910-1920," *Marxist Perspectives,* Table 3, p. 101; Wilkie, *The Mexican Revolution...,* Table 6-5, p. 141; Alcántara, *Modernizing Mexican Agriculture...,* Table 19, p. 61.

46. Alcántara, *Modernizing Mexican Agriculture...,* pp. 64-72.

47. José Lázaro Salinas, *La Emigración de Braceros—Vision Objectiva de un Problema Mexicano* (México: CUAUHTEMOC, 1955), pp. 44-47.

48. Ifigenia M. de Navarrete, "Income Distribution in Mexico," in *Mexico's Recent Economic Growth: The Mexican View,* translated by Marjory Urquidi, University of Texas, Institute of Latin American Studies, Monograph no. 10 (Austin: University of Texas Press, 1970), Table 14, p. 165.

49. Roger D. Hansen, *The Politics of Mexican Development* (Baltimore: Johns Hopkins University Press, 1971) p. 75; Grindle, *Bureaucrats, Politicians . . . ,* p. 80.

50. Reynolds, *The Mexican Economy...;* for population see Table 2.4, p. 64, and for rural share of GDP see Table 2.7, p. 72.

51. A good example of this phenomenon is found in Cline, *Mexico: Revolution to Evolution...,* who allocates the six core sending states to three different regions.

52. Navarrete, "Income Distribution in Mexico," *Mexico's Recent Economic Growth...,* Table 7, p. 146.

53. Reynolds, *The Mexican Economy...,* Table 3.3, p. 98, and Table 3.6, p. 103.

54. México, Dirección General de Estadística, *Anuario Estadístico de los Estados Unidos Mexicanos, 1964-1965* (México: 1967), pp. 362, 366, our calculations.

55. Alcántara, *Modernizing Mexican Agriculture...,* Tables 38 and 39, pp. 110-113.

56. México, *6º censo... 1940;* México, *Septimo censo general de población, 6 de junio de 1950* (México: 1952-1953); México, *VIII censo... 1960.*

57. México, *50 Años de Revolución...,* p. 21.

58. México, *6º censo... 1940;* México, *VIII censo... 1960.*

59. CDIA, *Estructura Agraria...* cites the 1963 Banco de México study which found the average agricultural family to consist of 5.4 individuals, while the nonagricultural family had 5.1 people.

60. CDIA, *Estructura Agraria...,* table on p. 312.

61. For wages see Martin Luis Guzmán Ferrer, "Coyuntura actual de la agricultura mexicana," *Comercio Exterior,* 25(5): 575 (May 1975). For numbers of landless see Alcántara, *Modernizing Mexican Agriculture...,* p. 130.

62. Eloisa Alemán Alemán, *Investigación socioeconomica directa de los ejidos de San Luis Potosí* (México: Instituto Méxicano de Investigaciones Económicas, 1966), passim.

63. CDIA, *Estructura Agraria...,* pp. 480-481.

64. Ibid., p. 200.

65. From *Noveno censo general de población, 1970,* cited in Grindle, *Bureaucrats, Politicians...,* Table 13, p. 81.

66. Rubén Mújica Vélez, "Las zonas de riego: acumulación y marginalidad," *Comercio Exterior,* 29(4): 407 (April 1979); CDIA, *Estructura Agraria...,* pp. 451-466, 477; Alcántara, *Modernizing Mexican Agriculture...,* surveys in Sonora indicated that by the mid-1960s, 80 percent of ejidal lands in the Yaqui River valley were rented, pp. 210-214.

67. Banco de México, S.A., *Review of the Economic Situation of Mexico,* 49(570): 169 (May 1973); Alcántara, *Modernizing Mexican Agriculture...,* p. 130.

68. México, *VIII censo... 1960;* México, *IX censo general de población, 1970* (Mexico City: 1971-1973).

69. Alcántara, *Modernizing Mexican Agriculture...,* p. 133.

70. México, *6º censo... 1940;* México, *IX censo... 1970.*

71. México, *Anuario Estadístico... 1964-1965,* p. 50.

72. Wayne A. Cornelius, *Politics and the Migrant Poor in Mexico City* (Stanford, Calif.: Stanford University Press, 1975), Chapter 2, pp. 16-52 discusses the process of rural/urban movement to Mexico City.

73. México, *Anuario Estadístico... 1964-1965,* pp. 48-58.

74. México, *VIII censo... 1960.* For further analysis of internal migration to Mexico City see Richard W. Wilkie, "Urban Growth and the Transformation of the Settlement Landscape of Mexico, 1910-1970," in *Contemporary Mexico...,* pp. 99-134; Humberto Muñoz, et al., "Internal Migration to Mexico City and its Impact upon the City's Labor Market," in *Migration Across Frontiers: Mexico and the United States,* eds., Fernando Camara and Robert Van Kemper, vol. 3 of Contributions of the Latin American Anthropology Group (Albany: State University of New York, Institute of Mesoamerican Studies, 1979), pp. 35-64.

75. University of Arizona, Department of Anthropology, *Mexican Migration,* eds. Thomas Weaver and Theodore E. Downing (Tuscon: Bureau of Ethnic Research, 1976), Table 3.9, p. 47.

Chapter 3 Notes

1. Simpson, *The Ejido*...

2. Lesley Bird Simpson, "Review of Howard Cline's *Mexico: Revolution to Evolution, 1940-1960,*" in *Hispanic American Historical Review,* 43(2): 295-297 (May 1963).

3. Informant, Ramón Beteta, Mexico City, 1964, in WOHI.

4. Calculations derived from tables in Wilkie, *The Mexican Revolution*..., pp. 208-219, 299; and México, *Anuario Estadístico... 1964-1965.*

5. Sue E. Hayes, "Farm and Non-Farm Wages and Farm Benefits, 1948-1977," in *Technological Change, Farm Mechanization and Agricultural Employment,* University of California, Division of Agricultural Sciences, Priced Publication no. 4085 (July 1978), pp. 60-61.

6. California Legislature, *The Bracero Program and Its Aftermath: An Historical Summary* (Sacramento: April 1965), pp. 1-2.

7. Richard B. Craig, *The Bracero Program: Interest Groups and Foreign Policy* (Austin and London: University of Texas Press, 1971), p. ix, erroneously assumes that the total number of contracts equals the total number of individuals who took them. In fact an undetermined number of people worked more than once in this country as a bracero, and as a result, precise enumeration of the total number of Mexicans so employed is impossible.

8. Whetten, *Rural Mexico,* pp. 267-270.

9. Ibid., Table 51, p. 269.

10. Henry P. Anderson, *The Bracero Program in California* (New York: Arno, 1976, reprinted), pp. 8-9.

11. Ibid., pp. 6-7.

12. Whetten, *Rural Mexico,* Plate IX.

13. Anderson, *The Bracero Program in California,* p. 9.

14. Belshaw, *A Village Economy*..., p. 400, shows loans and interest rates for his village; Luis González y González, *San José de Gracia: Mexican Village in Transition,* trans. John Upton (Austin: University of Texas Press, 1972), p. 240, found the loans there to have varied between 1,000 and 1,500 pesos with interest rates of 200 percent.

15. Belshaw, *A Village Economy*..., p. 126. Belshaw had not realized the importance of the bracero program to the village until he had already begun field work, and as a result, he only interviewed six, five of which he translated and published (pp. 126-133); González, *San José de Gracia*..., p. 241.

16. Belshaw, *A Village Economy*..., pp. 128-131.

17. Bruce S. Meador, *Wetback Labor in the Lower Rio Grande Valley* (San Francisco: R & E Research Associates, reprinted, 1973), p. 11.

18. Julian Samora and Patricia Vandel Simon, *A History of the Mexican American People* (Notre Dame, Ind.: University of Notre Dame Press, 1977), pp. 144-145; Wayne A. Cornelius, *Mexican Migration to the United States: Causes, Consequences, and U.S. Responses,* Massachusetts Institute of Technology, Center for International Studies (Cambridge: July 1978), p. 7.

19. Cline, *The United States and Mexico,* p. 392.

20. George O. Coalson, *The Development of the Migratory Farm Labor System in Texas: 1900-1954* (San Francisco, Calif.: R & E Research Associates, 1977), p. 67.

21. González, *San José de Gracia*..., p. 219.

22. Samora and Simon, *A History of the Mexican American People,* calculations based upon Table 2, p. 140.

23. Anderson, *The Bracero Program in California,* p. 151.

24. Richard H. Hancock, *The Role of the Bracero in the Economic and Cultural Dynamics of Mexico: A Case Study of Chihuahua* (Stanford, Calif.: Stanford University Press, 1958), Table 2, p. 20.

25. See for example the first three tables accompanying the text of Ramesh Kumar et al.,

"Estimates of the Impact of Agricultural Mechanization Development on In-Field Labor Requirements for California Crops," in *Technological Change...*, pp. 169-171.

26. U.S., Department of Agriculture, Economic Research Service, *Power and Equipment on Farms in 1964, 48 States,* Statistical Bulletin no. 457 (Washington, D.C.: 1970), p. 22.

27. James R. Tavernetti and H.F. Miller, *Studies on Mechanization of Cotton Farming in California,* Bulletin no. 747 (Berkeley: California Agricultural Experiment Station, University of California, Division of Agricultural Sciences, 1954), Table 1, p. 6.

28. Loc. cit.

29. Ibid., using 1948-1949 for one set of averages and 1951-1952 for the other.

30. Texas, Employment Commission, *Annual Report, 1948* (Austin: 1949), p. 15. By 1966 the same report revealed that the season had been extended a month at either end.

31. U.S., Department of Agriculture, *Power and Equipment...,* p. 18; "Mechanization and the Texas Migrant," Table B, unpaginated.

32. Hayes, "Farm and Non-Farm...," in *Technological Change...,* p. 61.

33. Eastin Nelson and Frederic Meyers, *Labor Requirements and Labor Resources in the Lower Rio Grande Valley of Texas* (Inter-American Education: Occasional Papers, no. 6, 1950), p. 23.

34. "Mechanization and the Texas Migrant," Table B, and pp. 1-2.

35. Ibid., p. 1.

36. Kenneth R. Jones, *The Movement Toward Mechanization* (California, Department of Agriculture: 1966), p. 1.

37. *The California Tomato Grower,* 22(6): 8 (June 1979). The sources used for their estimate were the working sheets from the growers' field offices and hence are the most reliable.

38. California, Legislature, *The Bracero Program...,* p. 5.

39. Orville E. Thompson and Ann F. Scheuring, *From Lug Boxes to Electronics: A Study of California Tomato Growers and Sorting Crews,* California Agricultural Policy Seminar, Monograph no. 3 (Davis: Department of Applied Behavioral Sciences, University of California: December 1978), p. 24.

40. Hayes, "Farm and Non-Farm...," in *Technological Change...,* p. 64.

41. Thompson and Scheuring, *From Lug Boxes...,* p. 24.

42. Hayes, "Farm and Non-Farm...," in *Technological Change...,* pp. 62-63 ff.

43. Stanley L. Robe, *Azuela and the Mexican Underdogs* (Berkeley: University of California Press, 1979), includes a major reconsideration of Azuela's novel based upon Robe's ability to locate a "first edition" run of the 1915 newspaper which published it.

44. The phrase is Frank Brandenburg's; see his *The Making of Modern Mexico,* passim.

45. For contemporary accounts of the *Sinarquistas* from a U.S. perspective, which in turn was reinforced by the Mexican government, see Betty Kirk, *Covering the Mexican Front: The Battle of Europe vs America* (Norman: University of Oklahoma Press, 1942), pp. 314-328; See also Whetten, *Rural Mexico,* pp. 484-522.

46. Jean Meyer, *Le Sinarquisme: un fascisme mexicain? 1937-1947* (Paris: Librairie Hachette, 1977), passim.

47. Lorenzo Meyer, *México y los Estados Unidos en el Conflicto Petrolero, 1917-1942,* seg. ed. (México: Colegio de México, 1972), pp. 347-467 [pp. 173-228 in English-language version. See Bibliography for citation]; J. Richard Powell, *The Mexican Petroleum Industry 1938-1950* (Berkeley: University of California Press, 1956), pp. 112-113; Joe C. Ashby, *Organized Labor and the Mexican Revolution under Lázaro Cárdenas* (Chapel Hill: University of North Carolina Press, 1967), pp. 245-271.

48. Kirk, *Covering the Mexican Front...,* p. 315.

49. Ibid., p. 314.

50. Whetten, *Rural Mexico,* p. 521.

51. See Appendix 3.

52. Vicente Fuentes Díaz, "Los partidos políticos en México," vol. 2 (México: D.F.: 1956), pp. 81-122; Kenneth Johnson, *Mexican Democracy: A Critical View* (Boston: Allyn & Bacon, 1971), pp. 122-126; Meyer, *Le Sinarquisme...;* for a village-level view of the withering away of the Sinarquistas, see González, *San José de Gracia...,* pp. 208-209.

53. Foster, *Tzintzuntzan: Mexican Peasants...,* p. 277.

54. Richard Mines, "Résumé of Research Findings: Impact of Migration on a Village Migrant Community," unpublished paper (University of California, Berkeley, nd).

55. González, *San José de Gracia...,* pp. 239-242.

56. Belshaw, *A Village Economy...,* p. 123.

57. Zarrugh, "Gente de mi Tierra...," pp. 22-23.

58. Josh Reichert and Douglas S. Massey, "Patterns of Migration from a Rural Mexican Town to the United States: A Comparison of Legal and Illegal Migrants," paper presented at the Pacific Anthropological Association (March 1979), Table 2, unpaginated; Cornelius, *Mexican Migration...Responses,* pp. 33-34.

59. Anderson, *The Bracero Program in California,* p. 166, found that a Mexican national's preference for alcoholic beverages and beer increased with his work experience in the U.S.

60. Pontones, "La Migración en México," in *Contemporary Mexico...,* cuadro 1, p. 138.

61. González, *San José de Gracia...,* p. 219. In *Views Across the Border: The United States and Mexico,* ed. Stanley R. Ross (Albuquerque: University of New Mexico Press, 1978), see Jorge A. Bustamante, "Commodity Migrants: Structural Analysis of Mexican Immigration to the United States," p. 198; Vernon M. Briggs, Jr., "Labor Market Aspects of Mexican Migration to the United States in the 1970s," p. 207; and Tad Szulc, "Foreign Policy Aspects of the Border," p. 234.

62. Based upon average Mexican family size of 5.5 persons in 1960, subtracting the bracero himself from that number, rounding down to obtain discrete as opposed to partial human beings, and assuming that half the remainder were males, we then estimated that each returning worker influenced two other potential workers. Source of family size: CDIA, *Estructura Agraria...,* p. 312.

63. Pontones, "La Migración en México," in *Contemporary Mexico...,* cuadro 1, p. 138, has a run of contracts and remittances from 1943-1967. When compared with Cline, *Mexico: Revolution to Evolution...,* Table XIX, p. 354 for selected years in the 1950s, and México, *Anuario Estadístico...1964-1965,* cuadro 16.2, p. 595, for selected years in the 1960s, a high degree of reliability is found. Since the peso was devalued from 8.5 to 12.5 to the dollar halfway through the Bracero Era, we have used a conversion rate of 10 to 1 to achieve the 7 billion pesos figure.

64. González, *San José de Gracia...,* p. 242.

65. CDIA, *Estructura Agraria...,* p. 479.

66. Nelson, *The Waiting Village...,* p. 39, recounted that the wording of the local village official on a *permiso* included the phrase a "good and honorable man, a worker and not an ejidatario."

67. Belshaw, *A Village Economy...,* p. 173.

68. See the following: Richard Mines, "The Workers of Las Animas: A Case Study of Village Migration to California," unpublished research essay for the Department of Agriculture and Resource Economics (University of California, Berkeley: 1978), pp. 9-11; Foster, *Tzintzuntzan: Mexican Peasants...,* pp. 275-277, 286-288; González, *San José de Gracia...,* pp. 241-243; Díaz, "Tonalá...," p. 25; Nelson, *The Waiting Village...,* pp. 37-41, found a local school teacher offering to obtain bracero permits from the mayor in return for the contributions of villagers to his school. Exposure of the fraud led to the loss of the villagers' money, no *permisos* obtained by the donations, and the resignation of the mayor. The prestige of the teacher increased.

69. Singer, *Growth, Equality and the Mexican Experience,* p. 103.

70. González, *San José de Gracia...*, p. 243.

71. Whetten, *Rural Mexico*, pp. 268, 270.

72. Lázaro Salinas, *La Emigración de Braceros...*, p. 11.

73. Jorge Vera Estañol, "The Results of the Revolution," in *Is the Mexican Revolution Dead?* ed. Stanley R. Ross (New York: Knopf, 1966), pp. 210-216, see p. 214.

74. Francisco Jiménez, "The Circuit," in *The Arizona Quarterly*, 29(3): 246-252 (Autumn, 1973); Francisco Jiménez, "Arado sin Buey," *The Bilingual Review*, 1(3): 277-278 (September-December, 1974).

75. U.S., Congress, Senate, Committee on the Judiciary, Select Commission on Immigration and Refugee Policy, *U.S. Immigration Law and Policy: 1952-1979*, 96th Cong., 1st sess. (Washington, D.C.: U.S. Library of Congress, Congressional Research Service, May 1979), p. 35; Ernesto Galarza, *Merchants of Labor: The Mexican Bracero Story* (Charlotte, N.C. and Santa Barbara, Calif.: McNally & Loftin, 1964), passim.

76. Coalson, *The Development of the Migratory Farm Labor...*, pp. 78-95.

77. U.S., Congress, Senate, Committee on the Judiciary, Select Commission on Immigration..., *U.S. Immigration Law and Policy...*, pp. 37-38.

78. Ibid.; Paul Ehrlich et al., *The Golden Door: International Migration, Mexico, and the U.S.* (New York: Ballantine, 1979), pp. 218-220, 302.

79. Craig, *The Bracero Program...*, pp. 151-197.

80. U.S., Congress, Senate, Committee on the Judiciary, Select Commission on Immigration..., *U.S. Immigration Law and Policy...*, p. 41.

81. Craig, *The Bracero Program...*, pp. 151-197.

82. *California Farmer*, 222(2): 4 (January 16, 1965), cited in California, Legislature, *The Bracero Program and its Aftermath*, pp. 10-11.

Chapter 4 Notes

1. Cornelius, *Mexican Migration...Responses*, p. 18.

2. Samora, *Los Mojados...*, Table 8, p. 85.

3. There is a growing literature on the upsurge of the late 1960s best summarized in Cornelius, *Mexican Migration ... Responses*, pp. 8-13; México, CENIET, *La Encuesta Nacional de Emigración...*, passim.

4. John Mamer and Varden Fuller, "Employment on California Farms," in *Technological Change...*, p. 2.

5. Hayes, "Farm and Non-Farm...," in *Technological Change ...*, pp. 62-63, 68.

6. Donald Rosedale and John Mamer, *Labor Management for Seasonal Farm Workers: A Case Study*, Division of Agricultural Sciences, leaflet no. 2885 (University of California, Berkeley: April 1976), p. 6.

7. Thompson and Scheuring, *From Lug Boxes...*, pp. 1, 8, 24.

8. Jones, *The Movement Toward Mechanization*, p. 10.

9. Rosedale and Mamer, *Labor Management for Seasonal Farm Workers...*, Table II, p. 19.

10. Interview with Jack Lloyd, Manager, Coastal Growers Association, June 20, 1979.

11. Rosedale and Mamer, *Labor Management for Seasonal Farm Workers...*, Table II, p. 19.

12. John Mamer, "The California Farm Labor Market: A Challenge to Management and Leadership," unpublished text of speech (University of California, Berkeley: 1977) p. 10.

13. Interview with Jack Lloyd, June 20, 1979.

14. Mamer, "The California Farm Labor Market...," p. 9. In 1978 the workers voted to join the United Farm Workers Union, and while relations have been good between labor and management, benefits accruing to the workers have been mixed. The UFW has maintained the seniority system since it exceeds their standards, but it has eliminated the paid vacation in Mexico; interview with Jack Lloyd, June 20, 1979.

15. Hayes, "Farm and Non-Farm...," in *Technological Change...*, pp. 68-69.

16. Mamer, "The California Farm Labor Market...," p. 11.

17. Ibid., pp. 4-5; Mamer's comments follow Glen G. Cain, "The Challenge of Segmented Labor Market Theories to Orthodox Theory: A Survey," *Journal of Economic Literature,* 14(4): 1215-1257 (December 1976).

18. Texas, Good Neighbor Commission, *Texas Migrant Labor: An Overview* (Austin: 1966), p. 66.

19. Interview with Sue E. Hayes, June 26, 1979.

20. Texas, Governor's Office of Migrant Affairs, *Migrant and Seasonal Farmworkers in Texas* (Austin: July 1976), pp. 2-18. A sample of 1,609 households were contacted and interviewed for the study.

21. Richard Mines, "Impact of Migration on a Village Migrant Community," unpublished interim report (University of California, Berkeley: February 1979), Table 12, p. 17, found that of his study of Animas, Zacatecas, only 29.7 percent and 40.5 percent of people in the 16 to 39- and 40 to 54-year age groups respectively were employed in agriculture. The remainder were in low- to high-wage urban jobs; Zarrugh, "Gente de mi Tierra...," pp. 36-41, relates that the majority of villagers in her study came to urban areas in California where they worked either as garbagemen or horticulturists.

22. U.S., Congress, Joint Economic Committee, Subcommittee on Inter-American Economic Relationships, *Recent Developments in Mexico and Their Economic Implications for the United States,* 95th Cong., 1st sess., 1977, Statement of Honorable Raul H. Castro, Appendix "D," p. 236.

23. Cornelius, *Mexican Migration... Responses,* Table 5, p. 54.

24. Jay Merrill, *Border Area Development Study: Profile of Undocumented Migration to the California Border Region,* computerized (Sacramento: Southwest Regional Border Commission, 1978), appendix, unpaginated. Employment in "Eating and Drinking Places" has been reclassified under services instead of "Wholesale and Retail Trade" for purposes of clearer economic sector analysis.

25. U.S., Congress, Senate, Committee on the Judiciary, Select Commission on Immigration..., *U.S. Immigration Law and Policy...,* pp. 51-58.

26. Ibid., pp. 63-64.

27. Ibid., appendix III, pp. 98-109, contains the text of the bill.

28. Robert D. Shadow, "Differential Out-Migration: A Comparison of Internal and International Migration from Villa Guerrero, Jalisco (Mexico)," in *Migration Across Frontiers...,* p. 72.

29. The generalizations in the text are based upon the following village studies: Mines, "Impact of Migration...," pp. 9-11; Zarrugh, "Gente de mi Tierra...," pp. 6-26, 36-38, and 119-123; James Stuart and Michael Kearney, "Migration from the Mixteca of Oaxaca to the Californias: A Case Study," paper presented at the symposium "Migration into the Californias: Conservatism and Change in Retrospect and Perspective," at the annual meeting of the American Anthropological Association (Los Angeles: 1978), passim.

30. California, Assembly, Committee on Human Resources, hearing, *Undocumented Persons: Their Impact on Public Assistance Programs,* testimony of Conrad C. Jamison, Security Pacific National Bank (Los Angeles: 1977), pp. 116-119, see p. 118.

31. Banco Nacional de Comercio Exterior, "La Economía Latinoamerica en 1978/ Comisión Económica Para América Latina," *Comercio Exterior,* 29(3): 355 (March 1979); for maize prices see Table 15 in Chapter 5.

Chapter 5 Notes

1. Cline, *Mexico: Revolution to Evolution...*, p. 233.
2. Norris Clement and Louis Green, "The Political Economy of Devaluation in Mexico," *Inter-American Economic Affairs*, 32(3) (Winter, 1978), Table 1, p. 48.
3. Loc. cit.
4. Appendini and Salles, "Algunas consideraciones...," *Foro Internacional*, p. 404; United Nations, Food and Agriculture Organization, *Production Yearbook 1977* (Rome: 1977), pp. 77-79.
5. Calculated from the sources used for Appendix 4.
6. Appendini and Salles, "Algunas consideraciones . . . ," *Foro Internacional*, Table 3, p. 426. In contrast, the Banco Nacional de México estimated only a 14 percent shortfall in maize production for 1975. See *Review of the Economic Situation of Mexico*, 52(603) (February 1976), p. 53.
7. Vélez, "Las zonas de riego," *Comercio Exterior*, graph 1, p. 409; Alcántara, *Modernizing Mexican Agriculture . . . ,*p. 224.
8. Compare New York and Chicago wheat and maize prices in *Review of the Economic Situation of Mexico*, 52(602) (January 1976), p. 8, with the prevailing guaranteed prices in Mexico in *Review of the Economic Situation of Mexico*, 52(603) (February 1976), p. 52, and Table 15 of this study.
9. Alcántara, *Modernizing Mexican Agriculture . . .* , Table 26, p. 93, from data of CONASUPO (Compañia Nacional de Subsistencia Populares—National Staple Products Company).
10. United Nations, *Production Yearbook 1977*, p.100; Appendini and Salles, "Algunas consideraciones . . . ," *Foro Internacional*, Table 3, p. 426.
11. México, *Quinto censo agrícola, ganadero y ejidal, 1970* (Mexico City, 1975), passim. Appendini and Salles, "Algunas consideraciones . . . ," *Foro Internacional*, p. 417.
12. México, *IX censo . . . 1970*.
13. Wellhausen, "The Agriculture of Mexico," *Scientific American*, p. 139.
14. *Review of the Economic Situation of Mexico*, 49(470) (May 1973), p. 169. See also Ina R. Dinerman, "Patterns of Adaptation Among Households of U.S.-Bound Migrants from Michoacán, Mexico," *International Migration Review*, 12(4) (Winter, 1978), p. 492, for decline in real agricultural wages in a sending state.
15. *Review of the Economic Situation of Mexico*, 52(605): 114-117 (April 1976), see p. 114.
16. Ibid., 49(569) (April 1973), p. 154.
17. International Labour Office, *Yearbook of Labour Statistics, 1978* (Geneva: 1978), p. 548.
18. Hayes, "Farm and Non-Farm . . . ," *Technological Change . . .*, Table 3, p. 43.
19. Clement and Green, "The Political Economy of Devaluation in Mexico," *Inter-American Economic Affairs*, Table 1, p. 48.
20. Ibid., passim.
21. Banco Nacional . . . , "La Económia Latinoamerica . . .," *Comercio Exterior*, p. 355.
22. Luis Angeles, "Notas sobre el comportamiento reciente de la inversión privada en México," *Comercio Exterior*, 28(1): 11-23 (January 1978), see p. 17, which discusses the real minimum wages in the 1970s and the fact that agricultural laborers rarely receive the official government minimum wage.
23. United Nations, Economic Commission for Latin America, *Anuario Estadístico de América Latina* (United Nations, 1977), Table 417, p. 409; compared to economically active, México, *IX censo . . . 1970*.
24. The literature provides many estimates of the numbers of "new" unemployed each

year. These range from 200,000 to 500,000 annually. Our figure is calculated by using a job growth rate for 1978-1979 of 3 percent; see *Los Angeles Times,* "Mexico: Crisis of Poverty/ Crisis of Wealth" (Sunday, July 15, 1979), pp. 1-4. Labor force from United Nations, *Anuario Estadístico de América Latina,* Table 417, p. 409.

25. Luis Gómez Oliver, "Crisis agrícola, crisis de los campesinos," *Comercio Exterior,* 28(6): 714-727 (June 1978), see Table 6, p. 721.

26. David Gordon, "Mexico: A Survey," *The Economist* (April 22, 1978), p. 4.

27. David Ibarra Muñoz y Armando Labra Manjarrez, "Tercer Congreso Nacional de Economistas," *Comercio Exterior,* 29(4): 466-472 (April 1979), see p. 472; Dilmus D. James and John S. Evans, "Conditions of Employment in Mexico as Incentives for Mexican Migration to the United States: Prospects to the End of the Century," *International Migration Review,* 13(1): 4-24 (Spring, 1978), see p. 7.

28. Muñoz y Manjarrez, "Tercer Congreso . . . ," *Comercio Exterior,* p. 471; Grindle, *Bureaucrats, Politicians . . . ,* p. 80. See also Barbara H. Tuchman, "The Green Revolution and the Distribution of Agricultural Income in Mexico," *World Development,* 4(1) (January 1976), p. 23, who delineates a regional differentiation in the relative decline of income for the lower half of the population between 1960 and 1969.

29. Figures from 1960 from México, *Anuario Estadístico . . . 1964-1965,* pp. 48-51; 1980 figures estimated from 1976 population in United Nations, *Demographic Yearbook 1977* (New York: 1978).

30. United Nations, *Demographic Yearbook 1977;* border cities' growth rate of 5 percent from Jorge A. Bustamante, "El estudio de la zona fronteriza México-Estados Unidos," *Foro Internacional,* 29(3): 471-516 (January-March 1979), see p. 485.

31. México, *IX censo . . . 1970.*

32. México, CENIET, *Análisis de algunos resultados . . . ,* Table 2.2, p. 27.

Chapter 6 Notes

1. See, for example, Leo Grebler, et al., *The Mexican-American People: The Nation's 2nd Largest Minority* (New York: The Free Press, 1970).

2. Cornelius, *Mexican Migration . . . Responses;* Zarrugh, "Gente de mi Tierra . . ."; Jorge A. Bustamante, "Undocumented Immigration from Mexico: Research Report," *International Migration Review,* 11(2): 149-177 (Summer, 1977); David S. North and Marion F. Houstoun, *The Characteristics and Role of Illegal Aliens in the U.S. Labor Market: An Exploratory Study,* report prepared for the Employment and Training Administration, U.S., Department of Labor (Washington, D.C.: Linton and Co., 1976); Merrill, "Border Area Development Study . . ."

3. México, CENIET, *Relaciones entre indocumentados y "coyotes"* (Mexico: nd), passim.

4. Marta Tienda, "Familism and Structural Assimilation of Mexican Immigrants in the United States," paper prepared for the Center for Demography and Ecology, Working paper no. 79-11 (University of Wisconsin, Madison: 1979), Table 1, p. 23.

5. Howard Twining, "Report of Progress of the Patzcuaro Project," unpublished (Ukiah, California: February 1979), p. 2.

6. James Sandos and Harry Cross, research in progress on a growing association in Ventura County, California (1980); for urban/rural discussion see R. Wilkie, "Urban Growth . . . ," in J. Wilkie, et al., *Contemporary Mexico . . . ,* pp. 99-134.

7. Zarrugh, "Gente de mi Tierra . . . ," p. 37.

8. David S. North, *Fraudulent Entrants: A Study of Malafide Applicants for Admission at Selected Ports of Entry on the Southwest Border and at Selected Airports,* study prepared for

the U.S., Department of Justice, Immigration and Naturalization Service, Office of Planning and Evaluation (April 1976), Table 3, p. 22.

9. Refugio I. Rochin, "Illegal Mexican Aliens in California Agriculture: Some Theoretical Considerations," paper presented at Primer Simposium Internacional sobre los problemas de los trabajadores migratorios en México y los Estados Unidos de Norte América (Universidad de Guadalajara: July 11-14, 1978), p. 19; Vernon Briggs, Jr., *Chicanos and Rural Poverty*, Policy Studies in Employment and Welfare, no. 16 (Baltimore: Johns Hopkins University Press, 1973), p. 34.

10. Richard Mines, "The Workers of Las Animas: A Case Study of Village Migration to California," unpublished research essay for the Department of Agriculture and Resource Economics, University of California, Berkeley (May 8, 1978).

11. Harry Cross and James Sandos, field work in San Ysidro, California (August 1979).

12. Richard Mines, personal communication (August 1979).

13. Kenneth Johnson and Nina M. Ogle, *Illegal Mexican Aliens in the United States: A Teaching Manual on Impact Dimensions and Alternative Futures* (Washington, D.C.: University Press of America, 1978), pp. 32-37; Samora, *Los Mojados...*, pp. 1-3.

14. Ehrlich et al., *The Golden Door...*, pp. 306-310; See also, Cross and Sandos, field work in San Ysidro, California (August 1979).

15. Bill Ott, "Controversy Flares at Border Patrolman's Trial Over Firing From Covina Police Job," *San Diego Union* (November 28, 1979), pp. B-1 and B-4; Jack Jones, "Border Patrol Agent Admits Striking Aliens," *Los Angeles Times,* San Diego County ed. (November 27, 1979), Part II, pp. 1, 4; Jack Jones, "Border Beating Told By Surprise Witness," *Los Angeles Times,* San Diego County ed. (November 29, 1979), Part II, pp. 1, 6.

16. John Ehrlichman, "Mexican Aliens Aren't a Problem...They're a Solution: Observations from a Prison Camp in Arizona," *Esquire,* 92(2): 54-64 (August 1979).

17. México, CENIET, *Análisis de algunos resultados...*, p. 21.

18. For example see Grebler et al., *The Mexican American People...*, pp. 605-608; U.S., Bureau of the Census, *Census 1970.*

19. Shadow, "Differential Out-Migration....," *Migration Across Frontiers...;* Mines, "The Workers of Las Animas..."

20. Zarrugh, "Gente de mi Tierra..."

21. Stuart and Kearney, "Migration from the Mixteca of Oaxaca to the Californias..."; Ellwyn R. Stoddard, "Illegal Mexican Aliens in Borderlands Society," *South Texas Journal of Research and the Humanities,* 2(2): 197-213 (Fall, 1978).

22. Zarrugh, "Gente de mi Tierra..."

23. México, CENIET, *Análisis de algunos resultados...*, Table 5.5, p. 54; Orange County, Task Force on Medical Care for Illegal Aliens, *The Economic Impact of Undocumented Immigrants on Public Health Services in Orange County: A Study of Medical Costs, Tax Contributions, and Health Needs of Undocumented Immigrants,* mimeograph (1978), p. 17.

24. Lesko Associates, "Final Report: Basic Data and Guidance Required to Implement a Major Illegal Alien Study During Fiscal Year 1976," report prepared for the U.S., Immigration and Naturalization Service (Washington, D.C.: October 1975), passim; Ehrlich et al., *The Golden Door...*, pp. 181-190; Kenneth Roberts et al., "The Mexican Numbers Game: An Analysis of the Lesko Estimates of Undocumented Migration from Mexico to the United States" (Austin: University of Texas, Bureau of Business Research, April 1978), passim; Cornelius, *Mexican Migration...Responses,* pp. 10-13.

25. Roberts et al., "The Mexican Numbers Game...," have the best discussion of Lesko's "got-away-at-entry" ratio, pp. 7-8 and passim.

26. Roberto Ham Chávez and Jorge A. Bustamante, "Las expulsiones de indocumentados Mexicanos," *Demografía y Economía,* 13(2): 185-207 (1979).

27. Michael J. Piore, *Birds of Passage and Promised Lands* (Cambridge: Cambridge University Press, 1979), passim.

28. Vernon M. Briggs, Jr., "Illegal Immigration and the American Labor Force: The Use of 'Soft' Data for Analysis," *American Behavioral Scientist,* 19(3): 351-363 (January-February 1976).

29. Cornelius, *Mexican Migration... Responses,* p. 58.

30. Briggs, "Illegal Immigration...," *American Behavioral Scientist,* p. 360.

31. Merrill, "Border Area Development Study...," Table 20, np.

32. North and Houstoun, *The Characteristics and Role...,* p. 130.

33. Barton Smith and Robert Newman, "Depressed Wages Along the U.S.-Mexico Border: An Empirical Analysis," *Economic Inquiry,* 15(1): 51-66 (January 1977).

34. Merrill, "Border Area Development Study...," Table 20, np.

· 35. James Sandos, field research.

36. M.D. Van Arsdol et al., *Non-Apprehended and Apprehended Undocumented Residents in the Los Angeles Labor Market: An Exploratory Study,* prepared for the Employment and Training Administration (U.S., Department of Labor, contract no. 20-06-77-16) (Los Angeles: May 1979), pp. 172-173. Our calculations.

37. Interview with Richard Mines, University of California, Berkeley (June 1979).

38. Interview with Herbert Grant, Assistant District Director for Investigations, U.S. Immigration and Naturalization Service, San Diego (November 7, 1979).

39. Harry Bernstein and Mike Castro, "Bid to Give Illegal Aliens' Jobs to Americans Failing," *Los Angeles Times* (July 3, 1975), Part 1, p. 1.

40. Manuel Vic Villalpando, *A Study of the Impact of Illegal Aliens on the County of San Diego on Specific Areas* (San Diego: Human Resources Agency, November 5, 1975), p. 59.

41. Presentation and participation by Jorge A. Bustamante in "Rural Poverty in Mexico as the Source of Emigration Pressure," seminar by the Center for Ethics and Social Policy, Graduate Theological Union, Berkeley (July 21, 1979).

42. U.S., Congress, Senate, Committee on Labor and Human Resources, Hearings, *Farmworker Collective Bargaining,* 96th Cong., 1st sess. (Washington, D.C.: April-May, 1979), see testimony of Cesar Chavez and "Summary from Log of United Farm Workers Report to Immigration and Naturalization Service."

43. North and Houstoun, *The Characteristics and Role...,* p. 143.

44. U.S., Congress, House, Committee on International Relations, Subcommittee on Inter-American Affairs, Hearings, *Undocumented Workers: Implications for U.S. Policy in the Western Hemisphere,* 95th Cong., 2nd sess. (Washington, D.C.: May-August, 1978), see testimony of Leonel J. Castillo, Commissioner, Immigration and Naturalization Service, p. 4.

45. The Villalpando study is not as precise as several others, as its question asked workers if their employers had made payroll deductions. The kind of tax or contribution was not specified in the report.

46. See for example, Stoddard, "Illegal Mexican Aliens...," *South Texas Journal of Research and the Humanities,* passim.

47. David S. North, *Interactions Between Illegal Alien Respondents and the Social Security Tax Collection System: Some Preliminary Findings* (Washington, D.C.: Trans Century Corporation for the Social Security Administration, July 1976), Table 6, p. 20; North and Houstoun, *The Characteristics and Role...,* p. 143, where less deductions were taken from agricultural workers' wages.

48. North, *Interactions Between Illegal Alien Respondents and the Social Security Tax Collection System...,* Table 5, p. 18.

49. México, CENIET, *Tabla de Estancia en los Estados Unidos para Trabajadores Mexicanos Indocumentados* (México: 1979), Table 2.3, p. 13 and Table 2.6, p. 19.

50. Orange County, Task Force on Medical Care for Illegal Aliens, *The Economic Impact...*, pp. 17-20.

51. For length of stay see Van Arsdol et al., *Non-Apprehended and Apprehended Undocumented Residents in the Los Angeles Labor Market...*, Tables 9 and 10, pp. 46-48.

52. See Appendix 9, Table 9-1.

53. Van Arsdol et al., *Non-Apprehended and Apprehended Undocumented Residents in the Los Angeles Labor Market...*, p. 174.

54. Ibid., p. 171.

55. Avante Systems, Inc., and Cultural Research Associates, *A Survey of the Undocumented Population in Two Texas Border Areas,* prepared for the Texas Advisory Committee of the U.S. Commission on Civil Rights (San Antonio: September 1978), p. 41. In the North and Houstoun Study, one in five Mexicans filed for income tax returns; see North and Houstoun, *The Characteristics and Role...*, p. 145.

56. David Carliner, *The Rights of Aliens: The Basic ACLU Guide to an Alien's Rights* (New York: Avon, 1977), p. 159 and passim; Kenneth F. Johnson, "Stranded Mexican Aliens in Missouri and Illinois: A Spectrum of Livability and Human Rights Issue," unpublished paper presented at the Rocky Mountain Council on Latin American Studies (El Paso, Texas: May 1979), p. 12.

57. Avante Systems, Inc., and Cultural Research Associates, *A Survey of the Undocumented Population...*, p. 41; Van Arsdol et al., *Non-Apprehended and Apprehended Undocumented Residents in the Los Angeles Labor Market...*, p. 173.

58. Orange County, Task Force on Medical Care for Illegal Aliens, *The Economic Impact...*, p. 7.

59. North and Houstoun, *The Characteristics and Role...*, p. 69.

60. Orange County, Task Force on Medical Care for Illegal Aliens, *The Economic Impact...*, pp. 13, 16-17.

61. México, CENIET, *Análisis de algunos resultados...*, Table 5.5, p. 54.

62. Van Arsdol et al., *Non-Apprehended and Apprehended Undocumented Residents in the Los Angeles Labor Market...*, pp. 162, 169. The figure for numbers of children is a *minimum* since the last choice in the question was "seven children or more," for which there were 159 positive responses.

63. Ibid., Table 10, p. 47.

64. Ibid., Table 25, p. 87. Our calculations.

65. County of Los Angeles, Department of Public Social Services, "Fact Sheet on Aliens" (Los Angeles: March 22, 1977), p. 2.

66. Van Arsdol et al., *Non-Apprehended and Apprehended Undocumented Residents in the Los Angeles Labor Market...*, Table 26, p. 89.

67. In the North and Houstoun sample 44 percent had hospitalization payments withheld from their paychecks. See North and Houstoun, *The Characteristics and Role...*, p. 142.

68. For length of stay see México, CENIET, *Análisis de algunos resultados...*, Table 5.5, p. 54.

69. The CENIET sample of deportees did not include another type of health care user from Mexico: the pregnant woman who enters the United States on an I-186, a 72-hour border crossing permit, and has her child in a U.S. medical facility. She then may legally cross back into Mexico. The child is an American citizen and can enter the country at age 21. University Hospital in San Diego, California has encountered several of these cases. Source: Interview with Joseph Nalven, Community Research Associates (CRA), February 28, 1980. CRA was commissioned by the San Diego Board of Supervisors in late 1979 to do a community impact study of San Diego County, in part to update the earlier Villalpando study.

70. See Van Arsdol et al., *Non-Apprehended and Apprehended Undocumented Residents in the Los Angeles Labor Market...*, Table 26, p. 89.

71. Telephone interview with a member of the statistical bureau of Medi-Cal Administration, State of California, (Sacramento: September 7, 1979).

72. Orange County, Task Force on Medical Care for Illegal Aliens, *The Economic Impact...*, pp. 10-12.

73. California, Assembly, Committee on Human Resources, Public Hearings, *Undocumented Persons: Their Impact on Public Assistance Programs* (Los Angeles: November 9, 1977), see testimony of Dr. Joseph Brooks, UCLA Sepulveda Medical Training Program, pp. 140-141.

74. Ibid., see testimony of Richard Cordova, Department of Health Services, County of Los Angeles, pp. 29-32.

75. Ibid., see testimony of David Odell, Director, Human Services Agency, County of Orange, to Assemblyman Bruce Nestande, Santa Ana, p. 163.

76. Villalpando, *A Study of the Impact of Illegal Aliens...*, pp. 118-119. Our calculations.

77. See also, California, Health and Welfare Agency, Department of Social Welfare, *State Social Welfare Board Position Statement, Issue: Aliens in California* (Sacramento: January 1973), pp. 34-35, 54.

78. Orange County, Task Force on Medical Care for Illegal Aliens, *The Economic Impact...*, pp. 20-21.

79. County of Los Angeles, Department of Public Social Services, Bureau of Special Operations, "Alien Status Verification Activity Quarterly Report, January-March, 1979" (Los Angeles: May 1, 1979), Part 1, p. 1.

80. *HispanoAmericano,* 72(1860) (December 26, 1977), p. 11.

81. Solvieg Torrik, "Learning in a Pinch: How Migrant Kids Fare," *San Francisco Chronicle* (July 27, 1979), p. 4.

82. Cornelius, *Mexican Migration...Responses,* pp. 24-27; for his views on the more settled population see "The Future of Mexican Immigration in California: A New Perspective for Public Policy," unpublished draft, passim.

83. Ibid., p. 26.

84. Orange County, Task Force on Medical Care for Illegal Aliens, *The Economic Impact...*, p. 17.

85. Two striking examples of this are the case of a 38-year-old Mexican who has lived and worked in Texas since she entered the country at age 6, and the California case of a 93-year-old who has been living in the U.S. since 1923. Avante Systems..., *A Survey of Undocumented Population...*, p. A7; Orange County, Task Force on Medical Care for Illegal Aliens, *The Economic Impact...*, p. 51.

86. Grebler et al., *The Mexican American People...*, pp. 132-135; Esther Estrada, Mexican American Legal Defense and Educational Fund (MALDEF), *Hispanics and the 1980 Census,* p. 3, asserts that the Hispanic population in the U.S. increased 33 percent between 1970-1979, while the nation's overall population grew by only 6.1 percent.

87. Herman Baca, Committee on Chicano Rights, Lecture, University of California, San Diego, March 10, 1980. The general remarks made in the text are drawn from 10 years of combined field work in the U.S. and extensive conversations with members of the community of Mexican ancestry and most scholars who study it.

88. Gamio, *Mexican Migration...Adjustment,* pp. 129 ff.

89. Ibid., Appendix III, pp. 208-216, especially p. 212.

90. Johnson, "Stranded Mexican Aliens...," passim; see also, Johnson, *Mexican Democracy...,* passim.

91. Ehrlichman, "Mexican Aliens...," *Esquire, pp. 54-64.*

92. Fernando R. Zazueta, "Attorneys Guide to the Use of Court Interpreters, With an English and Spanish Glossary of Criminal Law Terms," *8 Davis Law Review,* pp. 471-522 (1975).

93. MALDEF, *Statement of Position Regarding the Administration's Undocumented Alien Legislative Proposal* (San Francisco, Calif.: 1977), passim.

94. Gamio, *Mexican Migration... Adjustment,* Table II, pp. 3-6.

95. Juan Díez-Canedo, "Mexican Migration to the United States," paper submitted for the Workshop on Cooperative Labor Movements, Center for European Studies, Harvard University (Cambridge, Mass.: October 14-16, 1977), pp. 17 ff.

96. Mines, "Impact of Migration...," p. 2.

97. See Cornelius, *Mexican Migration... Responses,* p. 46; México, CENIET, *Análisis de algunos resultados...,* pp. 65-67. For more on impact on Mexico see John H. Moore, "Illegal Aliens: The View from a Mexican Village," proceedings of the Central States Anthropological Society, Selected Papers, vol. I (1975), passim.

98. Díez-Canedo, "Mexican Migration to the United States," passim.

99. Gamio, *Mexican Migration... Adjustment,* pp. 183-184, and Appendix VII, pp. 235-241.

100. Loc. cit.

101. See for example, Dinerman, "Patterns of Adaptation...," *International Migration Review,* passim; Raymond E. Wiest, "Wage-Labor Migration and Household Maintenance in a Central Mexican Town," *Journal of Anthropological Research,* 29(3) (Autumn, 1973), passim.

102. Josh Reichert and Douglas Massey, "Socio-Economic Stratification in a Mexican Community: The Effect of Migration to the United States," paper presented at the annual meeting of the Population Association of America (Denver, Colo.: April 1980).

Chapter 7 Notes

1. Appendini and Salles, "Algunas consideraciones...," *Foro Internacional,* p. 404, note 6.

2. See Harry Cross and James Sandos, *The Impact of Undocumented Mexican Workers on the United States: A Critical Assessment,* Battelle Memorial Institute, Population and Development Policy Program, Working Paper no. 15 (Washington, D.C.: November 1979).

3. "Attorneys Guide to the Use of Court Interpreter...," *8 Davis Law Review,* passim.

4. Howard Twining, various reports on the Patzcuaro Project, unpublished (Ukiah, Calif.: 1977-1979).

5. Mario M. Carrillo-Huerta, "Determinants of the Adoption of Agricultural Innovations," *The American Economist,* 22(2): 50-55 (Fall, 1978).

6. The information on Programa de Inversiones para el Desarrollo Rural (hereafter, PIDER) is from Michael M. Cernea, *Measuring Project Impact: Monitoring and Evaluation in the PIDER Rural Development-Mexico* (Washington, D.C.: World Bank Staff Working Paper no. 332, June 1979), and a presentation by August Schumacher of the World Bank in Washington, D.C. (November 29, 1979).

7. However, pegging the minimum wage to inflation does not necessarily solve the problem since perhaps as many as 50 percent of Mexico's working force do not even receive the minimum wage. José Luis Reyna, "El movimiento obrero en una situación de crisis," *Foro Internacional,* 19(3): 390-401 (January-March 1979), see pp. 394-395.

8. *Comercio Exterior,* "Cuestiones económicas y sociales de México," 29(7) (México: July 1979); Clement and Green, "The Political Economy of Devaluation in Mexico," *Inter-American Economic Affairs,* p. 70, note 1.

9. See John Crewdson, "The 'Time Bomb' on the Border: Imperial Valley Pollution," *San Francisco Chronicle/Examiner,* "This World" section (Sunday, September 9, 1979), p. 33.

10. John S. Nagel, "Mexico's Population Policy Turnaround," *Population Bulletin,* 33(5): 20 (December 1978).

11. Ibid., pp. 20-24.

12. Alfredo Gallegos et al., "Recent Trends in Contraceptive Use in Mexico," *Studies in Family Planning,* 8(8) (August 1977), Table 3, p. 199.

13. U.S., Bureau of the Census, *Country Demographic Profiles: Mexico,* Population Division (Washington, D.C.: September 1979), Table A-6, p. 30.

14. Coordinación del Programa Nacional de Planificación Familiar, *Bases para la Programación en Planificación Familiar, 1979-1982* (Mexico: 1979), Table A, p. 97.

15. Population Reference Bureau, Inc., "1979 World Population Data Sheet" (Washington, D.C.: 1979).

16. Promotora de Planificación Familiar, *Family Planning in Mexico: A Comprehensive Marketing Study of Awareness, Attitudes, and Practices among Consumers and Retailers* (México: 1979), p. 85.

17. Memo from Raúl A. Roca to Luis de la Macorra, Director of PROFAM, "House to House Sampling of Contraceptive Products, Ciudad Netzahualcoyotl, México, D.F., October-December, 1979" (Mexico City: January 18, 1980).

18. Ibid.

19. Coordinación del Programa Nacional de Planificación Familiar, *Encuesta Nacional de Prevalencia en el Uso de Metodos Anticonceptivos: Informe de Resultados* (México: 1979), p. 7.

20. Personal communication with Luis de la Macorra, Director of PROFAM, Washington, D.C. (March 7, 1980).

21. U.S., Bureau of the Census, *Country Demographic Profiles: Mexico,* Table 2, p. 5.

22. Ibid., Table 6, p. 9.

23. Nagel, "Mexico's Population...," *Population Bulletin,* p. 8.

Appendix 7 Notes

1. For an example of sound research on legal Mexican immigrants see Marta Tienda, "Familism and Structural Assimilation of Mexican Immigrants in the United States," Working Paper no. 79-11 (Madison: University of Wisconsin, Center for Demography and Ecology, 1979), passim.

2. Orange County, Task Force..., *The Economic Impact...;* Van Arsdol et al., *Non-Apprehended and Apprehended...;* and Villalpando, *A Study of the Socio-Economic Impact....*

3. Richard Mines, work in progress; also, see papers listed in the Bibliography, Unpublished Sources.

4. Thomas Weaver and Theodore Downing, *Mexican Migration* (Tucson: Bureau of Ethnic Research, 1976), passim.

5. Norris Clement and Louis Green, "The Political Economy...," in *Inter-American Economic Affairs,* pp. 47-73.

6. Delmus D. James and John S. Evans, "Conditions of Employment and Income Distribution in Mexico as Incentives for Mexican Migration in the United States: Prospects to the End of the Century," in *International Migration Review,* 13(1): 4-24 (Spring, 1979).

Appendix 8 Notes

1. Gregory J. Robinson, "Estimating the Approximate Size of the Illegal Alien Population in the United States by the Comparative Trend Analysis of Age-Specific Death Rates," paper

presented at the annual meeting of the Population Association of America (Philadelphia: April 26-28, 1979), pp. 1-3, 21, and Table 7, Appendix.

2. Clarise Lancaster and Frederick J. Scheuren, "Counting the Uncountable Illegals: Some Initial Statistical Speculations Employing Capture-Recapture Techniques," in *1977 Proceedings of the Annual Meeting of the American Statistical Association,* pp. 68-72, 74.

3. David Heer, "What is the Annual Net Flow of Undocumented Mexican Immigrants," pp. 419-422, and "The Annual Net Flow of Undocumented Mexican Immigrants to the United States," in Van Arsdol et al., *Non-Apprehended and Apprehended...,* pp. 105-112, and Table 32, p. 114.

4. See, for example, CENIET, *La Encuesta Nacional de Emigración a la Frontera Norte del País...,* Table 2 in Appendix, where the sample of 25,138 apprehendees included 2,314 (9.2 percent) women and 6,207 (24.7 percent) male youths under the age of 20. A study of non-apprehended living in the U.S. (Van Arsdol et al., see Heer, note 6) found that 35.4 percent of their sample of 2,905 were females, and that 10.5 percent were over the age of 44. See pp. 162, 164.

5. Lancaster and Scheuren, "Counting the Uncountable Illegals...," p. 73, in North and LeBel reference, note 9.

6. Heer, "The Annual Net Flow of Undocumented Mexican Immigrants...," in *Non-Apprehended and Apprehended...,* pp. 115-119.

7. Lancaster and Scheuren, "Counting the Uncountable Illegals...," p. 70.

8. These data are available in the *INS Annual Reports.*

9. David S. North and Allen LeBel, *Manpower and Immigration Policies in the United States* (Washington, D.C.: National Commission for Manpower Policy, special report no. 20, 1978); and a project by David North entitled "Analyzing the Apprehension Statistics of the Immigration and Naturalization Service," which has been submitted to the Department of Labor.

Appendix 10 Notes

1. California, Assembly, Committee on Human Resources, *Undocumented Persons: Their Impact on Public Assistance Programs* (Los Angeles: 1977), see testimony of Keith Comrie, Director, Los Angeles County Department of Public Social Services, pp. 18-21.

2. County of Los Angeles, "Alien Status Verification Activity Quarterly Report: January-March, 1979," p. 1.

3. See, for example, County of Los Angeles, "Fact Sheet on Aliens," p. 6, for costs of supporting citizen children of undocumented parents.

4. "Immigrants Inundate Los Angeles," in *The Futurist,* 11(2): 123 (April 1977).

5. Green cards are routinely purchased in Mexico and the U.S. for as low as $80. See Refugio I. Rochin, "Illegal Mexican Aliens in California Agriculture...," paper presented at Primer Simposium..., pp. 14-19; personal communication with Richard Mines, Department of Agricultural Economics, University of California, Berkeley (August 1979).

Bibliography

Published Sources

Alba, Francisco. "Mexico's International Migration as a Manifestation of its Development Pattern." *International Migration Review* 12(4): 502-513. Winter 1978.

Alcántara, Cynthia Hewitt de. *Modernizing Mexican Agriculture: Socioeconomic Implications of Technological Change 1940-1970.* Geneva: United Nations Research Institute for Social Development, 1976.

Alemán Alemán, Eloisa. *Investigación socioeconómica directa de los ejidos de San Luis Potosí.* México: Instituto Mexicano de Investigaciones Económicas, 1966.

Anderson, Henry P. *The Bracero Program in California.* Reprinted. New York: Arno Press, 1976.

Anderson, Richmond K., et al. "Nutrition Appraisals in Mexico." *American Journal of Public Health and the Nation's Health* 38(8): 1126-1135. August 1948.

Angeles, Luis. "Notas sobre el comportamiento reciente de la inversión privada en México." *Comercio Exterior* 28(1): 11-23. January 1978.

Appendini, Kirsten A. de, and Salles, Vania Almeida. *Agricultura Capitalista y Agricultura Campesina en México.* México: El Colegio de México, 1977.

_____. "Algunas consideraciones sobre los precios de garantía y la crisis de produdión de los alimentos básicos." *Foro Internacional* 19(3): 402-428. January-March 1979.

Appendini, Kirsten A. de; Murayama, Daniel; and Domínguez, Rosa María. "Desarrollo desigual en México, 1900 y 1960." *Demografía y Economía* 6(1): 1-39. 1972.

Ashby, Joe C. *Organized Labor and the Mexican Revolution under Lázaro Cárdenas.* Chapel Hill: University of North Carolina Press, 1967.

Avante Systems, Inc., and Cultural Research Associates. *A Survey of the Undocumented Population in Two Texas Border Areas.* San Antonio: U.S. Commission on Civil Rights, Texas State Advisory Committee, September 1978.

Banco Nacional de Comercio Exterior. *Comercio Exterior.* 29 vols. México: 1950-1979.

Banco Nacional de México. *Review of the Economic Situation of Mexico.* 55 vols. México: 1924-1979.

Bazant, Jan. *Cinco haciendas mexicanas: Tres siglos de vida rural en San Luis Potosí.* México: Colegio de México, 1975.

_____. "Peones, arrendatarios y aparceros en México, 1851-1853." *Historia Mexicana* 23(2): 330-357. October-December 1973.

Behrens, Steve, ed. *Questions and Answers on U.S. Immigration and Population.* Washington, D.C.: Zero Population Growth, 1978.
_____. *U.S. Population Fact Sheet.* Washington, D.C.: Zero Population Growth, 1978.
Belshaw, Michael. *A Village Economy: Land and People of Huecorio.* New York and London: Columbia University Press, 1967.
Bernstein, Harry, and Castro, Mike. "Bid to Give Illegal Aliens' Jobs to Americans Failing." *Los Angeles Times.* July 3, 1975.
Brading, David A. *Haciendas and Ranchos in the Mexican Bajío: León, 1700-1860.* Cambridge and Great Britain: Cambridge University Press, 1978.
Brandenburg, Frank. *The Making of Modern Mexico.* Englewood Cliffs, N.J.: Prentice-Hall, 1964.
Briggs, Vernon M., Jr. *Chicanos and Rural Poverty.* Policy Studies in Employment and Welfare, No. 16. Baltimore: Johns Hopkins University Press, 1973.
_____. "Illegal Immigration and the American Labor Force: the Use of 'Soft' Data for Analysis." *American Behavioral Scientist* 19(3): 351-363. January-February 1976.
Brown, Lyle C. "The Politics of United States-Mexican Relations: Problems of the 1970s in Historical Perspective." In Wilkie, et al., eds., *Contemporary Mexico...*, pp. 471-493.
Bustamante, Jorge A. "Commodity Migrants: Structural Analysis of Mexican Immigration to the United States." In Ross, ed., *Views Across the Border...*, pp. 183-203.
_____. "El estudio de la zona fronteriza México-Estados Unidos." *Foro Internacional* 19(3): 471-516. January-March 1979.
_____. "Undocumented Immigration from Mexico: Research Report." *International Migration Review* 11(2): 149-177. Summer 1977.
Cabrera Ipiña, Octaviano, and Cabrera Ipiña, Matilde. *Una Hacienda Potosina: San Francisco Javier de la Parada.* San Luis Potosí, México: Editorial Universitaria Potosina, 1978.
Cain, Glen G. "The Challenge of Segmented Labor Market Theories to Orthodox Theory: A Survey." *Journal of Economic Literature* 14(4): 1215-1257. December 1976.
California. Assembly. Committee on Human Resources. Hearings. *Undocumented Persons: Their Impact on Public Assistance Programs.* Los Angeles: November 9, 1977.
_____. Health and Welfare Agency. Department of Social Welfare. *State Social Welfare Board Position Statement. Issue: Aliens in California.* Sacramento: January 1973.
_____. Health and Welfare Agency. Department of Health Services. California Center for Health Statistics. *California's Medical Assistance Program Annual Statistical Report,* Calendar Year 1978. Report No. 0542-001. Sacramento: July 1979.
_____. Legislature. *The Bracero Program and Its Aftermath.* Sacramento: April 1965.
_____. University. *Technological Change, Farm Mechanization, and Agricultural Employment.* Berkeley: Division of Agricultural Sciences, 1978.
The California Tomato Grower 22(6). Stockton: The California Tomato Growers Association, June 1979.
Camara, Fernando, and Kemper, Robert Van. *Migration Across Frontiers: Mexico and the United States.* Vol. 3 of *Contributions of the Latin American Anthropology Group.* Institute for Mesoamerican Studies. Albany: State University of New York, 1979.
Cardenas, Gilberto. "United States Immigration Policy Toward Mexico: An Historical Perspective." *Chicano Law Review* 2: 66-91. Summer 1975.
Carillo-Huerta, Mario M. "Determinants of the Adoption of Agricultural Innovations." *The American Economist* 22(2): 50-55. Fall 1978.
Carliner, David. *The Rights of Aliens: The Basic ACLU Guide to an Alien's Rights.* New York: Avon Books, 1977.

Carr, E.H. *A History of Soviet Russia.* 9 vols. in 11 and continuing. London and New York: Macmillan, 1950-1971.

Centro de Investigaciones Agrarias [CDIA]. *Estructura Agraria y Desarrollo Agrícola en México.* México: Fondo de Cultura Económica, 1974.

Cernea, Michael M. *Measuring Project Impact: Monitoring and Evaluation in the PIDER Rural Development-Mexico.* Staff Working Paper no. 332. Washington, D.C.: World Bank, June 1979.

Chamberlin, William Henry. *The Russian Revolution, 1917-1921.* 2 vols. Reprinted. New York: Grosset and Dunlap, 1965.

Clement, Norris, and Green, Louis. "The Political Economy of Devaluation in Mexico." *Inter-American Economic Affairs* 32(3): 47-73. Winter 1978.

Cline, Howard F. *Mexico: Revolution to Evolution, 1940-1960.* New York: Oxford University Press, 1963.

_____. *The United States and Mexico.* New York: Atheneum, 1963.

Coalson, George O. *The Development of the Migratory Farm Labor System in Texas, 1900-1954.* Reprinted. San Francisco: R & E Research Associates, 1977.

Cockcroft, James D. *Intellectual Precursors of the Mexican Revolution, 1900-1913.* Austin: University of Texas Press, 1968.

Conard, Jane Reister. "Health Care for Indigent Illegal Aliens: Whose Responsibility?" 8 *Davis Law Review,* 107-126. Davis: University of California, 1975.

Cook, Sherburne F., and Borah, Woodrow. *Essays in Population History: Mexico and the Caribbean.* Vol. 1. Berkeley: University of California Press, 1971.

_____. *Essays in Population History: Mexico and California.* Vol. 3. Berkeley and Los Angeles: University of California Press, 1979.

Coordinación del Programa Nacional de Planificación Familiar. *Bases para la Programación en Planificación Familiar, 1979-1982.* México: 1979.

_____. *Encuesta Nacional de Prevalencia en el Uso de Metodos Anticonceptivos: Informe de Resultados.* México: 1979.

Cornelius, Wayne A. *Mexican Migration to the United States: Causes, Consequences, and U.S. Responses.* Cambridge: Massachusetts Institute of Technology, Center for International Studies, 1978.

_____. *Mexican Migration to the United States: The View from the Rural Sending Communities.* Cambridge: Massachusetts Institute of Technology, Center for International Studies, 1976.

_____. *Politics and the Migrant Poor in Mexico City.* Stanford, Calif.: Stanford University Press, 1975.

Corwin, Arthur F. Editor. *Immigrants—and Immigrants: Perspectives on Mexican Labor Migration to the United States.* Westport, Conn.: Greenwood Press, 1978.

_____. "Mexican Emigration History, 1900-1970: Literature and Research." *Latin American Research Review* 8(2). Summer 1973.

Craig, Richard B. *The Bracero Program: Interest Groups and Foreign Policy.* Austin and London: University of Texas Press, 1971.

Crewdson, John M. "The 'Time Bomb' on the Border: Imperial Valley Pollution." *San Francisco Chronicle/Examiner,* "This World" Section. September 9, 1979.

Cross, Harry E. "Debt Peonage Reconsidered: A Case Study in Nineteenth Century Zacatecas, Mexico." *Business History Review* 53(4): 473-495. Winter 1979.

_____. "Living Standards in Rural Nineteenth Century Mexico: Zacatecas, 1820-1880." *Journal of Latin American Studies* 10(1): 1-19. May 1978.

Cross, Harry E., and Sandos, James A. *The Impact of Undocumented Mexican Workers on the United States: A Critical Assessment.* Battelle Memorial Institute, Population and

Development Policy Program, Working Paper no. 15. Washington, D.C.: November 1979.

Cumberland, Charles C. *Mexican Revolution: The Constitutionalist Years*. Austin: University of Texas Press, 1972.

_____. *Mexico: The Struggle for Modernity*. New York: Oxford University Press, 1968.

Dagodag, W. Tim. "Source Regions and Composition of Illegal Mexican Immigration to California." *International Migration Review* 9(4): 499-511. Winter 1975.

Davis, L. Harlan. "Appropriate Technology: An Explanation and Interpretation of its Role in Latin America." *Inter-American Economic Affairs* 32(1): 51-66. Summer 1978.

DeWalt, Billie R. *Modernization in a Mexican Ejido: A Study in Economic Adaptation*. Cambridge and Great Britain: Cambridge University Press, 1979.

Dinerman, Ina R. "Patterns of Adaptation Among Households of U.S.-Bound Migrants from Michoacán, Mexico." *International Migration Review* 12(4): 485-501. Winter 1978.

Ehrlich, Paul; Bilderback, Loy; and Ehrlich, Anne. *The Golden Door: International Migration, Mexico, and the United States*. New York: Ballantine Books, 1979.

Ehrlichman, John. "Mexican Aliens Aren't a Problem...They're a Solution: Observations from a Prison Camp in Arizona." *Esquire*, August 1979, pp. 54-64.

Ericson, Anna-Stina. "The Impact of Commuters on the Mexican-American Border Area." *Monthly Labor Review* 93(8): 18-27. August 1970.

Finkler, Kaja. "From Sharecroppers to Entrepreneurs: Peasant Household Production Strategies under the *Ejido* System of Mexico." *Economic Development and Cultural Change* 27(1): 103-120. October 1978.

Flores, Roy, and Cardenas, Gilbert. *A Study of the Demographic and Employment Characteristics of Undocumented Aliens in San Antonio, El Paso, and McAllen*. A report submitted to the Southwestern Regional Office of the U.S. Commission on Civil Rights. August 23, 1978.

Foster, George M. *Tzintzuntzan: Mexican Peasants in a Changing World*. Boston: Little, Brown and Co., 1967.

Frisbie, Parker. "Illegal Migration from Mexico to the United States: A Longitudinal Analysis." *International Migration Review* 9(4): 3-13. Spring 1975.

Fromm, Erich, and Maccoby, Michael. *Social Character in a Mexican Village*. Englewood Cliffs, N.J.: Prentice-Hall, 1970.

The Futurist. "Immigrants Inundate Los Angeles." 11(2): 123-124. April 1977.

Galarza, Ernesto. *Merchants of Labor: The Mexican Bracero Story*. Charlotte, N.C. and Santa Barbara, Calif.: McNally and Loftin, 1964.

Gallegos, Alfredo, et al. "Recent Trends in Contraceptive Use in Mexico." *Studies in Family Planning* 8(8): 197-204. August 1977.

Gamio, Manuel. *Mexican Immigration to the United States: A Study of Human Migration and Adjustment*. Chicago: University of Chicago Press, 1930. Reprinted by Dover, 1971.

García y Griego, Manuel. *El volumen de la migración de mexicanos no documentados a los Estados Unidos: Nuevas hipotesis*. Mexico, D.F.: Centro Nacional de Información y Estadísticas del Trabajo, 1980.

Gil, Carlos B. Editor. *The Age of Porfirio Díaz*. Albuquerque: University of New Mexico Press, 1977.

_____. "Rosendo Peña, Hacienda Laborer in West-Central Mexico." In Gil, ed., *The Age of Porfirio Díaz*, pp. 156-163.

Goldschmidt, Alfonso. *Tierra y Libertad: El desarrollo campesino en México*. México: Edicíon y Distribucíon Ibero-Americana de Publicaciones, 1940.

Gómez Oliver, Luis. "Crisis agrícola, crisis de los campesinos." *Comercio Exterior* 28(6): 714-727. June 1978.

González y González, Luis. *San José de Gracia: Mexican Village in Transition.* Translated by John Upton. Austin: University of Texas Press, 1974.

Gordon, David. "Mexico: A Survey." *The Economist,* Supplement, April 22, 1978.

Grebler, Leo; Moore, Joan W.; and Guzman, Ralph C. *The Mexican American People: The Nation's Second Largest Minority.* New York: The Free Press, 1970.

Grindle, Merilee Serrill. *Bureaucrats, Politicians, and Peasants in Mexico: A Case Study in Public Policy.* Berkeley and Los Angeles: University of California Press, 1977.

Guzmán Ferrer, Martin. "Coyuntura actual de la agricultura mexicana." *Comercio Exterior* 25(5): 572-584. May 1975.

Ham Chávez, Roberto, and Bustamante, Jorge. "Las expulsiones de indocumentados mexicanos." *Demografía y Economía* 13(2): 185-207. 1979.

Hancock, Richard H. *The Role of the Bracero in the Economic and Cultural Dynamics of Mexico.* Stanford, Calif.: Stanford University Press, 1958.

Hansen, Roger D. *The Politics of Mexican Development.* Baltimore: Johns Hopkins University Press, 1971.

Hayes, Sue E. "Farm and Non-Farm Wages and Farm Benefits, 1948-1977." In California, University, *Technological Change, Farm Mechanization and Agricultural Employment,* pp. 33-72.

Heer, David M. "The Annual Net Flow of Undocumented Mexican Immigrants to the United States." In Van Arsdol, et al., eds., *Non-Apprehended and Apprehended Undocumented Residents in the Los Angeles Labor Market,* pp. 103-129.

Herrera-Sobek, María. *The Bracero Experience: Elitelore versus Folklore.* Los Angeles: University of California, Latin American Center, 1979.

Hirschman, C. "Prior U.S. Residence among Mexican Immigrants." *Social Forces* 56(4): 1179-1202. June 1978.

HispanoAmericano. 72(1860). December 26, 1977.

Hoffman, Abraham. *Unwanted Mexican Americans in the Great Depression: Repatriation Pressures, 1929-1939.* Tucson: University of Arizona Press, 1974.

International Labour Office. *Yearbook of Labour Statistics, 1978.* Geneva: International Labour Office, 1978.

James, Dilmus D., and Evans, John S. "Conditions of Employment and Income Distribution in Mexico as Incentives for Mexican Migration to the United States: Prospects to the End of the Century." *International Migration Review* 13(1) 4-24. Spring 1979.

Jasny, Naum. *The Socialized Agriculture of the U.S.S.R.: Plans and Performance.* Stanford, Calif.: Stanford University Press, 1949.

Jenkins, J. Craig. "The Demand for Immigrant Workers: Labor Scarcity or Social Control? *International Migration Review* 12(4): 514-535. Winter 1978.

_____. "Push/Pull in Recent Mexican Migration to the U.S." *International Migration Review* 11(2): 178-189. Summer 1978.

Jiménez, Francisco. "Arado sin Buey." *The Bilingual Review* 1(3): 277-278. September-December 1974.

_____. "The Circuit." *The Arizona Quarterly* 29(3): 246-252. Autumn 1973.

Johnson, Kenneth F., and Ogle, Nina M. *Illegal Mexican Aliens in the United States: A Teaching Manual on Impact Dimensions and Alternative Futures.* Washington, D.C.: University Press of America, 1978.

Johnson, Kenneth F. *Mexican Democracy: A Critical View.* Boston: Allyn and Bacon, 1971.

Jones, Jack. "Border Patrol Agent Admits Striking Aliens." *Los Angeles Times,* San Diego County ed. November 27, 1979.

_____. "Border Beating Told By Surprise Witness." *Los Angeles Times,* San Diego County ed. November 29, 1979.

Jones, Kenneth R. *The Movement toward Mechanization.* Sacramento: California Department of Agriculture, 1966.

Jones, Lamar B. "Alien Commuters in United States Labor Markets." *International Migration Review* 4(3): 65-86. Summer 1970.

Kemmerer, Edwin W. *Inflation and Revolution: Mexico's Experience of 1912-1917.* Princeton, N.J.: Princeton University Press, 1940.

King, Allan G., and Rizo-Patrón, Jorge. "A Model of Texas Labor Markets: Towards Assessing the Impact of Illegal Migration." Austin: University of Texas, Bureau of Business Research Report, 1977.

King, Jonathan. "Interstate Migration in Mexico." *Economic Development and Cultural Change* 27(1): 83-102. October 1978.

Kirk, Betty. *Covering the Mexican Front: The Battle of Europe vs. America.* Norman: University of Oklahoma Press, 1942.

Korns, Alexander. "Coverage Issues Raised by Comparisons Between CPS and Establishment Employment." In *1977 Proceedings of the Annual Meeting of the American Statistical Association.* Washington, D.C.: 1978.

Kumar, Ramesh; Chancellor, William; and Garrett, Roger. "Estimates of the Impact of Agricultural Mechanization Developments on In-field Labor Requirements for California Crops." In California, University, *Technological Change, Farm Mechanization and Agricultural Employment,* pp. 157-198.

Lancaster, Clarise, and Scheuren, Frederick J. "Counting the Uncountable Illegals: Some Initial Statistical Speculations Employing Capture-Recapture Techniques." In *1977 Proceedings of the Annual Meeting of the American Statistical Association.* Washington, D.C.: 1978.

Lázaro Salinas, José. *La emigración de Braceros: visión objetiva de un problema mexicano.* México: CUAUHTEMOC, 1955.

Lewin, M. *Russian Peasants and Soviet Power: A Study of Collectivization.* Translated by Irene Nove. Evanston, Ill.: Northwestern University Press, 1968.

Lewis, Oscar. *Pedro Martínez: A Mexican Peasant and His Family.* New York: Vintage Books, 1964.

Los Angeles. City. Community Development Department. Community Analysis and Planning Division. *Population, Employment, and Housing Survey, 1977.* 4 vols. 1978-1979.

Mamer, John, and Fuller, Varden. "Employment on California Farms." In California, University, *Technological Change, Farm Mechanization and Agricultural Employment,* pp. 1-32.

Martínez, Oscar J. *Border Boom Town: Ciudad Juárez Since 1848.* Austin: University of Texas Press, 1978.

Martínez Cerda, Carlos. *El Algodón en la Región de Matamoros, Tamaulipas.* México: Banco Nacional Crédito Ejidal, 1954.

Meador, Bruce S. *Wetback Labor in the Lower Rio Grande Valley.* San Francisco: R & E Research Associates, 1973.

Merrill, Jay. *Border Area Development Study: Profile of Undocumented Migration to the California Border Region.* Sacramento: Southwest Regional Border Commission, 1978.

Mexican American Legal Defense and Education Fund (MALDEF). *Hispanics and the 1980 Census.* San Francisco: 1979.

_____. *MALDEF Statement of Position Regarding the Administration's Undocumented Alien Legislative Proposal.* San Francisco: 1977.

México. Departamento Agraria. *Memoria.* México, D.F.: 1945-1946.

_____. Dirección General de Estadísticas. *Censo general de Republica Mexicana, verificado el 20 de octubre de 1895.* 31 parts. México: Oficina de la Secretaría de Fomento, 1897.

_____. *Censo general de la Republica Mexicana, verificado el 28 de octubre de 1900.* 34 parts. México: Oficina de la Secretaría de Fomento, 1901.

_____. *Tercer censo de población de los Estados Unidos Mexicanos, verificado el 27 de octubre de 1910.* 3 vols. México, D.F.: 1918-1920.

_____. *Censo general de los inhabitantes, 30 noviembre 1921.* 30 parts. México, D.F.: 1925-1928.

_____. *Quinto censo de población, 15 mayo 1930.* 34 parts. México, D.F.: 1932-1936.

_____. *Anuario estadístico de los Estados Unidos Mexicanos, 1939.* México: Talleres Gráficos de la Nación, 1941.

_____. *Segundo censo agrícola ganadero de los Estados Unidos Mexicanos, 1940, Resumen general.* México, D.F.: 1951.

_____. *6º censo de población, 1940.* 30 parts. Mexico City: 1943-1948.

_____. *Séptimo censo general de población, 6 de junio de 1950.* 33 parts. Mexico City: 1952-1953.

_____. *VIII censo general de población, 1960.* 35 parts. Mexico City: 1962-1964.

_____. *Anuario Estadístico de los Estados Unidos Mexicanos, 1964-1965.* Mexico City: 1967.

_____. *IX censo general de población, 1970.* 35 parts. Mexico City: 1971-1973.

_____. *Quinto censo agrícola, ganadero de los Estados Unidos Mexicanos, 1970.* Mexico City: 1975.

_____. Nacional Financiera. *50 Años de Revolución Mexicana en Cifras.* México, D.F.: 1963.

_____. Partído Nacional Revolucionario. *La cuestión agraria Mexicana.* México, D.F.: 1934.

_____. Secretaría de Recursos Hidráulicos. *Informes de Labores, 1974-1975.* México, D.F.: 1975.

_____. *El riego en México.* México, D.F.: 1975.

_____. Secretaría del Trabajo y Previsión Social. Centro Nacional de Información y Estadísticas del Trabajo. CENIET. *Análisis de Algunos Resultados de la Primera Encuesta a Trabajadores no Documentados Devueltos de los Estados Unidos, CENIET, Octubre 23-Noviembre 13 de 1977.* No. 1. México, D.F.: 1978.

_____. *Primera Encuesta a Trabajadores Mexicanos no Documentados Devueltos de los Estados Unidos (Octubre-Noviembre de 1977): Análisis de Algunas Variables y Cuadros de Resultados.* No. 2. México, D.F.: nd.

_____. *Relaciones Entre Indocumentados y "Coyotes."* No. 3. México, nd.

_____. *Tabla de Estancia en los Estados Unidos para Trabajadores Mexicanos Indocumentados.* No. 4. México, D.F.: 1979.

_____. *La Encuesta Nacional de Emigración a la Frontera Norte del País y a los Estados Unidos: Descripción del Proyecto y Hallazgos de la Segunda Etapa* (Agosto, 1978). No. 5. México, D.F.: 1979.

Meyer, Jean. *La Cristiada.* Translated by Aurelio Garzón del Camino. 3 vols. 2nd ed. México, D.F.: Siglo Veintiuno Editores, 1974.

_____. *The Cristero Rebellion: The Mexican People Between Church and State 1926-1929.* Condensed English-language version of *La Cristiada,* translated by Richard Southern. Cambridge and Great Britain: Cambridge University Press, 1976.

_____. *Le Sinarquisme: un fascisme mexicaine? 1937-1947.* Paris: Librairie Hachette, 1977.

Meyer, Lorenzo. *México y Estados Unidos en el Conflicto Petrolero, 1917-1942.* 2nd ed. México: Colegio de México, 1972. English-language version *(Mexico and the U.S. in the Oil Controversy, 1917-1942)* translated by Muriel Vasconcellos. Austin and London: University of Texas Press, 1977.

Meyer, Michael C., and Sherman, William L. *The Course of Mexican History.* New York: Oxford University Press, 1979.

Moore, John H. "Illegal Aliens: The View From a Mexican Village." *Proceedings of the Central States Anthropological Society: Selected Papers.* Vol. 1. 1975.

Mújica Vélez, Rubén. "Las zonas de riego: acumulación y marginalidad." *Comercio Exterior* 29(4): 404-410. April 1979.

Mumme, Stephen P. "Mexican Politics and the Prospects for Emigration Policy: A Policy Perspective." *Inter-American Economic Affairs* 32(1): 67-94. Summer 1978.

Muñoz, David Ibarra, and Manjarrez, Armando Labra. "Tercer Congreso Nacional de Economistas." *Comercio Exterior* 29(4): 466-472. April 1979.

Muñoz, Humberto; Oliveira, Orlandina de; and Stern, Claudio. "Internal Migration to Mexico City and Its Impact upon the City's Labor Market." In Camara, ed., *Migration Across Frontiers: Mexico and the United States.*

Nagel, John S. "Mexico's Population Policy Turnaround." *Population Bulletin* 33(5): 1-39. December 1978.

Navarette, Ifigenia M. de. "Income Distribution in Mexico." In *Mexico's Recent Economic Growth: The Mexican View.* Translated by Marjory Urquidi. Institute of Latin American Studies, Monograph no. 10. Austin and London: University of Texas Press, 1970.

Nelson, Cynthia. *The Waiting Village: Social Change in Rural Mexico.* Boston: Little, Brown and Co., 1971.

Nelson, Eastin, and Meyers, Frederick. *Labor Requirements and Labor Resources in the Lower Rio Grande Valley.* Occasional Papers, no. 6. Austin, Tex.: Inter-American Education, 1950.

North, David S. *The Border-Crossers: People Who Live in Mexico and Work in the United States.* Prepared for the Manpower Administration, U.S. Department of Labor, contract no. 81-09-69-08. Washington, D.C.: Trans Century Corporation, 1970.

_____. *Fraudulent Entrants: A Study of Malafide Applicants for Admission at Selected Ports of Entry on the Southwest Border and at Selected Airports.* Study prepared for the U.S. Department of Justice, Office of Planning and Evaluation, Immigration and Naturalization Service. Washington, D.C.: April 1976.

_____. *Illegal Aliens: Final Report Outlining a Rationale for a Preliminary Design of a Study of the Magnitude, Distribution, Flow, Characteristics and Impacts of Illegal Aliens in the United States.* Washington, D.C.: Linton and Co., Inc., 1975.

_____. *Illegal Aliens: Research Design.* Washington, D.C.: Linton and Co., Inc., 1975.

_____. *Interactions Between Illegal Alien Respondents and the Social Security Tax Collection System: Some Preliminary Findings.* Prepared for the U.S. Social Security Administration. Washington, D.C.: Trans Century Corporation, July 1976.

North, David S., and Houstoun, Marion F. "A Summary of Recent Data on and Some of the Public Policy Implications of Illegal Immigration." In Piore, ed., *Illegal Aliens: An Assessment of the Issues.*

_____. *The Characteristics and Role of Illegal Aliens in the U.S. Labor Market: An Exploratory Study.* Report prepared for the Employment and Training Administration, U.S. Department of Labor, contract no. 20-11-74-21. Washington, D.C.: Linton and Co., Inc., 1976.

North, David S., and LeBel, Allen. *Manpower and Immigration Policies in the United States.* Special Report No. 20. Washington, D.C.: National Commission for Manpower Policy, 1978.

Nove, Alec. *An Economic History of the U.S.S.R.* London: Penguin, 1972.

Nye, Peter. "Illegal Aliens: An Urban People Problem." *Nation's Cities* 15(7): 15-18. July 1977.

Orange County, California. *The Economic Impact of Undocumented Immigrants on Public Health Services in Orange County: A Study of Medical Costs, Tax Contributions, and Health Needs of Undocumented Immigrants.* Orange County: Task Force on Medical Care for Illegal Aliens, 1978.

Ott, Bill. "Controversy Flares at Border Patrolman's Trial Over Firing from Covina Police Job." *San Diego Union,* November 28, 1979.

Piore, Michael J. *Birds of Passage and Promised Lands.* Cambridge: Cambridge University Press, 1979.

_____. Editor. *Illegal Aliens: An Assessment of the Issues.* Washington, D.C.: National Council on Employment Policy, October 1976.

Pontones, Eduardo. "La Migración en México." In Wilkie, et al., *Contemporary Mexico...,* pp. 135-163.

Population Reference Bureau. "1979 World Population Data Sheet." Washington, D.C.: April 1979.

Powell, J. Richard. *The Mexican Petroleum Industry, 1938-1950.* Berkeley: University of Californi a Press, 1956.

Program for the Introduction and Adaptation of Contraceptive Technology (PIACT). *Condom Product Preference Among Mexico City Factory Workers.* Seattle, Wash.: PIACT, 1978.

Programa para la Introducción y Adaptación de Tecnología Anticonceptiva (PIATA). *Program Overview.* México: PIACT de México, 1979.

Promotora de Planificación Familiar. *Family Planning in Mexico: A Comprehensive Marketing Study of Awareness, Attitudes, and Practices among Consumers and Retailers.* México: 1979.

Quirk, Robert E. *The Mexican Revolution, 1914-1915: The Convention of Aguascalientes.* Reprinted. New York: W.W. Norton and Co., 1970.

Reed, John. *Insurgent Mexico.* New York: International Publishers, 1969.

Reisler, Mark. *By the Sweat of Their Brow: Mexican Immigrant Labor in the United States, 1900-1940.* Westport, Conn.: Greenwood Press, 1976.

Reubens, Edwin P. "Aliens, Jobs, and Immigration Policy." *The Public Interest* 51: 113-134. Spring 1978.

Reyna, José Luis. "El movimiento obrero en una situación de crisis: México 1976-1978." *Foro Internacional* 19(3): 390-401. January-March 1979.

Reynolds, Clark W. *The Mexican Economy: Twentieth Century Structure and Growth.* New Haven and London: Yale University Press, 1970.

Riquelme Inda, Julio. "Las cosechas de maíz en el año de 1916." *Boletín de la sociedad mexicana de geografía y estadística,* Quinta Época, 9: 131-137. 1919.

Robe, Stanley L. *Azuela and the Mexican Underdogs.* Berkeley: University of California Press, 1979.

Rosales, Francisco Arturo. "The Regional Origins of Mexicano Immigrants to Chicago During the 1920s." *Aztlan* 7(2): 187-201. Summer 1976.

Rosedale, Donald, and Mamer, John. *Labor Management for Seasonal Farm Workers: A Case Study.* Informational Series in Agricultural Economics, leaflet no. 2885. Berkeley: University of California, Division of Agricultural Sciences, April 1976.

Ross, Stanley R., ed. *Is the Mexican Revolution Dead?* New York: Alfred A. Knopf, 1966.

_____. *Views Across the Border: The United States and Mexico.* Albuquerque: University of New Mexico Press, 1978.

Salinas, Guadalupe, and Torres, Isaias D. "The Undocumented Mexican Alien: A Legal, Social, and Economic Analysis." *Houston Law Review* 13: 863-916. July 1976.

Samora, Julian. *Los Mojados: The Wetback Story.* Notre Dame, Ind.: University of Notre Dame Press, 1971.

Samora, Julian, and Simon, Patricia Vandel. *A History of the Mexican American People.* Notre Dame, Ind.: University of Notre Dame Press, 1977.

San Diego. Chamber of Commerce. "Economic Analysis of Mexican Citizen Activity in San Diego County." San Diego, Calif.: 1979.

Sax, Antimaco. *Los mexicanos en el destierro.* San Antonio, Tex.: International Printing Co., 1916.

Shadow, Robert D. "Differential Out-Migration: A Comparison of Internal and International Migration from Villa Guerrero, Jalisco (Mexico)." In Camara and Kemper, *Migration Across Frontiers...,* pp. 67-83.

Simpson, Eyler N. *The Ejido: Mexico's Way Out.* Chapel Hill: University of North Carolina Press, 1937.

Simpson, Leslie Bird. "Review of Howard Cline's *Mexico: Revolution to Evolution, 1940-1960.*" *Hispanic American Historical Review* 43(2): 295-297. May 1963.

Singer, Morris. *Growth, Equality, and the Mexican Experience.* Austin: University of Texas Press, 1969.

Smith, Barton A., and Newman, Robert J. "Depressed Wages Along the U.S.-Mexico Border: An Empirical Analysis." *Economic Inquiry* 15: 51-66. January 1977.

Smith, Robert F. *The United States and Revolutionary Nationalism in Mexico, 1916-1932.* Chicago: University of Chicago Press, 1972.

Stein, Walter J. *California and the Dust Bowl Migration.* Westport, Conn.: Greenwood Press, 1973.

Stoddard, Ellwyn R. "A Conceptual Analysis of the 'Alien Invasion': Institutionalized Support of Illegal Mexican Aliens in the U.S." *International Migration Review* 10(2): 157-189. Summer 1976.

_____. "Illegal Mexican Aliens in Borderlands Society." *South Texas Journal of Research and the Humanities* 2(2): 197-213. Fall 1978.

_____. "Illegal Mexican Labor in the Borderlands: Institutionalized Support of an Unlawful Practice." *Pacific Sociological Review* 19(2): 175-210. April 1976.

Tavernetti, James R., and Miller, H.F. *Studies on Mechanization of Cotton Farming in California.* California Agricultural Experiment Station, Bulletin no. 747. Berkeley: University of California, Division of Agricultural Sciences, 1954.

Taylor, Paul S. "Mexican Labor in the United States: Valley of the South Platte-Colorado." Vol. 1 of *Mexican Labor in the United States. University of California Publications in Economics* 6(2): 95-235. Berkeley: University of California Press, June 12, 1929.

_____. "Mexican Labor in the United States: Chicago and the Calumet Region." Vol. 2 of *Mexican Labor in the United States. University of California Publications in Economics* 7(2): 25-284. Berkeley: University of California Press, March 31, 1932.

_____. "Mexican Labor in the United States: Migration Statistics." Vol. 12, no. 1 of *Mexican Labor in the United States. University of California Publications in Economics.* Berkeley: University of California Press, January 10, 1933.

_____. "A Spanish-Mexican Peasant Community: Arandas in Jalisco, Mexico." *Ibero-Americana* 4: 38-39. Berkeley: University of California Press, 1933.

Texas. *Employment Commission Annual Report, 1948-1966.* Austin: 1949-1967.

_____. The Good Neighbor Commission. *Texas Migrant Labor.* Austin: 1966.

_____. Governor's Office of Migrant Affairs. *Migrant and Seasonal Farmworkers in Texas.* Austin: 1976.

_____. University. Institute of Latin American Studies. *Mexico's Recent Economic Growth: The Mexican View.* Monograph no. 10. Translated by Marjory Urquidi. Austin and London: University of Texas Press, 1970.

Thompson, Orville E., and Scheuring, Ann F. *From Lug Boxes to Electronics: A Study of California Tomato Growers and Sorting Crews.* California Agricultural Policy Seminar,

Monograph no. 3. Davis: University of California, Department of Applied Behavioral Sciences, December 1978.

Thompson, Wallace. *Trading with Mexico*. New York: Dodd, Mead and Co., 1921.

Tienda, Marta. "Familism and Structural Assimilation of Mexican Immigrants in the United States." Center for Demography and Ecology, Working Paper 79-11. Madison: University of Wisconsin, 1979.

Times, Los Angeles. Editorial. "Mexico: Crisis of Poverty, Crisis of Wealth." July 15, 1979.

Torrik, Solvieg. "Learning in a Pinch: How Migrant Kids Fare." *San Francisco Chronicle,* July 27, 1979, p. 4.

Tuchman, Barbara H. "The Green Revolution and the Distribution of Agricultural Income in Mexico." *World Development* 4(1): 17-24. January 1976.

United Farm Workers of America, AFL-CIO. "Report on Illegal Alien Farm Labor Activity in California and Arizona." Keene, Calif.: nd.

United Nations. Department of International Economic and Social Affairs. Statistical Office. *Demographic Yearbook, 1977.* New York: 1978.

_____. Economic Commission for Latin America. *Anuario Estadístico de América Latina.* United Nations: 1977.

_____. Food and Agriculture Organization. *Production Yearbook, 1977.* Rome: 1977.

United States. Bureau of the Census. "Country Demographic Profiles: Mexico." *Reports of the Population Division,* Washington, D.C.: September 1979.

_____. *Current Population Survey: March 1978.* P-20, no. 339. Washington, D.C.: June 1979.

_____. Congress. House. Committee on International Relations. *Undocumented Workers: Implications for U.S. Policy in the Western Hemisphere.* Hearings before the Subcommittee on Inter-American Affairs. 95th Congress, 2nd session. Washington, D.C.: 1978.

_____. Congress. Joint Economic Committee. Subcommittee on Inter-American Economic Relationships. *Recent Developments in Mexico and Their Economic Implications for the United States.* 95th Congress, 1st session. Washington, D.C.: 1977.

_____. Congress. Senate. Committee on Human Resources. *Hearings on Farm Worker Collective Bargaining: April 26, May 24, 1979.* 98th Congress, 1st session. Washington, D.C.: 1979.

_____. Judiciary Committee. *Hearings on Brewing and Liquor Interests and German and Bolshevik Propaganda.* Senate Document 62. 66th Congress, 1st session. Washington, D.C.: 1919.

_____.*U.S. Immigration Law and Policy: 1952-1979.* Report for the Select Commission on Immigration and Refugee Policy. 96th Congress, 1st session. [Joyce Vialet] Appendix II. "The Immigration and Nationality Act—Questions and Answers." Washington, D.C.: Library of Congress, Congressional Research Service, May 1979.

_____. Department of Agriculture. Economic Research Service. *Power and Equipment on Farms in 1964, 48 States.* Statistical Bulletin no. 457. Washington, D.C.: 1970.

_____. Foreign Agricultural Service. "U.S. Agricultural Imports and Exports, January-December Cumulative, 1979: Mexico." Washington, D.C.: 1980.

_____. "U.S. Agricultural Imports and Exports by Commodity Group, Calendar Years, 1972-1978: Mexico." Washington, D.C.: 1979.

_____. Library of Congress. Congressional Research Service. Education and Public Welfare Division. *Illegal Aliens: Analysis and Background.* Washington, D.C.: 1977.

_____. *Illegal Aliens and Alien Labor: A Bibliography and Compilation of Background Materials (1970-June 1977).* Washington, D.C.: 1977.

Van Arsdol, Maurice D., Jr.; Moore, Joan W.; Heer, David M.; and Haynie, Susan Paulvir. *Non-Apprehended and Apprehended Undocumented Residents in the Los Angeles Labor*

Market: An Exploratory Study. Report for the Employment and Training Administration, U.S. Department of Labor, Contract No. 20-06-77-16. Los Angeles: May 1979.

Vera Estañol, Jorge. "The Results of the Revolution." In Ross, Stanley R., ed. *Is the Mexican Revolution Dead?*, pp. 210-216.

Vernon, Raymond. *The Dilemma of Mexico's Development: The Roles of the Private and Public Sectors.* Cambridge, Mass.: Harvard University Press, 1963.

Villalpando, Manuel Vic. *Illegal Aliens: Impact of Illegal Aliens on the County of San Diego.* San Diego, Calif.: Human Resources Agency, 1977.

Weaver, Thomas, and Downing, Theodore, eds. *Mexican Migration.* University of Arizona, Department of Anthropology. Tucson: Bureau of Ethnic Research, 1976.

Wellhausen, Edwin J. "The Agriculture of Mexico." *Scientific American* 235(3): 128-150. September 1976.

Whetten, Nathan L. *Rural Mexico.* Chicago: University of Chicago Press, 1948.

Wiest, Raymond E. "Wage-Labor Migration and the Household in a Mexican Town." *Journal of Anthropological Research* 29(3): 180-209. Autumn 1973.

Wilkie, James W. *Elitelore.* Los Angeles: University of California, Latin American Center, 1973.

_____. *La Revolución Mexicana (1910-1976): Gasto federal y cambio social.* México, D.F.: Fondo de Cultura Económica, 1978.

_____. *The Mexican Revolution: Federal Expenditure and Social Change Since 1910.* 2nd ed., rev. Berkeley: University of California Press, 1970.

_____. "The Meaning of the Cristero Religious War Against the Mexican Revolution." *A Journal of Church and State* 8(1): 214-233. Spring 1966.

_____. Editor. *Statistical Abstract of Latin America, 1978.* Vol. 19. Los Angeles: University of California, Latin American Center, 1978.

Wilkie, James W.; Meyer, Michael C.; and Wilkie, Edna Monzón de, eds. *Contemporary Mexico: Papers of the Fourth International Congress of Mexican History.* Berkeley and Los Angeles: University of California Press, 1976.

Wilkie, Richard. "Urban Growth and the Transformation of the Settlement Landscape of Mexico, 1910-1970." In Wilkie, J. et al., *Contemporary Mexico....*

Womack, John. "The Mexican Economy during the Revolution, 1910-1920: Historiography and Analysis." *Marxist Perspectives* 1(4): 80-123. Winter 1978.

Zazueta, Fernando R. "Attorneys Guide to the Use of Court Interpreters with an English and Spanish Glossary of Criminal Law Terms." 8 *Davis Law Review,* 471-522. Davis: University of California, 1975.

Zubiran, Salvador, and Chávez, Adolfo. "Algunos datos sobre la situación nutricional en México." *Boletín de la Oficina Sanitaria Panamericana* 54(2): 101-113. February 1963.

Unpublished Sources

Archivo Cabrero Ipiña. Private Archive. San Luis Potosí, San Luis Potosí, México. ACI.

Archivo Gerardo Badillo. Private Archive. Guadalupe, Zacatecas, México. AGB.

Archivo Gordoa, Hacienda del Maguey. Private Archive. Zacatecas, Zacatecas, México. AGHM.

Archivo López, Hacienda de Trancoso. Private Archive. Trancoso, Zacatecas, México. ALHT.

Archivo Salvador Tello. Private Archive. Zacatecas, Zacatecas, México. AST.

Bailey, David C. "The Cristero Rebellion and the Religious Conflict in Mexico, 1926-1929." PhD dissertation, Michigan State University, 1969.

Bustamante, Jorge A. "National Survey on Outmigration in Mexico: Description and Preliminary Findings." Paper, Brookings Institution/Colegio de México Symposium on Structural Factors Contributing to Current Patterns of Migration in Mexico and the Caribbean Basin. Washington, D.C., June 29-30, 1979.

_____. Presentation and participation in "Rural Poverty in Mexico as the Source of Emigration Pressure," seminar sponsored by the Center for Ethics and Social Policy, Graduate Theological Union. Berkeley, California, July 21, 1979.

Cabrera Ipiña, Octaviano. "Datos Sobre las Haciendas de la Familia Ipiña en el Estado de San Luis Potosí." San Luis Potosí, México: author's manuscript, nd.

_____. "Fincas rústicas de los Cabrera Ipiña." San Luis Potosí, México: author's manuscript, 1960.

_____. "Las antiguas haciendas mexicanas." 6 vols. San Luis Potosí, México: author's edition, 1978.

Cardenas, Gilbert. "Manpower Impact and Problems of Mexican Illegal Aliens in an Urban Labor Market." PhD dissertation, University of Illinois, Champaign-Urbana, 1977.

Center for United States-Mexican Studies, University of California, San Diego. "Mexican Immigration: Elements of the Debate in the United States and Mexico." A briefing session sponsored by The Rockefeller Foundation, International Relations Division, June 10-12, 1979. Summary of the discussion by Ann L. Craig, Rapporteur. La Jolla, Calif.

Chiswick, Barry R. "Methodology for Estimating the Impact of Immigration on Unemployment in the United States." Report prepared under Immigration and Naturalization Service Contract CO-78-525, July 14, 1978.

Cornelius, Wayne A. "America in the 'Era of Limits': The 'Nation of Immigrants' Turns Nativist—Again." See Center for United States-Mexican Studies, University of California, San Diego.

_____. "The Future of Mexican Immigrants in California: A New Perspective for Public Policy." Paper presented at the Woodrow Wilson International Center for Scholars. Washington, D.C., February 27, 1980.

_____. "Harvest of Shame: United States Responses to Mexican Migration from Wilson to Carter." Discussion paper prepared for Council on Foreign Relations, Study Group on Immigration and U.S. Foreign Policy. Washington, D.C., June 8, 1978.

Cross, Harry E. "The Mining Economy of Zacatecas, Mexico in the Nineteenth Century." PhD dissertation, University of California, Berkeley, 1976.

_____. "Debt Peonage in Northern Mexico During the Nineteenth and Early Twentieth Centuries." Manuscript. Stanford University, 1978.

_____. "Rural Labor in North Central Mexico, 1880-1940." Manuscript in preparation.

Díaz, May N. "Tonalá: A Mexican Peasant Town in Transition." PhD dissertation, University of California, Berkeley, 1963.

Díez-Canedo, Juan. "Mexican Migration to the United States." Paper submitted for the Workshop on Comparative Labor Movements, Center for European Studies, Harvard University. Cambridge, Mass., October 14-16, 1977.

Dinerman, Ina. "Community Specialization in Michoacán: A Regional Analysis of Craft Production." PhD dissertation, Brandeis University, 1972.

Evans, John S., and James, Dilmus D. "Increasing Productive Employment in Mexico." Paper, Brookings Institution/Colegio de México Symposium on Structural Factors Contributing to Current Patterns of Migration in Mexico and the Caribbean Basin. Washington, D.C., June 29-30, 1979.

Fuentes Díaz, Vicente. "Los partídos políticos en México." 2 vols. México, D.F.: author's edition, 1956.

Gallart Nocetti, Antonietta. "El Cambio en la Orientación de la Producción Ganadera en San Miguel el Alto, Jalisco/sic/." Licenciado thesis, Universidad Iberoamericana, México, 1975.

Heer, David M. "What is the Annual Net Flow of Undocumented Mexican Immigrants to the United States?" Paper presented for U.S. Department of Labor contract no. 20-06, 77-16, 1978.

Hispanic American Conference on National and Inter-American Affairs. "Jobs for Hispanic Americans." Sponsored by the Labor Council for Latin American Advancement. Albuquerque, N.M., July 30-August 2, 1979.

Houstoun, Marion F., and North, David S. "The 'New Immigration' and the Presumption of Social Policy: A Commentary." Trans Century Corporation. Washington, D.C., May 1975.

Ingham, John M. "Culture and Personality in a Mexican Village." PhD dissertation, University of California, Berkeley, 1968.

Johnson, Kenneth F. "Stranded Mexican Aliens in Missouri and Illinois: A Spectrum of Livability and Human Rights Issues." Paper, Rocky Mountain Council on Latin American Studies. El Paso, Texas, May 1979.

Kearney, Michael. "U.S.-Mexico Migration and Economic Development Program (Draft)." Paper, Department of Anthropology, University of California, Riverside, nd.

King, Allan G. "A Brief for a Tax-Based Immigration Policy." Bureau of Business Research, University of Texas. Austin, 1978.

_____. "The Effect of Illegal Aliens on Unemployment in the United States." Bureau of Business Research, University of Texas. Austin, nd.

King, Allan G.; Rizo-Patrón, Jorge; and Roberts, Kenneth D. "An Estimate of the Number of Undocumented Mexican Workers Employed in U.S. Agriculture in 1970: An Instrumental Variable Approach." Bureau of Business Research, University of Texas. Austin, nd.

Lesko Associates. "Final Report: Basic Data and Guidance Required to Implement a Major Illegal Alien Study During Fiscal Year 1976." Report prepared for the U.S. Immigration and Naturalization Service. Washington, D.C., October 1975.

Lopez, Pedro. "A Study of Unapprehended and Apprehended Aliens in El Paso: Characteristics and Reported Reasons for Coming to the U.S." MA Thesis, University of Texas, El Paso, 1977.

Los Angeles. County. Department of Public Social Services. "Fact Sheet on Aliens." Los Angeles, March 22, 1977.

_____. Department of Public Social Services. Bureau of Special Operations. "Alien Status Verification Activity Quarterly Report, January-March, 1979." Los Angeles, May 1, 1979.

Mamer, John. "The California Farm Labor Market: A Challenge to Management and Leadership." Speech, Department of Agriculture and Resource Economics. University of California, Berkeley, 1977.

Martin, Philip L. "Illegal Immigration: An American Dilemma." The Brookings Institution. Washington, D.C., February 1979.

Mayio, Albert. "Rural Development Programs in Mexico and Illegal Mexican Immigration to the United States." The Brookings Institution. Washington, D.C., December 1977.

Mines, Richard. "Impact of Migration on a Village Migrant Community." Interim Report, Title V, Rural Development Act of 1972. Department of Agriculture and Resource Economics. University of California, Berkeley, February 1, 1979.

_____. "Resume of Research Findings: Impact of Migration on a Village Migrant Community." Department of Agriculture and Resource Economics. University of California, Berkeley, nd.

_____. "The Workers of Las Animas: A Case Study of Village Migration to California."

Research essay for the Department of Agriculture and Resource Economics. University of California, Berkeley, May 8, 1978.

Montañez Davis, Grace. "The Hispanic Population of the City of Los Angeles: Statistics and Trends." Deputy Mayor's Office, Los Angeles, California, nd.

North, David S. "The Migration Issue in U.S.-Mexico Relations." Paper prepared for presentation at Second Annual Symposium on Mexico-U.S. Economic Relations. Mexico City, May 23-25, 1979.

Pendleton, Edwin C. "History of Labor in Irrigated Agriculture in Arizona." PhD dissertation, University of California, Berkeley, 1950.

Project Patzcuaro. A Small Farmer Rural Development Project in the Lake Patzcuaro Region of the State of Michoacán, Mexico. Proposals and Progress Reports. Ukiah, Calif.: Farm Centers International, 1977-1979.

Reichert, Josh, and Massey, Douglas S. "Socio-Economic Stratification in a Mexican Community: The Effect of Migration to the United States." Paper presented at the annual meeting of the Population Association of America. Denver, Colo., April 1980.

_____. "Patterns of Migration from a Rural Mexican Town to the United States: A Comparison of Legal and Illegal Migrants." Paper presented at the Pacific Anthropological Association meeting, March 1979.

Research Seminar on the Problem of the Undocumented Workers. D.H. Lawrence Ranch of the University of New Mexico, San Cristóbal, August 9-11, 1978.

Reyes and Associates. "Illegal Alien Interview Forms" (2 parts). Prepared under contract to the Immigration and Naturalization Service, 1978. New Trans Century Foundation, Washington, D.C.

Roberts, Kenneth; Conroy, Michael E.; King, Allan G.; and Rizo-Patrón, Jorge. "The Mexican Migration Numbers Game: An Analysis of the Lesko Estimate of Undocumented Migration from Mexico to the United States." Bureau of Business Research, University of Texas, Austin, April 1978.

Robinson, Gregory J. "Estimating the Approximate Size of the Illegal Alien Population in the United States by the Comparative Trend Analysis of Age-Specific Death Rates." Paper presented at the annual meeting of the Population Association of America. Philadelphia, Penn., April 26-28, 1979.

Roca, Raúl A. "House to House Sampling of Contraceptive Products, Ciudad Netzahualcoyotl, México, D.F., October-December, 1979." Memo to Luis de la Macorra, Director of PROFAM. Mexico City, January 18, 1980.

Rochin, Refugio I. "Illegal Mexican Aliens in California Agriculture: Some Theoretical Considerations." Paper presented at Primer Simposium Internacional sobre los Problemas de los Trabajadores Migratorios en México y los Estados Unidos de Norte América. Universidad de Guadalajara, July 11-14, 1978.

Rubens, Edwin P. "Surplus Labor, Emigration and Public Policies: Requirements for Labor Absorption in Mexico." Paper, Brookings Institution/Colegio de México Symposium on Structural Factors Contributing to Current Patterns of Migration in Mexico and the Caribbean Basin. Washington, D.C., June 29-30, 1979.

San Diego, Calif., Chamber of Commerce, Economic Research Bureau. "The Baja California-San Diego County Linkage." nd.

Sandos, James A. "The United States and the Mexican Revolution, 1915-1917: The Impact of Culture Conflict in the Tamaulipas-Texas Frontier upon the Emergence of Revolutionary Government in Mexico." PhD dissertation, University of California, Berkeley, 1978.

Stoddard, Ellwyn R. "Illegal Mexican Aliens in Borderlands Society." Paper presented to the Society for the Study of Social Problems, Annual Meeting. San Francisco, Calif., September 2, 1978.

_____. "Selected Impacts of Mexican Migration on the U.S.-Mexico Border." Department of Anthropology-Sociology. University of Texas, El Paso, 1978.

Stuart, James, and Kearney, Michael. "Migration from the Mixteca of Oaxaca to the Californias: A Case Study." Paper presented at the symposium, "Migrations into the Californias: Conservatism and Change in Retrospect and Perspective." Annual meeting of the American Anthropological Association. Los Angeles, November 1978.

Sylvestre Terrazas Collection, Bancroft Library. University of California, Berkeley. STC.

Twining, Howard. "The Patzcuaro Project of Farm Centers International." Speech presented to Farm Centers International. Ukiah, Calif., 1979.

——————. "Report of Progress of the Patzcuaro Project." Farm Centers International. Ukiah, Calif., 1979.

Vogel, Linda; Lancaster, Clarise; Oh, H. Lock; and Scheuren, Frederick. "Selected Income Distribution Statistics Under Alternative Models for the Number of Illegal Aliens: Basic Tables and Related Backup Materials, Based on the March 1973 Current Population Survey Exact Match File." U.S. Social Security Administration. Washington, D.C., April 16, 1979.

Wiest, Raymond E. "Wage-Labor Migration and Household Maintenance in a Central Mexican Town." PhD dissertation, University of Oregon, 1970.

Wilkie, James W., and Monzón de Wilkie, Edna. Oral History Interviews, Bancroft Library. University of California, Berkeley. WOHI.

Zarrugh, Laura Hoffman. "Gente de mi Tierra: Mexican Village Migrants in a California Community." PhD dissertation, University of California, Berkeley, 1974.

Interviews

Cameron, Donald. Chief Patrol Agent, Border Patrol, U.S. Immigration and Naturalization Service. Chula Vista, California. August 6, 1979.

Grant, Herbert. Assistant District Director for Investigations, U.S. Immigration and Naturalization Service. San Diego, California. November 7, 1979.

Hayes, Sue E. Researcher, Department of Agricultural Economics, University of California, Berkeley. June 26, 1979.

Henning, Joseph. Agent, Border Patrol, U.S. Immigration and Naturalization Service. Chula Vista, California. August 5-6, 1979.

Lloyd, Jack. Coastal Growers Association. Oxnard, California. June 20, 1979, August 8, 1979.

de la Macorra, Luis. Director, PROFAM. Washington, D.C. March 7, 1980.

Mines, Richard. Doctoral candidate, Department of Agricultural Economics, University of California, Berkeley. June 1979, August 1979.

Williamson, Randolph. Agent, Border Patrol, U.S. Immigration and Naturalization Service. Chula Vista, California. August 6, 1979.

THE INSTITUTE OF GOVERNMENTAL STUDIES

One of the oldest research units in the University of California, the Institute of Governmental Studies conducts studies and service programs in such fields as public policy, politics, urban-metropolitan problems, and public administration. Its library houses one of the nation's major collections of ephemeral and nontrade publications on public affairs and policy, and offers in-depth reference services to the public as well as the University community. Institute activities include sponsorship of lectures, conferences, and workshops, and publication of books, monographs, bibliographies, periodicals, and a variety of reports dealing with local, state, and national issues.

SELECTED RECENT PUBLICATIONS

Health Policy

A Geriatric Medical Policy for California: Manpower and Setting. Robert L. Kane, et al. (California Policy Seminar Monograph No. 9) 1981. 27 pp. $3.75.

Surgical Care for Cardiovascular Disease in California: Present Status and Future Policy. Shan Cretin and Nigel K. Roberts (California Policy Seminar Monograph No. 8) 1981. 37 pp. $3.75.

Medical Life on the Western Frontier: The Competitive Impact of Prepaid Medical Care Plans in California. Lewis H. Butler, et al. (California Policy Seminar Monograph No. 6) 1980. 19 pp. $3.50.

Private Management of California County Hospitals. Ruth Roemer and William Shonick (California Policy Seminar Monograph No. 4) 1980. 27 pp. $3.75.

Environment and Energy

Coastal Conservation: Essays on Experiments in Governance. Stanley Scott, ed. 1981. 76 pp. $5.50.

Solar Energy for California's Residential Sector: Progress, Problems, and Prospects. Jennifer K. Hollon. Research Report 80–3. 1980. 71 pp. $4.50.

Policies for Seismic Safety: Elements of a State Governmental Program. Stanley Scott. 1979. 94 pp. $5.75.

Environmental Chemicals Causing Cancer and Genetic Birth Defects: Developing a Strategy to Minimize Human Exposure. Bruce N. Ames (California Policy Seminar Monograph No. 2) 1978. 28 pp. $3.50.

Housing, Land Use, Property Taxes

Proposition 13, Property Transfers, and the Real Estate Markets. Frederick E. Balderston, et al. Research Report 79–1. 1979. 56 pp. + Appendices. $3.00.

Allocating the One Percent Local Property Tax in California: An Analysis. Thomas Fletcher, et al. Research Report 79–2. 1979. 35 pp. + Appendices. $3.25.

Housing Conservation in Older Urban Areas: A Mortgage Insurance Approach. Kenneth F. Phillips and Michael B. Teitz. Research Report 78–2. 1978. 39 pp. $3.50.

Regulation v. Compensation in Land Use Control: A Recommended Accommodation, a Critique, and an Interpretation. John J. Costonis, et al. 1977. 91 pp. $3.50.

Other Public Policy Issues

The Impact of California's Legislative Policy on Public School Performance. Douglas E. Mitchell and Laurence Iannaccone (California Policy Seminar Monograph No. 5) 1980. 24 pp. $3.75.

Regulating Occupations in California: The Role of Public Members on State Boards. Howard G. Schutz, et al. (California Policy Seminar Monograph No. 7) 1980. 22 pp. $3.50.

Limiting State Spending: The Legislature or the Electorate. Frank M. Bowen and Eugene C. Lee. Research Report 79–4. 1979. 100 pp. + Appendices. $5.00.

Financing Capital Formation for Local Governments. Ann Robertson McWatters. Research Report 79–3. 1979. 51 pp. $3.00.

Monographs, bibliographies, research reports, and a full list of Institute publications are available from the Institute of Governmental Studies, 109 Moses Hall, University of California, Berkeley, California 94720. Checks should be made payable to the Regents of the University of California. Prepay all orders under $30. California residents add 6% sales tax; residents of Alameda, Contra Costa, and San Francisco counties add 6½% sales tax. Prices subject to change.